GOODBYE TEDDY

J D Stockholm

Goodbye Teddy
JD Stockholm

Based on a true story. Though names, places and dates may have been changed.

Contact

dearmrted@gmail.com

http://jdstockholm.com/

http://www.facebook.com/dearmrted

https://www.facebook.com/JDStockholmTeddy

These two sites have been invaluable to me throughout the last few years. I salute the many people on there, survivors, directors and above all, my friends. Thank you for the support at those times I needed it.

http://www.isurvive.org.uk

http://www.recoveryourlife.com/

ISBN-13:978-1492307242

ISBN-10:1492307246

Also by JD Stockholm

Thank You

This journey has been an odd one; I didn't even know I was on it. Dear Teddy was born out of a conversation with my therapist at the time, a way for the child to speak after so many years of silence and being locked away in the dark. Once I gave him a pen and told him it was okay for him to talk, he didn't stop. He had so much to say, and he did.

I have so many people to thank who have walked alongside him all the way and helped me to put the story out into the world. These thanks aren't in any order, and although I have decided not to use people's surnames, I am certain that those who I am thanking know exactly who they are.

Thank you to all of you. I don't have the words to express how grateful I am, but I will try.

Cynthia, you came along when I didn't really know I needed someone. You offered me help, not just with my book, but other things too - even just listening to me prattle on about the same thing for the millionth time. One day, I'll buy you coffee; I might even add some chocolate, but I hope you understand how grateful I am for everything you have done for me. Not just for the little boy in the books, but also for the crazy man who wrote them.

Ditter, for helping me make friends and to get Dear Teddy out there. For the constant nagging about seeing my feet and for just being that friend that can make me laugh when what I want to do is cry.

Azure, thank you for everything. I don't even remember how we became friends, just that it was through the first book and, for some reason, you adopted me as your odd English brother. Thank you for listening to me and supporting me. Thank you for still being there even when I am quiet and just need to be alone.

Teresa, it was a night so long ago, I don't even know why it came out, or why I chose to tell you the things I did. I don't think you'll ever know or comprehend how much your friendship has meant to me and your continued encouragement still does. You are a true friend and anyone is lucky to know you. Including me.

Thank you to the following for just being my friend: Gloria, Lois, Barbie, Sheila, Christopher, Nancy M and Nancy J, Jodie, Julie, Tonya, Pam, Dawn and so many more. These are just the names that come to mind. If I missed you off, it isn't personal, I promise.

Thank you to my beta readers, Vicki, Stephanie and Erica for all your help.

Tony, my thanks to you is very simple. Thank you for loving me.

Lastly, to Jamie, perhaps the most important of all. Thank you for everything. You survived.

One

(Age Eight)

My mum has cold hands. I hold them tight. They feel shiny. They are shiny because she cleans lots of things. It makes her hands very sore. Then she gets special cream for them. It is like magic. It makes her hands better. She gets it off the nice doctor. He likes my mum very much. My mum has long red nails. She doesn't get mad when I play with them. They are so long I can get my fingers under them.

My mum is sad. I don't like it when she is sad. It makes her cry. The nice doctor says my brother has a poorly heart. He has to go to the hospital to make it better. The nice doctor said he will telephone them and make it all better. My mum is very scared in her tummy about it. Maybe she needs Mr. Ted. He makes it better when I get scared in my tummy. But Andrew says grownups don't hug teddy bears. So I don't ask my mum. I hug him myself. I ask Mr. Ted if he makes my mum feel better and then she doesn't cry. He is very magic.

My mum is scared because the hospital people are mean. They took away my big brother when his head got hurt. His head got hurt because my mum throwed him at the fireplace. But she didn't mean it. She was very poorly too. She had to take medicine. But the hospital people gave my big brother away. Maybe they sold him in a shop. I ask Mr. Ted but he doesn't know. They just don't let him come and live in our house anymore. Maybe he is sad. Me and Mr. Ted are sad because we don't live in my mum and dad's house. They don't have lots of room for us. We have to live with my Nan. But she is very nice.

"It isn't my fault," my mum says. "He doesn't like to eat food. That's why he doesn't eat. They will think I am a liar."

I know my mum isn't a liar. Sometimes I am. I am a liar because I am bad. When I am bad, the bad man comes and he does the hurt thing. I try my hardest not to be bad. Mr. Ted tells me to be good. He tells the bad man I try to be good too.

My mum cries very hard. It makes me feel sad. But I don't let the crying get out. It keeps in my eyes. I am eight. I am big. I don't let the crying out.

"If they don't believe me, they'll send you both away. Then you'll go to a boys home with all the bad boys and you won't ever be able to see us again."

I don't want to go to the boys home. I don't want to go where I don't see my mum and dad. I tell my mum I promise. I will tell them the truth and then they don't send us away. I don't want to ever go away. I don't like it when I go away.

I had to go away to the play place. My mum and dad didn't know it was a trick. I don't tell them. It didn't be very nice. It made me cry because the people did lots of things that hurt very bad. I didn't get to take Mr. Ted or Andrew. Andrew is invisible. But he didn't like it. So he ran away.

"I'll tell them," I say to my mum. I make a big giant promise. I cross my heart and hope to die. I won't let them send us to the boys home.

"But you might say it wrong. Then they'll think you're a liar because you're like your Nan and she is deceitful. People can tell. And because you live there, the doctors will think it is because I don't want you. They don't understand, we don't have a bed at the house for you."

I tell my mum it is okay. I try to give her a big hug. But she doesn't want it. She moves away and then I don't get to hug her. She doesn't like my filthy arms. I forget about them. Maybe if I am good she will like all the hugs. She gets lots of hugs from my brother. He doesn't have the filthy arms. Maybe if I have a nearly heart attack like him, then she can give me lots of hugs too.

Me and Mr. Ted promise to tell the hospital people about my brother. He is scared about the food because he came out of my mum's tummy and he didn't breathe. He had lots of stuff in his mouth like snot. It was slimy and gooey. The doctor. Not the nice doctor. But a mean one. He put a tube in my brother's mouth and sucked all the snot stuff out so he didn't die.

Now my brother gets scared about the food part and then

maybe he has to get it out with a tube thing because it might get stuck and then he will die and go to heaven. I don't want him to go to heaven. Maybe he can get medicine like I do. My mum gives me medicine. It makes the sick come out all the time. It is to get my badness away because I got born from the devil. She gives it me lots of times. But it is spicy. I ask Mr. Ted. He thinks maybe it burns my brother's mouth off because it is too spicy. Maybe that is why she doesn't give it to him so the food doesn't get stuck.

I am glad I don't get a tube in my mouth. I don't like when the sick comes out. But the tube makes me scared in my tummy too. I don't ever want one.

"He knows if you tell lies," my mum says. "He watches everything. That's why he won't go away, because you attract the evilness."

I want my mum to shush. I hug Mr. Ted very tight. I don't want her to talk about him. I know she means the bad man. He gets mad when I tell someone. I don't be allowed to. Then he will come and maybe he makes everyone die. He is magic. He knows lots of things. He hears if I tell. He hears when I am bad too. Then he comes and makes it all hurt. I don't want him to be mad. My tummy turns upside down about it and my eyes want to cry. I don't tell lies. Not ever. I know the bad man can see everything. I tell Mr. Ted in my brain to tell the bad man I don't tell lies.

He knows everything. He will bite and scratch me and do the hurt thing.

If I am a good boy then he doesn't come. He doesn't come at my Nan's house anymore because I don't let the badness get out. Mr. Ted and Andrew tell me when things get bad. Then I make it stop. I tell my mum I won't tell lies. I say I promise. I make the letter P sound all big. Then it is a real promise. I feel the letter on my lips. I say it lots of times.

"Stop making stupid noises," my mum says. But I don't know how to make it stop. It keeps my badness away. I hug Mr. Ted more tight. Please don't let the bad man come.

"I have a picture of him," my mum says. "Because he won't go away. We got special people in the house who can see evil things. They set all the cameras up and then, when I put you to bed, you shouted and he was there, but we didn't see him. The people got a picture of him. They didn't let me see because he has such a bad face. Maybe you want to see it when we get home?"

I shake my head fast. So fast maybe it makes me dizzy and falls off. I don't ever want to look at it. Not ever. I wish it would go away. I promise I don't tell lies.

Two

I sit in the chair next to my brother's bed. I make my legs swing backwards and forwards. My mum tells me to stop it. It is annoying. I try to make it stop. Then I forget and I swing them again.

"Stop fidgeting," she says. She has her mad voice. I tell Mr. Ted we don't swing our legs anymore. My brother doesn't swing his legs. He sits on his big bed. It's a magic bed. It moves and bends in half. Then it is like a chair. I wish I had a bed like that. I don't be allowed to sit on the bed. I make it dirty with my shoes and then we will be in trouble.

My mum sits in the other chair next to me. She watches all the people. She sniffs lots of times. I try to give her a tissue. She doesn't want it. She is sad because she wants to go home. She doesn't like the outside places. They make her scared in her tummy. I tell her it is okay. She doesn't have to be scared. She whispers to me that she wants to go home. Maybe Mr. Ted could make the magic. But he doesn't know how. Outside places make her scared because bad people come and then they take her away. She doesn't like it. It makes her not be able to breathe. She tries not to cry about it.

I wish she didn't get scared about it. It is the hospital. They make people all better. They made my Nan all better when she tried to go to heaven by herself. They made her not sad inside. Maybe the hospital can make my mum not be scared inside.

When I am big, I am going to be a doctor. Then I will work in the hospital and I can make children better. Then they can go home and their mums and dads don't be sad about it. Maybe I can make my mum better.

It is very early in the morning. Maybe it is still night. It is dark outside. We had to get in very early. Before the sun got up and got his hat on. Maybe the sun is a lazy bones today. My brother is a lazy bones. He lies by the fire all the time with his baby bottle. Maybe the sun doesn't get up and get his hat on. I sing the song all the time. My mum tells me to shut up. So me and Mr. Ted sing it quiet. Andrew laughs about it. I tell my mum maybe the sun didn't get out of bed yet. "Sit down and be quiet," she says. I am being stupid. She says all my stories are stupid. But I like to make them. Me and Mr. Ted write them all the time. We have lots of fun. Andrew likes them too.

I don't tell my mum any more stories. I don't want her to be mad about it. She tells my dad when she gets mad about things. He shouts very loud; it makes me cry sometimes. I don't like it when he is mad with me. Sometimes it makes my badness come out and then he shouts at me more.

I like the room my brother gets to sleep in. He is very

lucky. There are lots of children. It is like a giant sleep over. But they are poorly too. I ask Mr. Ted about it. He says maybe they didn't eat like my brother and then it makes their heart attack them. Mr. Ted is very clever. He knows all the things. The children get breakfast on trays. I show Mr. Ted. We wish we had some. It makes my tummy very hungry inside. It growls very loud about it. I didn't get time to get any breakfast. We had to go very fast in the morning. My mum says if I am good I get something later.

The nurse comes to my brother and my mum. It is time for my brother's breakfast. But he doesn't get it on a tray like the others in his bed. He has to eat it in a special room. They want to show him that food doesn't be scary and he can eat it. My mum says she is coming too. Me and Mr. Ted don't know if we are allowed to go too. But the nurse asks if I want to go with them. She is nice. She has a big smile and she has stickers on her clothes. They are cats and dogs and lots of nice things. I don't have any stickers. Mr. Ted says he wants a sticker. Maybe Andrew can sneak some. We ask him about it. He likes to sneak in the hospital.

My mum doesn't know about it. I don't want my mum to get mad. I stand up and then I say yes. I ask Mr. Ted if it is okay and he says yes. I ask my mum in my brain. But she doesn't answer. She doesn't know how to do the talking in her brain thing.

I leave Mr. Ted with my bag at my brother's bed. He isn't allowed to come with us. I hope he doesn't get lost. I don't know if he knows where the house is to get back. I put him in the bag all deep inside and then he can't get out. I tell him I will be back soon.

We go to the special room. It has glass walls. It is like my mum and dad's new house. They have lots of glass walls all over. Like a greenhouse. But it doesn't have lots of flowers inside. There are lots of chairs too and a big giant television. There are lots of toys. They are in a box. Maybe I can get to play with them. But I don't ask about it.

I don't ask about the toys. Maybe they get mad about it. I wish I had Mr. Ted then I could ask him. He knows all the answers. I don't want to make anyone mad. Then I get shouted at. It makes me feel sad inside about it.

There are lots of tables. My mum and brother sit at the one where the tray is. I don't sit there. I sit at a different one. Then I don't get in the way. Sometimes my mum says I am a nuisance. I don't like to be.

The nurse sits down with my mum and brother. She has a bowl. It has my brother's breakfast in it. It smells very yummy. Like porridge. Maybe it is like the porridge my Gaga used to make me. But he went to heaven.

My brother doesn't want to eat the porridge. He hugs

himself tight and shakes his head about it. He says no very loud. No, no, no. He doesn't want it. My mum nods her head and folds her arms.

"See?" she says to the nurse. "He doesn't want to eat it."

The nurse puts the bowl down. Then she makes my brother get his arms undone. She tells him to sit up. But he doesn't want to. She tries to get the spoon in his mouth like my mum does to me. But she doesn't bash his teeth and make them bleed. He doesn't want it. He pushes the spoon away.

My brother starts to cry. He doesn't want the food. The nurse tries to get his hands away. But he makes himself all stiff then he slides on the floor and cries about it. My mum bends down and tells him it is okay. She picks him up and gives him a hug. My mum is mad. "I'm not staying here," she says. "He doesn't want to eat the food and I am not letting you force feed him."

The nurse says something to my mum. But I don't know what it is. It makes my mum mad. But she cries too. The nurse says my brother might eat if she isn't in the room. But she doesn't want to go out. Maybe she will shout at the nurse about it. Me and Andrew watch it. Andrew thinks my brother is very silly.

My mum shouts at the nurse. They are all liars. They want to make her bad. But she doesn't. She tries her best to get him to eat. But he doesn't want it. Another nurse comes in. She doesn't have stickers. She has a thing around her neck that listens inside. The nice doctor has one too. He lets me listen inside. He lets me listen inside Mr. Ted too. We listen to our hearts. They sound like trains inside. The nice doctor says Mr. Ted has a special bear heart. That is why we don't hear it very well. Because he is magic and it is a secret. I tell Mr. Ted. It makes him happy about it.

The nurse that doesn't have stickers tells my mum she has to leave the room. My mum starts to cry about it. I don't like it when she cries. I wish I could hug her. I wish I didn't have filthy arms. Maybe then, she doesn't cry. My Nan tries to hug me when I get the crying. But I don't let her. I make the crying go away. Maybe my mum can make the crying go away too.

My mum goes out of the room. There is another nurse outside. She stands with my mum and gives her a tissue to blow her nose. My mum cries all big. The nurse looks very nice. She rubs my mum's back. I don't know if I have to go too. No one tells me to go away.

My brother sits on the chair again. He swings his legs like I do and crosses his arms all over. The nurse shows him all her stickers. She has five of them. She asks him which one he likes the best. He likes the dog one. It looks like Sheba. I wish I had one. She asks him if he wants one. He says yes please. She tells him if he eats some breakfast he can have some. The breakfast is very nice. It has sugar and chocolate. She gets his spoon in it and then he opens his mouth. He eats it all up. Then she takes the sticker off her dress and she gives it to him. Maybe I can get porridge and I can get a sticker too.

The porridge makes my tummy rumble. I didn't get dinner too last night. I didn't have anything all day. My mum forgets about it because they had to go to the hospital. I know she will give me some food later. If I am good and she doesn't forget. She forgets lots of times. She is very busy.

The nurse smiles at me. It makes me smile too. She tells me I can come and sit at the table. I do. I climb on the chair next to her. "He likes his food," I say to her.

She nods her head. "Yes he does."

"He doesn't ever like food," I tell her. "He thinks it will make him choke like when he was a baby."

She asks me about it. I tell her that he doesn't eat the food at home. He doesn't ever like it. He only likes his baby bottle. I tell her maybe he thinks he is a baby. She laughs about it.

"Do you eat the food?" she asks me. I nod my head lots of times. I don't tell her about the badness. Then I don't get food. I don't want her to know I am bad inside.

"What did you have for breakfast?" she asks. I don't

know what to say about it. I didn't get any yet. I tell her I didn't eat it. We were too busy and then we had to come to the hospital.

She asks if my mum and dad are nice. I nod my head. They are the bestest mum and dad in the whole wide world. They give me lots of things and lots of food. But my brother doesn't like to eat it.

"Your mum is very sad about it," the nurse says to me. My mum is outside. She is still crying. I see her through the glass.

"My mum gets sad lots of times," I tell the nurse. She does all the things she can. But then we make it all a mess and she doesn't know what to do. She is very busy taking care of us. The nurse asks if my mum gets mad at me. Maybe the nurse knows about my badness. I don't want her to know about it. Not ever. No one gets to know. I shake my head big about it. But I make my arms hug me and then no badness gets out and she doesn't know about it.

"Do you know where the cafe is?" she asks. "You can get breakfast there."

I know I can't. My mum doesn't have lots of money. I don't be allowed to go. "I'm not hungry."

She gets the paper out of the pocket. She writes my name on it and then she writes her name on it too. She puts the words breakfast and lunch on it. "If you take this to the cafe, they will let you have breakfast and lunch," she says.

I look at my mum. I don't know if I get in trouble about it. I don't have Mr. Ted. I am very hungry. I don't want to say no. Maybe they have cereal there with the sugar on them. Maybe all the crying gets out. I don't know if it is bad to get the food paper.

The nurse puts it on the table. "It can be a secret," she says.

The other nurse doesn't see. She doesn't know the nice nurse gave me food paper. When she looks away, I take it very fast like Superman. It is mine and I get breakfast. I put it in my pocket. I don't tell anyone.

I put my finger on my mouth and whisper shush. I keep it a secret.

Three

My brother eats his breakfast all up. He is very good. The nurse says he can have another sticker. He smiles big about it. They write down what food he ate. They tell him he is a very good boy. The nice nurse asks me if I think he is a good boy. I smile very big and say yes. The other nurse says he is good too. Then she asks if she can listen inside his tummy. Maybe she wants to hear his breakfast. He lets her and lifts up his top.

Andrew says we have to look at the other nurse. Then we know what her face looks like. He knows how to be a spy. We do it when we get food. Then she doesn't catch us with the paper thing. Andrew says we can hide like real spies and then she doesn't see us and then we don't get in trouble about it. Maybe Andrew can have a paper thing for the food too.

The nice nurse asks me lots of questions. But I don't know the answer. Andrew doesn't know them too. I wish I had Mr. Ted and he doesn't be in my bag. He knows all the answers to everything. She asks me what time my brother goes to bed. Where he sleeps and if he has supper at bedtime. But I don't know. I don't sleep at their house at night time.

I tell the nurse I don't know about it. "I have sleep over's in my Nan's house," I tell her. She asks me why. It makes my tummy feel bad inside. I don't tell her my mum doesn't like me.

Then she makes me go away. I don't want the nurse to know I am bad inside. I am very bad. My brother is very good. My badness comes out and makes my mum sad. I don't get to sleep at my mum's house until I get better from the badness inside. "My Nan's house is next to my school and my mum doesn't have lots of room," I tell her. That is what my mum says about it.

She asks if I ever sleep at my mum's house. I nod my head about it. I tell her I do. She asks me lots of things. I get them all mixed up. I don't know why she asks me lots of things. Maybe she thinks I am bad. Then she wants to know.

My mum says people ask lots of things because they are nosey and they want to make trouble. It is like the nosey old bat lolly pop lady at the school. Lots of people stick their oar in. But I don't know what an oar is. It is bad. My mum gets very mad when they do it. She says my Nan does it too. But I don't ever see her have an oar. Maybe it is a secret. I ask Mr. Ted but he doesn't know either.

The nurse tells my brother she is very happy he eats all his food. He is big and clever about it. She asks him to promise to eat his lunch. He can have another sticker if he does. He promises. I want to tell her I eat my food. Then she gives me stickers too. But I don't. Maybe she gets mad about it because I get in the way.

The nurse says it is time to go back to the room where the

bed is. She says she will get some stickers for him. The nurse asks me if I know where the room is. I nod my head very big. Andrew knows the way. "Can you be a big brother and take him?" I say yes. I smile big about it. I like being big. I get up and then I hold my brother's hand. He doesn't want to. But he has to. Then he doesn't get lost. The nurse tells him he has to go with me back to our mum. My mum doesn't be outside the room. I didn't see her go away. Maybe she went far away.

The room isn't very far away. It has a long big corridor. There is Mickey Mouse on the wall and a big house. It looks very nice. Someone drew it very good. I like to draw. But I don't draw big like that. I take my brother to the room where the beds are. My mum is in there. She runs to my brother and picks him up. She gives him a big hug and asks him if he is okay. He shows her his dog sticker. My mum pushes my hand off. I don't be allowed to hold his hand. Maybe I make him have filthy arms. My mum tells me lots of times to get my filthy arms off her. My mum tells me to go away. I ask if I can play outside.

The nurse brings the book with the food things. She shows my mum. She wrote in it that my brother ate a bowl of porridge and he had a drink of juice. Then she put the time. She tells my mum how to do it. My mum is very happy that he ate all his food. I get my bag when my mum is talking. She looks at me with her mad eyes. I know I get in the way. I go away. Then she doesn't get sad I am there.

The hospital is very big. Maybe I can get lost. Maybe it is like a big house. Lots of people live there. The walls are green and the floor is green too. Like grass. But it isn't grass. Grass is only outside. It is shiny and clean. It is miles and miles long. I look all the way. But it is a long way. It is slippery. Mr. Ted says ready, set, and go, then we run very fast. I jump and make my feet slide. They slide along the floor and make a squeak sound. There isn't anyone there. They don't tell me off. I know the bad man sees. I look up at the roof. Maybe he has secret cameras and he can see me. I tell him I am sorry. I don't mean to be bad about it.

My dad doesn't like when I do the slide thing. He says I make my shoes have holes in them. He doesn't have the money to pay when I make things broken because I play stupid games. He has to work very hard and I don't care about it. I make everything broken.

I tell Andrew we don't slide anymore. He says we can look around. There are lots of corridors on the sides. They go to different places. They have signs that say their names. Maybe we can sneak in them and get lost. I try to get lost lots of time when I play on my bike. But I don't ever do it. I always get back home again. Mr. Ted says maybe if we do it with our eyes closed then we don't know where we are going. Then we get lost. I try it sometimes. But my eyes keep getting open because I don't want to fall over when I bash into things.

I make my eyes closed when I walk with my Nan. I hold her hand. Then I close my eyes. But I don't get lost. I try to make myself fall to sleep so I can sleepwalk. But my eyes open lots of times. There is one corridor that has a slope. It doesn't have a green floor. It has a white floor instead. It is shiny too. Then it goes around the corner. Andrew says maybe we can go down there. Maybe it is where they keep all the monsters. I tell Andrew we can bring skates in the morning time. We can stand on it and go very fast. He thinks it is a good idea.

The cafe is at the end of the long green corridor. It has a pattern on the floor. Like lots of bricks. Maybe it is the green brick road. Like the yellow one. I don't like the film with the witch in it. I watch it lots of times with my Nan. But I hide. I don't like when the witch hides in the trees. Then she jumps out with her scary face. She makes me get pictures about the bad man. It makes him come and get me. I watched it with my mum. But I had to go to the toilet. He hided upstairs. I didn't know about it.

Maybe the green brick road doesn't have witches. Maybe it has trolls and things. I don't like them too. My dad says trolls eat people up. They take them in their caves. Then they hang them up forever and eat them. Trolls are mean. Mr. Ted says maybe we can feed the witches to the trolls.

I walk up the stairs. They have metal on the edge. I make

the metal feel in the middle of my foot. It doesn't be allowed to feel anywhere else. It makes me feel bad if I do it wrong. Then I have to do it again. I count the stairs. But I don't say four. I never say four. Four is bad.

The cafe smells very nice. It makes my tummy get excited. It is very hungry. There are big doors. I push them open. Me and Andrew pretend we are doctors. There are lots of doctors in there. Maybe they think so too. I don't see the nurse.

There are lots of tables and chairs. I get to the food thing. It is like the one my Nan takes me to at the tower. Not like the one we get at school. At school, we stand in a line. We get a tray and then we get food. But I get a tray and then I get to pick the food. I can read very well. My mum showed me how to do it. Then I can read books and not get on her nerves. I read all the signs. It says I can pick one thing. There are lots of things though. I ask Mr. Ted what we should get. He doesn't know.

I get rice krispies. But I get the kind that has the sugar on them already. They don't need more sugar. Then the sugar doesn't get in the milk at the bottom. I don't like it when it does that. It tastes very bad. I get some orange juice too. It is nice and cold. It has lots of bits in it.

Graham used to get orange that had bits in it when I had sleepovers in his house. He let me have it at breakfast time. Graham said they squish lots and lots of oranges and make the orange juice. He said they come from trees. I don't ever see an orange tree. It makes me sad in my tummy. Mr. Ted gets sad too. Graham went to heaven. I wish he didn't go there.

I give the lady at the till the paper. She doesn't say anything about it. I don't want her to shout at me. But she doesn't. Andrew says we should sit all the way at the back. Then no one sees us. It is a good idea. I take my tray and I sit in the corner. No one sees me and no one thinks I am greedy. I filled my bowl big with krispies and then there is lots of milk on it. I try not to make it spill over when I walk. I don't want any to go away.

I take Mr. Ted out of my bag. I put him on the chair. No one sees him. He is magic. Andrew sits too. The cereal makes lots of popping noises. We listen to it until all the pops go away. Then I squish it down with my spoon. I make the milk get on my spoon but not the krispies. It tastes like krispies milk. It is very nice. I wish I had that all by itself. Mr. Ted likes krispies milk too. But I don't give him any. It makes his fur all soggy. Then he gets smelly and my mum will put him in the bin. I don't want him to get throwed away.

I don't eat any of the krispies. My mum tells me off when I do it at her house. But I don't let her see. I like to do it. I don't like to eat the krispies and milk together. They don't taste very nice. I like when the krispies are soggy and squishy. When all the milk is gone, I get the krispies on my spoon. I get a big giant spoonful then I put it in my mouth. I don't make it go down though. I put more in and then it is full. I get in trouble if I cough. Then the krispies go everywhere and my mum has to do lots of cleaning. But I don't let the cough out. I squish the krispies and make them all go inside my tummy. I drink my orange too. It is very nice. But it makes my face all scrunch up. It is cold inside. I feel sad when it is all gone. I don't have any more juice or krispies left. I wish I could go and get some more. But I don't.

Four

Mr. Ted says I have to put my tray in the pile with all the dirty ones. Then we can go out of the cafe. It is a nice sunny day. Maybe the lazy bones sun got up and got his hat on. We look out of the window. There are lots of trees and flowers. Andrew says we can play out there. Then there can be a jungle. We can hunt for lions and crocodiles and lots of things like that. I wish Sheba were here too. She is good at the hunting games. We like to live in the woods. Then she helps us do all the hunting things.

I put Mr. Ted in my bag again. I tell him I am sorry. It is just a little bit of time. Then he can come out and we can all play outside. We go to the corridor with the slope on it. I read the signs. It says about the heart place. There is an old lady on a bed in the hallway. She is sleeping. She has a funny mask on her face. There is a nurse there too. She smiles at me.

We walk all the way along the corridor. I don't know where it goes. Andrew says it is an adventure. There is a door at the end. We push it open and walk outside. There are lots of stones on the ground. They are crunchy when I walk on them. Me and Andrew run outside to play. There are lots of slopes and things. It will be very good when I get the skates tomorrow. We can go fast. Andrew has skates. But he doesn't be faster than me on them. I am the fastest.

The hospital is very big. It has lots of trees around it. There is a park too. But it is over the road. I don't be allowed to cross it. It is very busy. All the big cars go down it and maybe I get run over. There is a place with lots of trees too. But it has a fence around it. It says Zoo on the outside. Me and Andrew sneak to the fence. No one sees us because we hide behind the trees when we sneak there. Maybe we can see some animals. But we don't. Maybe they are hiding.

We pick up big sticks and we use them to walk. We need them, then we don't fall over. I bash mine on the ground when I walk. It makes lots of noise. We walk all around the hospital. I didn't know the place where my Nan goes was there. She doesn't be there now. She went there when she had to go in the ambulance. She tried to make herself go to heaven because she missed my Gaga. They gave her medicine then she didn't miss him and it didn't make her cry. I miss him too. It doesn't make me cry. Me and my Nan go and put flowers on the place in the cemetery. I ask my Nan if he is all muddy in there. She said maybe he is. My mum doesn't know we go. I am not allowed. My Nan makes me sneak there. I like to go. Me and Mr. Ted read all the things. There are lots of dead people there.

It is boring outside. Me and Andrew walk around lots. Maybe it takes all day long. We go back to my brother. He is sleeping. He lies in his bed. He has a poorly tummy. Maybe his tummy didn't like the food. The sick came out. It is in a bowl next to my mum. I don't make lots of noise. I don't want to be in trouble if I wake him up.

I look around the room. There is a little baby at the other side. He has a bed by the door. His mum and dad doesn't be there. He cries lots and no one comes. Maybe he is sad because his mum and dad don't be there. It makes me sad in my tummy. No one comes when I cry too. Me and Andrew go to his bed to look at him. He has a baby bed with bars on it. But he isn't a baby. He is just little. He has a nappy on. He has a pipe in his nose and a needle in his hand. He has lots of wires. The machine next to him makes lots of bleep noises. Maybe he cries because he doesn't like it. I don't like it when I get all tied down and I don't get to move. It makes me cry too. I cry when lots of things hurt very bad. I hug Mr. Ted and make it all go away.

"Hello," I say to the baby. But he doesn't say hello back. Maybe he can't hear me because his crying is loud. I ask him what his name is. But he doesn't say it. I tell him my name. I show him Mr. Ted. Mr. Ted waves at him. The nurse comes and she writes in his book. It hangs on the bottom of his bed. Maybe she writes about his food too. I ask her if he is poorly like my brother.

She says that he has poorly eyes. They don't work and he can't see anything. I ask Mr. Ted. Maybe that is why he is sad. Maybe that is why he cries. She says the special pipe makes him breathe properly. Maybe it is like when my face gets squished and I don't breathe properly. I don't like it when that happens. My dad makes my face all squished when he does the hurt thing.

I ask where his mummy is. "He doesn't have a mummy," she says to me. Me and Mr. Ted feel very sad about that. It is not nice when there is no mummy. I cry very bad when my mum goes away. I miss her lots and lots it makes it all hurt inside. Maybe he misses his mum too.

The nurse says he is called Tommy, then she goes away. But he still cries. He has lots of toys in the cot too. But he doesn't play with them. Maybe he doesn't want to. I put my hand in the cot and I pick them up. They are like keys. They don't be real. I use them on pretend. I shake them. I say his name and I make them shake so he hears them. But he doesn't do anything about it.

I make the keys jingle at his nose. He doesn't grab them or take them away. Peter's mum has a baby. When we played with the toys, his sister grabbed them. Then she tried to eat them. But Tommy doesn't. Maybe he doesn't want to play. I tickle the keys on his tummy. He stops crying. But my arm gets sore and tired. It might fall off. I put the keys down. But then Tommy starts to cry again. I whisper shush to him. Then I make the keys jingle. I tell him he can have them if he wants. Maybe he wants to play with them.

I get his dummy. It lies by his head. I put it in his mouth. He pinches it very fast in his mouth and it bounces up and down when he sucks it. He falls to sleep. Then I can put the keys down. My arm is very tired. Maybe it wants to go to sleep too. The nurse comes back. She says I am very nice to get him to sleep. But maybe he was very tired.

Me and Mr. Ted can read him stories. I ask Mr. Ted about it. He says yes. We can write lots of them when we get home. Maybe we can write a story and Tommy gets to be in it too. Maybe he wants to play with me and Mr. Ted. I tickle his tummy and say bye-bye to him. I hope he doesn't get sad that I go home when he wakes up. I ask the nurse if she will tell him I have to go home to my mum's house. But I will come back and then I can tell him stories. She promises she will. She says he is very happy I got to play with him today.

I have to go home in the evening time. My dad comes. But my brother is sleeping. He didn't want to eat his supper. They take him away and I didn't be allowed to go too. But he didn't want any food. The nurse put it all in his book about it. She said he didn't eat lots of food. He wanted his baby bottle. But the nurse said he can't have it. It is for babies

Tommy doesn't have a baby bottle. He has a bag thing. It hangs up. That is why he has the needle thing in his hand. The nurse said it is for his food.

I have to go home with my dad. I don't go to my Nan's house. We have to go back to the hospital in the morning time. My mum is going to sleep over. Then my brother doesn't get scared all by himself about it. I hope she doesn't get scared in her tummy too. I try to give my mum a hug goodbye. But she doesn't want it. She tells me to get off and stop it. I hug Mr. Ted instead.

My dad came in the car. He has Sheba too. She doesn't be allowed in the hospital because she is a dog. It is for people. My dad says I have to go and sit with her because he doesn't want to leave her in the car. He has to talk to my mum. Maybe they talk about boring things. He tells me the car isn't locked up. "Don't let her get on the road," he says. "She will get run over." I promise I don't.

It is dark outside. The sun has gone to bed. Sheba wags her tail and stomps her feet when we get outside. She barks very loud. I give her a big hug when I get in the car. She licks my face about it. We can play while we wait for my dad. We can be monsters with swords and chop people all up. There is a big building. It has a cross on it. My dad says it is where they keep all the dead people. Me and Sheba try to look inside the windows. But I don't be able to see anything. Maybe the dead people will jump up and bash the window to scare us.

It is very cold outside. It makes me shiver. I tell Sheba to get in the car. We can play lots of times later. I wish my dad would hurry up. I am bored. I don't want to stay at the hospital. I want to go home then me and Mr. Ted can write lots of stories.

I sneak back in the hospital. We walk all bent down then no one sees. We look for my dad. So then we can run back to the car and he doesn't know I am inside. We sneak up to where my brother is. But we don't go in. We hide at the corner. Tommy is awake. He doesn't cry. I tell him in my brain about the stories. Maybe he can like them in the morning. I tell him we don't make them scary.

My mum is crying because my dad has to go home. He gives her a big hug about it. It makes me cry too. I don't like when she cries. I don't want her to be sad about it. I stay at the door. Then I don't get in the damn way all the time. I don't make a scene and I don't get on their nerves. I always get on her nerves. She says I get on her wick. But I don't know what that is. When I asked my Nan, she said it was like nerves. I don't mean to. When my dad finishes hugging my mum I run back to the car. Then he doesn't know.

He lets me sit in the front seat. Sheba is big. She lies on the back seat. She takes it all up. I don't like the house. It is all dark. Maybe the bad man hides in there. I don't like the bedroom. My mum and dad say it is mine. I am going to live with my mum and dad again. But I don't get to yet because I don't have a bed. The house is very big. It has lots of glass walls inside. It has big wooden stairs in the middle. They are like steps. I sit on them and put my legs through the holes.

The front room is very big. It has a giant fire and two sofas. Mr. Ted thinks maybe we have to sleep on the sofa with Sheba. But I don't want to because the walls are all glass. I can see all the way to the kitchen. Maybe the bad man can hide there and he can see me in the windows and when my dad goes to bed he can come and get me.

My dad says I can have dinner with him. He didn't get time to get any yet. He got me some fish cakes. I like them very much. Mr. Ted likes them too. My dad puts them in the grill. My dad tells me to set the table. I do and then I sit at it and wait for my food. I sit there with Andrew and Mr. Ted. Then we write the story for Tommy. We write about witches and monsters. But I don't make it scary because he is little. I don't want him to be scared about it.

My dad gives me the fish cakes when they are cooked. I don't want anything with them. But he gives me some of his potatoes and vegetables. I ask if I can have some red sauce. But he says no. That is my brother's. I don't be allowed any. My dad says if I eat all my dinner, I can have some special drink. I don't like the whiskey. But it doesn't be that. He has lots of red wine. It is very strong. He makes it himself. He has it in the attic in big tubs. It has a glass pipe at the top and bubbles come out. My dad says it has to stay there for a long time. Then all the juice in it makes wine. He drinks it lots of times.

My dad gives me a big glass of it. It makes me all warm inside. I ask Mr. Ted if he wants some. But he doesn't drink wine. It feels funny in my mouth. I drink it all up and I eat all my food. I take my plate and my dad's in the kitchen. I have to scrap them into the bin. We don't wash the dishes. My mum gets mad about it if we do. She says we make everything broken and smashed. Then we wash the plates all wrong too.

My dad is going to watch television. He likes the detective programs. He doesn't wear a police uniform. He wears a suit with a tie. He has a funny moustache. He is old. My dad has read all the books. He likes them very much. My dad lets me sit on the sofa with him and then me and Mr. Ted write more stories.

I am sleepy inside. My eyes want to go to sleep. Me and Andrew and Mr. Ted lie down on the sofa. My dad doesn't get mad about it. Sheba lies on the floor by the fire. She likes it because it is warm. I don't know I go to sleep. It is on surprise. Sometimes I do that at my Nan's house too when the bad man comes. I don't know I go to sleep then. When I wake up it is all sore inside.

I don't know my dad got my clothes open too. I didn't feel it. I don't tell him that I waked up. Maybe he gets mad if he knows about it. He puts his mouth on me and I don't like it. It feels funny. I don't want Sheba or Mr. Ted to see. I hug him tight and then I roll over. Maybe my dad thinks I rolled over in my sleep. But my dad doesn't let me. He pulls me down and then he makes me roll back again. He takes all my clothes off. I don't let the shivers start. He lifts me off the sofa and puts me on the floor. He makes me lie on my tummy. I don't look at the glass walls because then I can see. They are like big giant mirrors. I don't want to look. My dad takes his clothes off too and then he puts his thing inside and does the hurt thing. I look at the television so I don't see it. But the television doesn't have the police thing on anymore. My dad has films about lots of people doing the hurt thing. I don't want to see that too. My dad likes it. He watches it all the time. He tells me that I will like it when I am big. But I won't. He says when I get all grown up then I will do it to people. I tell Mr. Ted I don't. Not ever.

I try not to look at anything. Maybe I can fall asleep. Then I don't have to know about things. My dad says I am a good boy. When he makes all his noises. He tells me to go to the bathroom to get ready for bed. He says I can sleep in the bed with him because my mum doesn't be there and my brother is in the hospital. I tell him thank you. I don't have to hide from the bad man.

Five

We wake up very early. We are going back to the hospital to see my mum and brother. My dad doesn't stay. He has to go to work. Or we don't get any money. He says no one else does it if he doesn't then we all starve to death and sleep outside. We wake up at 6 am. It is very early. The sun is just getting up too. My dad gets out of bed. He wants to get a shower before he goes to work. He lets my hands get untied. I have to get dressed too and I don't be allowed to take a long time.

My hands are sore because they were all tied up. My dad tied them up in the nighttime when he did the hurt thing lots of times. I falled to sleep. I forgot to get my hands open from the rope. My arms are stuck. Maybe it is like when I pull a funny face and my Nan says it will stick that way if the wind changes. Maybe the wind changed when I was sleeping. Now my hands are stuck in the air. Mr. Ted thinks it will look very silly if I don't get them down again.

I rub them and make them not sore. I pull the covers on. I wish I could go away. I feel bad inside. I wish I didn't have the badness. I don't let the crying out. It is not allowed. I am bad. I get my nails. I make them scratch on my arms about it. Then maybe it gets away all the bad parts.

My dad says I have to get a shower too. But not at the

same time. I have to wait until my dad finishes. I don't like to move. It makes it hurt inside. I feel the smell too. I don't like how it smells. Maybe everyone can smell it and know that I am bad.

The bathroom is downstairs. The house is back to front. It is a nice bathroom. It is green too like the hospital. It has a bath and a shower. I didn't ever get a real shower before. Peter has one at his house. It has special doors that close. It looks like a Tardis from Dr. Who. I like it very much. I get in the bathroom and take my clothes off. I don't look at the mirror. I don't want to see all the badness there. I get in the shower. Maybe I can wash it all away. My dad has special brushes. He uses them to get all the dirt from his nails. It is very hard. I put soap on it. Then I rub it all over. I want to make the badness go away. It is inside. It doesn't wash away with soap. I make the brush hard. It hurts very bad. Good. It should hurt. I am bad. I want it to hurt bad and make it all go away. I don't let the crying out. Stupid boys cry. I don't cry. But I am stupid and bad. Bad boys don't ever get to cry. It is my fault I am too bad. No one else has to do it and my brother is sick and it is all my fault because my mum is too busy looking after all my badness. I do everything wrong. I make the brush get harder. It makes my legs all red and bleeding. Good. They should bleed. Maybe all the blood can get out and then I can go away and everyone will be happy.

I don't be able to get the smell away. It is there. In my nose. I wash my mouth inside too. I don't use the brush, but I get the water in there. I don't like how it tastes. My dad put his thing in there when I was tied up. But I didn't let the sick get out. I swallowed it all. I keeped it in like my dad said. My dad says I was good when I did it. But it makes my tummy do the turn over thing and I don't like it. But the sick didn't get out and I didn't make a mess.

I have been a long time in the bathroom. My dad knocks on the door. "Hurry up," he says to me. We have to go. My mum has called. She wants some clothes and other things.

We have to go very fast. I don't get time to get any breakfast. My dad forgets about it. He eated his when I was in the shower. I was too slow. It is tough. If I didn't take very long then I could have some. But I don't want any anyway. I am too bad to eat it. My tummy feels hungry inside. I tell it good. I get my notebooks and my paper. I put them in my bag with Mr. Ted. I don't talk to Mr. Ted. He thinks I am bad inside too.

Maybe Tommy doesn't think I am bad. I am going to read him a story. I hope he likes it very much. Maybe he will think it is silly. My mum thinks my stories are too silly. She tells me they are very bad. But I like to write them. I write about spies and things. Me and Andrew like spies and police. We play it all the time. They get to be big and special. Like the police we watch at my Nan's house. They get to ride motorbikes and catch all the bad people. My dad has motorbikes. But he doesn't catch bad people. He just likes to ride them with his friends. I don't be allowed to touch them. I will make them broken.

I put my skates in a bag too. I don't tell my dad about it. Maybe if it is a sunny day I can play on them outside. Then I don't get in everyone's way and then they don't tell me to go away. Maybe I can skate inside too if no one gets to see it. I wrote Tommy a story about skating too.

We drive to the hospital. I am excited in my tummy about the stories. Tommy is awake when we get in my brother's room. He is crying. My mum says that bloody child has been screaking all night long. She didn't get to sleep because he makes so much noise. No one comes and makes him shut up. I feel bad inside my tummy. Maybe he was sad and scared of the dark. No one was here. Maybe my mum would let me stay and I can make him not sad about it.

I say his name when I go to his bed. But he cries lots of times. The nurse changes the bag on his needle thing. The other bag is empty. Maybe he is very hungry.

My mum says his mum took bad medicine when he was in her tummy. That is why he can't see. She was selfish and she took all the drugs. I don't know why that made him blind. Medicine makes people better. Maybe bad medicine makes people poorly. I tickle his tummy with my fingers and I tell him I have a story for him. I have Mr. Ted. Mr. Ted says hello too.

Mr. Ted is very happy to see him. Tommy bangs his arms and legs about. Maybe he doesn't like Mr. Ted. I tell him that Mr. Ted isn't scary. He keeps all the bad people away. He does lots of nice things and he wrote lots of stories with me. I whisper Tommy the shush sound like my mum did when my brother was a baby. She does it if he hurts himself very bad. It makes all the hurt parts go away. She doesn't do it to me. I am too bad. It is good when I hurt myself. My brother gets sad about it.

I get the chair and I sit next to Tommy. Me and Mr. Ted read the stories to him. We read lots of times. Maybe he doesn't know what I am saying because I laugh about it. Then the words don't come out. My mum gets mad. She comes over and tells me to shut up. I disturb everyone. I don't mean to. I tell her I am sorry. Tommy stops the crying part. I put my hand on his tummy too and I make it go all around. I sing the song to him, round and round the garden, like a teddy bear. It makes him fall to sleep again. Mr. Ted says maybe he is tired because he didn't sleep in the nighttime. I get very tired when I don't sleep at the nighttime because I am very scared inside.

The side of the cot is very high. I don't be able to reach over it properly. I have to stand on my toes to make myself big. Mr. Ted says I can stand on the chair. Then I can see Tommy without the bars. His eyes are closed. He snores very loud. I tell Mr. Ted about it. Maybe we can look after Tommy forever and then he doesn't ever get sad. Tommy has lots of wires and stickers. Not stickers with dogs on them. He has special ones. They get wires stuck to them. I ask the nurse about them. She says that they listen inside. Then his heart makes the machine beep very loud. It is like magic.

I ask Andrew about it. If we run away then no one does the hurt thing and we can live in a cave. I ask Tommy if he wants to live in a cave too. Maybe there are bats in there. I like bats. They look funny. I know how to live in a cave. I watch it on the television with my Nan. We watch about making the fires and then we get fish from the water and cook it. It looks like a very good time. Maybe when Tommy is better and doesn't have to be in hospital we can do it.

I don't tell my mum about it. She will tell me it is stupid. I am stupid lots of times. She says my head lives in the clouds. I don't know what she means.

I ask my mum to look after Tommy. He is sleeping. Me and Andrew are going to play outside on the skates. The lazy bones sunshine has got out of bed and come outside to play.

Six

We go and see my brother every day. It is very boring. I wish I get to go to my Nan's. But I don't want to make Tommy sad about it. I read him lots of stories and tell him lots of things. I write about my brother too. He has to have the needle in his hand like Tommy. The nurse put it in and then he has a bag of water too. It drips into it and then goes into his hand. It makes his tummy filled up inside. He eats some food too. But not lots of it. My mum says he is getting better. Maybe now he doesn't go to heaven.

The nice doctor phoned the hospital to see if he was better. My mum gets a big smile about it. Maybe he really wanted to talk to her. Maybe it was his secret plan. My mum knows he likes to talk to her lots of times. But he can't because of his mean wife. I wish she would go away. Then my mum doesn't get sad about her. He was very sad that my brother had to get the needle in his hand. My mum doesn't cry about it now.

The nurse shows my mum the special book. It has to be filled in when we are at home. There will be a lady that comes to see my brother. She wants to check that he eats all his food. Then she knows he doesn't get poorly again. I don't want him to get poorly again. I don't want him to go to heaven. I write down all my brother's things too. Then I know he doesn't go away. I make one for Tommy too. I write about them. I write what they eat and what they do. I show Mr. Ted the book. He thinks they are getting better. I am very glad.

My brother is allowed to get off the bed. He gets toys to play with. I take him to see Tommy. But my mum gets mad about it. She tells me off. I make too much damn noise all the time. I shouldn't be making my brother go to see that bloody child. I don't mean to make my mum mad. I tell her I am sorry. Tommy is nice. But she says he cries and cries all the time. She wishes he would just shut up. Maybe his mum can come and get him. She says it is his mum's fault. She is too selfish. "People like her should have their children taken off them and given away," she says. "Not people like me who look after their children." The nurses need to fix him with medicine. I tell my mum he just misses his mummy. She tells me not to be so bloody stupid.

I miss my mum when she goes away. She goes away all the time. She doesn't stay at my Nan's house. She goes away at the nighttime. Sometimes she doesn't say goodbye. It makes me cry and be sad about it. I tell my mum I get sad. I miss my mum. But she doesn't believe me. If I really missed my mum then I would be good all the time. I try. I try not to let the badness out. But it just happens.

I am from the devil. My brother doesn't be. The devil

tells me to say all the lies and do all the bad things. She can't wait until I get big and then I can live by myself. It makes me scared in my tummy. I don't want to live by myself. Maybe the bad man will come and get me. I don't know how to make food too. My mum tried to get the badness away with the medicine. But she doesn't give it to me anymore. Maybe that is why my badness comes back. Because I don't get medicine. Maybe the nurse has medicine for badness too.

It gets to be day five. It is a very long time. I write all the days in my book for my brother and Tommy. Me and my dad go to the hospital again. I am excited because I made Tommy a big giant story. I want to read it to him. Me and Mr. Ted made it. It is very special. We drawed all the pictures too. I drawed the cave and the sea and lots of sunshine. I try to run. But I don't be able to. It hurts all inside from the hurt thing with my dad. We did it lots of times in the nights. It makes me have tummy ache. But I don't tell my mum about it. She knows I am bad inside. I make my dad do the hurt thing.

We have to use the stairs to get to where my brother is. I don't be allowed to use the lift because that's lazy. The stairs don't be so big. But they make my tummy hurt and where my dad does the hurt thing. I try not to cry about it. But it feels all scratchy inside and then maybe I got all chopped to pieces and I didn't know about it. Sometimes the blood comes out. Not lots of it. Just a little bit and then I have to make it all cleaned away in the shower.

My dad walks fast. He leaves me on the stairs. He tells me to catch up. If I want to be slow I can do it by myself. I tell him I am sorry. I don't mean to be slow. I don't bring my skates today. I wanted to play inside with them. I found a place where there doesn't be anyone and Andrew said we could skate there. But it hurts too bad to ride on my skates. I tell Andrew I am sorry. I didn't mean to make my dad do the hurt thing to me.

My brother sits in his bed. He is watching the television. It is a special one on wheels. They have cartoons on it. I watch cartoons at my Nan's house. But I don't be allowed to watch them at my mum and dad's house. Then I have to let my brother watch the television because he gets bored.

My mum and dad talk about things. I go to Tommy's bed to show him the pictures I made. He likes it when I come. The nurse says I make him happy when I read stories and tickle his tummy. But he doesn't be there. His bed is empty.

I don't know where he is. I look around. But he doesn't be there. The bed covers are all gone. His toys don't be there. Maybe he will come back. Maybe he got better. I hug Mr. Ted. I don't know where Tommy is. It makes my tummy hurt. The nurse comes in. She has the breakfasts on the trays. I sit on the chair next to Tommy's bed. Maybe he comes back soon.

The nurse comes over to me. She asks me if I am okay. I

don't be able to make the crying go away. I don't know where Tommy is gone. I have a story for him. I ask the nurse where Tommy is. She kneels down in front of me. She gives me a tissue for my face. I don't want her to see that I get the crying out. It is bad when I cry. My dad says I am just a big baby. But I don't be able to help it.

She tells me he has gone away. But he didn't say goodbye. It makes me cry very bad about it. No one says goodbye. They all sneak away. Maybe I am too bad. I don't mean to be. I try to be nice lots of times. Maybe he doesn't like my stories. He didn't tell me that he was going to go away. I tell her he didn't say that he was going away. He didn't tell me about it. No one ever tells me when they are going away. I hug myself tight. I don't know why he didn't tell me. I didn't be bad. I didn't make him mad at me. He was my friend.

The nurse says he didn't know he was going away. He would have said goodbye if he knew. But it was a surprise. She told me that he misses me very much too. He liked all the nice things I did for him. He liked all the stories and things that I told him. She says his toys are in her office. Maybe I would like one. He said I can have one if I want it.

I don't want to take Tommy's toys. Maybe he comes back for them because he misses them. He likes the keys when they go on his tummy. I do that lots of times and I make them tickle all to his hands. I ask the nurse if she knows where he lives. She says yes. I ask her if she can send him the story. I made it for him and the pictures. Maybe he likes them. She says I am very nice.

She looks at Mr. Ted. She asks me who he is. He looks very nice. I tell her he is Mr. Ted. He helps me write the stories. She asks if he makes good stories. I nod my head very big about it. "Mr. Ted likes to write lots of stories."

"You are very lucky to have a Mr. Ted," she says. "I hope you look after him."

I do. I promise. I never let any bad things happen to Mr. Ted. I tell the nurse I am going to go and play outside. She smiles about it and tells me not to forget to give her the story for Tommy. I promise I don't forget.

I go for a walk in the hospital. Then I go away and don't get on my mum's nerves. I don't walk very fast because it hurts inside and I don't go very fast because I feel sad. I wish I got to say goodbye to Tommy. Maybe I will see him again. Andrew says maybe we can make him a goodbye card and we can draw on it. I think that is a good idea.

We go to the cafe place. The nurse always gives me the paper thing for the food. I sit in the back and I eat my food and I don't let anyone see because it is a big secret. I don't want her to get in trouble about it. Me and Andrew draw him a picture. We draw me and Mr. Ted and Andrew and Sheba and Tommy. He didn't ever see Sheba, but she is nice and she wanted to see him. I asked her and she said yes. We draw it all in a picture and then we tell him that we miss him very bad. Maybe if I put my address on it then he can draw me a picture back too. When he is bigger and he knows how to draw things. I give Tommy special glasses in the picture. They are special because they make him see things. He can see everything. Even through walls. When he comes back, we can make them and we can be spies like the stories. Then he will be able to see and we can play all day long together. I hope he wants to.

I take the picture when I am finished and give it to the nurse. I ask her if she will give it to Tommy. I tell her she doesn't be allowed to read it. It is a surprise. She gives me a sticker. She says she will give it to Tommy and she says thank you.

I go back to my mum and brother. I sit on the chair. I don't move all day. It is lots of hours. My brother is happy. Maybe he is nearly better. There is another baby in Tommy's bed. He is sat up. He has his mummy and daddy. I tell him in my brain he doesn't be allowed there. It is Tommy's bed not his. He can look after the bed until Tommy comes back again.

Seven

I wish Tommy didn't go away. I wish I got to say goodbye to him. I think about him lots. I talk to Mr. Ted about him. I hug Mr. Ted tight. It makes me cry. I ask my dad about it too when he drives the car to go home. My dad says maybe he went home with his mummy. I ask Mr. Ted. Mr. Ted thinks so too. I tell Mr. Ted Tommy doesn't be sad if his mummy came back.

My mum is happy that Tommy is gone. Then she can go to sleep at night. Because he doesn't cry all the time. After my dinner, I go to bed in my mum and dad's bed again. I don't put any pyjamas on. My dad does the hurt thing lots of time. He gives me his special drink in bed. It makes my head sleepy. Maybe Tommy is sad that he didn't get to say goodbye. I squeeze my eyes all tight and tell him in my brain.

I fall to sleep in my mum and dad's bed. I hug Mr. Ted. I don't think about the hurt part. When it gets to morning time, I don't have any stories or pictures to take. I sit on the sofa and wait for my dad. He is in the shower. I wish my brother comes out of hospital soon. I don't like going there. I ask my dad if I can go to my Nan's house. But he says I don't be allowed. She is a nosy cow. He doesn't like it when she gets in all his things. I don't be allowed to go there again.

My mum says I am going to live at their house. She has got me the room that is at the top of the stairs. It is all mine. They are going to get my Gaga's bed from my Nan's house. They don't have lots of money to buy a new one. It is old and blue. It is dusty because my granddad went to heaven on it. But then no one ever used it. My mum says it is fine for me to use. I never had a bed before. Not all to myself. I didn't ever have a bedroom. My dad says I am eight years old. It is time to get into my own room and stop sharing with everyone.

My brother has a cot thing in their bedroom. It is by the door. He doesn't get to sleep in my room with me. I don't know why he doesn't get one of the other bedrooms. There are five bedrooms in the house. Some of them are downstairs. My dad got one for his books and his office. But there is two more near the bathroom. My dad says I can sleep in one of them and then my brother can have my room. But I don't want it all the way at the back. Maybe the bad man will come and it is at the back of the house. No one will hear and come and help me when he gets me. Maybe he can get in from the window. The window is at the back of the house and no one can see. I tell my mum I don't want one. So my brother has to sleep in their room and then I get one all to myself.

I don't have it yet. It is all filled with boxes of things. My mum and dad have lots and lots of things. The telephone rings and I have to answer it because my dad doesn't come out of the bathroom yet. It is early. I say hello and it is my mum.

"Get your dad right now," she says to me and I do. I run all the way to the bathroom and tell him to come quickly. My mum needs him on the telephone right now. He comes out of the shower. He is all soapy and wet. But he runs to the phone with no clothes on and no towel. He talks to my mum. I don't be able to hear what he says.

He tells me to go away and sit back in the front room. When he finishes on the telephone, he doesn't say anything. He looks all mad at me. He has his angry eyes. He goes back to the bathroom and finishes his shower and then he comes back. He moves very fast and I don't be able to get away. He smacks me very hard across my legs. I cry and tell him I am sorry. I don't know what I did. He grabs my arm and lifts me off the sofa. He pulls my pants down and then he smacks my leg very hard. It makes a noise and it stings very bad. I try to get away but he doesn't let me. He is mad and he shouts at me.

I made him scared. I told him to come right now and he didn't need to. He doesn't know why I am so bad. "Why did you make it sound like something was wrong," he says to me and I didn't. I didn't mean to make him scared. I just said what my mum said. He tells me I am a liar. "You don't mess with people like that," he says then he smacks me again and tells me to stand there. I don't be allowed to move.

He goes to his front room. It is one of the bedrooms. It has all his books. He goes there a long time and I don't move. Like a statue. I stand still. My legs get all the pins and needles in them. It is a long time. I watch my dad come out later. He goes to the kitchen. It is lunchtime. He makes his lunch and he sits at the big table in the dining room. He doesn't give me any. I need to go to the bathroom but I don't ask him.

He tells me to go anyway. We are going to the hospital. My brother is coming home today. We didn't need to go there all early. I don't let the crying out when I try to move my legs. They hurt all bad because maybe they were stuck that way when I didn't move. I tell my dad I am sorry. He tells me I am bad.

My brother gets to come home. He eats all his food like he is supposed to. My mum keeps it in a book. The lady from the hospital is going to come every three days and make sure that he is eating his dinner up. My mum says he is going to start school. He didn't start school already because he was poorly and maybe he wouldn't like it there.

He doesn't go to the same school as me. My dad says the school I go to is for people that don't be very clever. It is not a nice place. He doesn't want him to be there where I make my brother all bad. He is going to go to a new school that is far away. He has to drive in the car. My dad is going to take him. I don't be allowed to sleep in. I have to be up very early or I make my brother late for school. I promise I will try not to.

I don't go back to my Nan's house. She doesn't want me there anyway. My dad said so. I am too much of a burden. I don't know what a burden is. But I miss my Nan. Maybe she is sad I go away. But she says she is okay. She goes to a club place in the daytime with her friends. I don't mean to be a burden to my Nan.

When we get to the hospital, my brother is ready. He is very excited. I don't be allowed to stay in the ward. I stay outside with Sheba. My mum says I will make it all bad with the nurses. I tell the nurse goodbye and then I go to the car where Sheba is. My dad says I can let her out. But I don't be allowed to let her on the road. She might be hit by a car and then she will go to heaven too. I don't want her to go to heaven. I keep her very safe. Me and Andrew play in the trees with her. We tell her no when she tries to go to the cars.

I sit in the back of the car with Sheba. Not on the seats. My brother sits there. He has his bags and his special things. Me and Sheba sit in the boot. I like it in there. I can see all the cars. I lie on Sheba; she doesn't get mad about it.

We stop at the shop. My dad wants to buy my brother a special thing for being very brave. He got the needles out of his hand and now he eats lots of food. They throwed his baby bottles in the rubbish bin. He doesn't be allowed them anymore.

My dad buys him some books. I don't be allowed to

touch them. They are my brother's not mine. My dad tells me very loud don't touch them. They aren't yours. I tell him I won't. I don't want to make him mad about it. My dad doesn't buy me any books. I wish he did. But I don't be brave and I don't do anything good.

We get to the house; my mum sits with my brother. She is very happy he is home. I ask my dad if I can play outside. He tells me I can. Then I don't get in the way. I don't know anyone near my mum and dad's house. But there are lots of children. I have a tennis ball. Me and Sheba play with it. She runs and gets it. I can't do it because I am sore inside. The other children stare at me. Maybe they know I am bad.

There is a girl. She comes to me. She says she is called Faye. She asks me what my name is. I tell her. She asks me if that is my dog. I tell her it is. She has a dog too. It is just little. It is her mum's dog. She lives in the house across the road. She has a sister and a brother. She asks if I have any brothers and sisters. I tell her about my brother. But he isn't very well. He was just in the hospital. She asks me if I want to play cricket with them. I tell her yes please.

Faye is very nice. I like her very much. Her brother is big. He comes and plays too. There are lots of children. We all play together outside. We play cricket. I have a very fun time. I like them all lots. Maybe they can be my friends and they don't ever know I am bad inside. I won't ever tell them.

Eight

(Age Nine)

My dad says he will put new paper on the walls in my bedroom. But I like it. It is mine and Mr. Ted's. There is some paper there. But it is peeling off. Some of the walls have wood on them. I am allowed to put pictures there. But I don't be allowed to put them on the paper parts. Not even the broken paper parts. I have to use the blu-tak. I don't get to use tape. Me and Mr. Ted draw lots of pictures. We put them on the wall. We drawed one of Tommy at the hospital. He is with his mummy. He smiles very big. He doesn't have lots of wires anymore.

My room is big. It is at the front. The window sticks out from the roof outside. It has a door. The door is made out of glass. I have a big wardrobe too. Me and Mr. Ted look inside it. It is made into the wall. It has a shelf with a pole in it. Maybe we can hide in there. Me and Mr. Ted can climb all the way to the shelf and sit on it. No one ever finds us.

I have a sink too. It is green. It is in my room. My mum says I don't be allowed to use it very much. My dad says he will put some shelves on the wall. I have lots too many books. I need to put them all there. He says he will do it when I get new paper. I get to pick the paper. I am very excited. I get a new room and lots of new things. I get to make it look all nice like my friends have. I don't know what to make it look like.

My dad gived me his old desk. He has a new one. The old one is scratched. But I like it very much. Me and Mr. Ted put a pot on it. We have lots of pens and paper. We write lots of stories at it and draw lots of pictures. Then we put them on the wall. It looks very nice.

My mum says I can have sleepovers too. Peter is coming to sleep. I can't wait. He doesn't ever see my room before. His mum is going to bring him in her car. I look out of my window. Maybe he comes very soon.

I get bored waiting for him. My window is very high. I have to stand on the table next to my bed to look out of it. I let Mr. Ted look too. But not too much. I don't want him to fall out of the window. Then he goes away and gets stuck on the roof at the bottom. Then I never get him back and he gets scared about it.

My mum and dad's room is next to mine. It is very big too. It has a big bed and my brother's cot thing. It has a sink too. My mum has the box that I sleeped on when we lived at my Nan's house. No one sleeps on it now. My dad puts his garage clothes on it when he gets changed. My mum doesn't let him stay in his overalls. She says he makes everything dirty when he does. He has to get a shower too. He takes his clothes off in the bedroom. Then I see him go past my door. He is going for his shower. He doesn't wear any clothes when he does that.

I wait for my dad to shut the door downstairs. I can hear it. Then he goes to the bathroom. I sneak into my mum and dad's room. I look in my dad's pocket. He has lots of money. Maybe he is rich. Andrew comes too. He listens for my dad coming back. There are lots of notes all rolled in a tube. I wish they were mine. I could buy lots of things. Maybe I can buy sweets. I ask Mr. Ted if my dad knows about all the money. But he doesn't think so. We take fifty pence. I put it in my pocket and go back to my room. Maybe he will know I got it and then he will be mad about it. Maybe he can see it in my room. But I don't give it back.

Peter comes and I am very excited. I put Mr. Ted on my bed. Then he has to stay there. He doesn't come to play with us outside. Peter comes in my room. I show him all the things. He likes it very much. I tell him my granddad died on the bed. Then I laugh when he gets all scared about it. He is scared about ghosts. But my granddad doesn't be a ghost. He is in heaven.

I tell Peter I have to go to my mum and dad's room. My dad has finished his shower and he had all his dinner. I didn't get any. They forget again. But it is okay. I don't need lots of food. I tell Peter I don't be allowed in there really. I ask him to listen for my mum and dad. He says yes. He stands and listens for them. I sneak into their room again. I walk on my toes like a real burglar and they don't know about it. I take one of the notes from my dad's pocket. I put it in mine folded up then he doesn't see it.

I can buy lots of things to eat with it. Then when my badness goes away, I don't cry about the hungry parts. It feels bad in my tummy to take the money. Maybe the bad man sees it. But he didn't come for a long time. Maybe he doesn't come anymore. I ask Mr. Ted in my brain to tell him I am sorry. If he wants I will put it back. But he doesn't say anything about it. Maybe I am too bad now. I take the money because of my badness.

Me and Peter go to the shop. We don't buy lots of things with it. I don't want my mum or dad to see that we have sweets and drinks. Then she will ask how we got it and I don't want to tell her. When we go to the lady at the counter, I think about my mum. Maybe the shop lady knows my mum and she will ask her about the things we buy. Maybe she will call her and tell her that I stole some money. I think the lady might know that we steal the money. But she doesn't say anything about it. Maybe everyone knows that I am bad and I steal. Maybe I should just go away. I really am bad like they say.

I tell Peter we have to put the things in our clothes and then my mum and dad doesn't see it because I am not allowed any sweets. I think maybe my mum can see them there. But she doesn't. We get them into the house and then we take them into my bedroom. We hide them in the box that is near my wardrobe. We can eat them later when everyone is in bed sleeping.

I don't want my mum to get mad at me again. Then maybe she will send me away. I don't want her to send me to the place at the weekend times. I like when Peter is there. Then I can't go. I don't ask my mum about it because maybe she forgot about it. I don't want to go there. I have lots of pictures in my brain about it. But I don't ever tell anyone. I don't tell my mum.

I don't tell Peter about the place. Maybe he will think I am bad about it. I don't want to ask him. But maybe his dad does the hurt thing too. I don't ask that either. I don't think Peter is bad to get the hurt thing. I don't want to make my dad do it if he finds that we stole some money and then we got sweets with it. My dad will be very mad. It is not Peter's fault it is mine because I am so bad.

My mum doesn't like Peter's mum any more. She says that Peter's mum causes trouble. It's because she has bright red hair. My brother doesn't like her hair. My mum wishes she would go away. Everyone gets in the way all the time. She asks lots of times about my brother and all his food. She should shut up and mind her business.

It gets dark. My mum says we have to go to my bedroom. We sit in the bed and we get the sweets. We play games and we eat them all up. But we hide them in the bed so my mum doesn't come in and see them. We play games all night. My mum tells us to go to sleep when it gets to past midnight. My dad has gone to bed. He is very tired. The hospital lady is coming in the morning. If I am very good, then Peter can sleep at my room again.

In the morning, the lady from the hospital comes. Me and Peter sit on the floor. We keep out of the way. We are very good like my mum says. We smile about it.

The hospital lady asks about my brother's food and then she wants to see the book. We sit and watch. I write what my brother eats too and then he can't go to heaven. Not if he eats lots of food. I have sweets he can eat and then he has some food. But I don't tell him about it because he might tell on me that I have sweets hiding in my room. I don't be allowed any food up there.

The hospital lady is very happy with my brother. He has eaten lots of food. She makes him stand on the scales and he makes it go higher. Sometimes my dad says that is because he is fat. He says I am fat too. But I don't be. I can see all my skeleton inside. When I squish my tummy in, it all goes inside. But my dad says that anyone can do that. Now my brother will be big and fat like me and then he will be stupid. But he doesn't tell the hospital lady that. He just tells my brother he is fat all the time. Sometimes my brother cries about it. Sometimes I tell my brother he is fat too and I make him cry. He doesn't like to be fat. But my mum makes him eat lots of food and then he doesn't get taken away. He has big giant plates of food and maybe so much it will make him pop. He doesn't need to eat my sweets. He is already big and fat. My dad says so.

Nine

I am good all week long. I don't let any badness come out. My mum says Peter can stay again. I like it when he sleeps at my house. We are very excited when it is home time from school. His mum isn't going to pick him up. He gets to come home with me from school and he has his sleepover things in his bag. We put them in my room. I tell Peter to stay there. I go in my mum and dad's room again and I take some of the coins out of my dad's pocket. Peter doesn't know about it. I don't even tell Mr. Ted. He thinks it is bad to steal things. But I can't help it. It is my badness inside.

I tell Peter I have some money to go and get some sweets for the sleepover. We stay out for a long time. We play with the ball and the bikes and things. We have to go inside when it gets dark. My mum says that we have to go and get showers. It is Friday and we smell like school. My dad tells me that we can go and get one together.

I don't ever have a shower with Peter before. I got to have them lots of times at the play place. But I don't like them there. We had to do lots of things and the people took pictures about it. I don't want to take pictures with Peter. I don't want him to see all the bad things. Maybe he knows that my dad does the hurt things lots of times. I don't get to shower in the mornings. Then I have to go to school and I smell it all bad on me. But Peter doesn't ask about it.

My mum says we have to use the towel that is in the bathroom already. It is big and green. My dad uses it. It is a little bit wet. But we don't mind. The bathroom door is made from glass. It has a blind over it. I close it and then no one gets to see when we are in the shower.

The bathroom is near my dad's study place. Maybe he can hear the things we do in there. I tell Andrew to go away. Then he doesn't see us in the shower. It feels bad in my tummy. I have to take my clothes off and I don't want Peter to see. Peter takes his off. He doesn't mind about it. He gets in the shower. My eyes keep wanting to look at his thing. But it feels bad inside to look. My dad says that I like it. That's why he does the hurt thing. Then I will like it when I am all big. He makes me feel tingly when he touches me and then it is all nice and warm inside. Maybe Peter does that too with his dad.

I take my clothes off too and I make them into a pile for my mum so she doesn't get mad I didn't do it right. I get in the shower and then I close the door and we stand in the water together and get our hair all wet.

I feel all my badness inside. It makes me want to do all the bad things like my dad. I ask Peter if he wants me to wash his hair and he says yes. His mum does it lots of times. He doesn't do it right. My dad washes mine sometimes. I get the shampoo and I make his hair all soapy. I don't get it in his eyes. But he makes his eyes all closed and then it doesn't sting.

Peter washes my hair too. He washes it nice. I think about the place. When we had to wash each other all over. Maybe I can do that with Peter. Maybe he likes it too. I ask him if he wants me to make his back soapy and he says yes.

He doesn't say anything when I get my hands on him like my dad does. I get my hand down. He closes his eyes about it. My dad says it is nice to do it to people. Maybe I can make Peter hurt me like my dad does. Maybe it is the badness inside and it has come out.

Peter doesn't make it hurt like my dad does. He doesn't do the inside part. He gets his hands all soapy and he does the same as me. I put his hand on my thing and I tell him to do it like I do. He does. But he is not mean like my dad. He doesn't make it all hurt. I want him to make it all hurt inside. But he doesn't. It makes me feel sad inside because he can't do it right and I don't know how to tell him to do it right.

Peter makes all the sounds like my dad does and then I get my hand away from his thing. I get my hand off and then I get a cup and fill it with water from the shower. I pour the water on Peter to get all the soap away. He doesn't say anything to me. He takes his hand off. It makes me want to shout at him because he doesn't do it right. He never gets it right. He has to. He has to make the badness inside go away. I feel it all big and it is there and if he doesn't do the thing like my dad does it won't go away. I turn the shower up to hot. I fill the cup and I pour it all on me so it makes my skin all hot and it burns. I ask Peter if he will do it for me. He nods his head about it.

I tell him to put his hand back and make all the water very hot at the same time. He does it. He doesn't get mad at me. I tell him he does it all right. He smiles all big about it.

I hold his hand like my dad does to me. I show him what he has to do because he doesn't know. Maybe his dad doesn't show him properly. I make him do it until it feels all funny inside like when my dad does it. But I don't let the sounds all out.

I want Peter to go away. I don't want him to see. I am so bad. I made him do the things like my dad. My dad is right. He said I like it. I do. I don't mean to. I am bad inside. Very bad. I feel it all. It is dirty. I want to make it go away. I tell Peter to go away. I don't let him see the crying parts. I tell Peter to go and get dressed. I have tummy ache. I will come in a minute.

He says okay and he gets dressed. He goes out of the bathroom. I make the door locked behind him. I look in the mirror. I am so bad. I see it all there. I make myself get back in the shower. I turn the water all hot. I make my nails scratch it all away. The crying wants to come out but I don't let it. It isn't allowed. I am bad and then I made Peter bad too. I am sorry. I didn't mean to.

It gets all washed away and then I get dressed too. I make the bathroom all clean again and my mum doesn't get mad. Peter is sat in the lounge when I go there. He is on the sofa with my brother. They are watching cartoons. I get my dirty clothes and I take them to the kitchen to my mum. She tells me to put them on the floor. I don't look at her. Maybe she knows that I am so bad inside. Maybe she knows what I made Peter do.

I don't look at my dad too when I go back to Peter. But Peter isn't mad. He asks me what I want to do. He asks if we can play cards or a game. My dad tells him he shouldn't play with me. I always cheat. It's the only way I can win. I cheat at everything. I don't tell Peter my dad is lying. He isn't. I know how to cheat at all the games. But I don't let anyone know about it.

We play cards. We play a game called fish. My dad tells me to sit with him. He slides me between his legs. I sit on the floor. I can feel his thing behind me. But I don't move. He tells Peter all the cards I have. Peter thinks it is funny and then I lose the game because my dad cheats. I get mad at my dad. I try to stand up but he holds me there and he doesn't let me go. He laughs about it. I cry and shout. I want him to let me go. But he doesn't do it. Peter thinks it is funny too because I get mad about nothing at all. He squeezes me all tight and I don't be able to breathe. He tells my brother to go and play with Peter because I don't be able to play with my friends. I am a baby. I get mad because Peter wins. That's what he says. He tells me to go to my room now and I don't be allowed to move. I tell him I hate him and I don't keep the tears away. I am a baby like he says.

Ten

I go to my room. I don't keep the crying away. Peter plays with my brother. They make the Lego on the big table in the dining room. I don't be allowed to play. I am just too bad all the time. I make everything bad. I go to my room because my dad told me to. I don't hug Mr. Ted. I don't hug Sheba and I don't talk to Andrew. I sit on the floor where I don't be near the door. Then no one can get me. I fold my arms up. My dad always makes me mad. He makes me want to shout at him. I don't know why he does it. Then I get mad and I get in trouble. I don't mean to. Maybe I should go back to my Nan's house and then everyone gets to be happy.

I hear my dad come up the stairs. He has big heavy feet. They stomp on the stairs and make lots of banging noises. I look at the glass door. It is all wavy. I don't be able to see out of it properly. But I can see my dad. He stands there and then he knocks. I don't say hello. I don't tell him to come in.

He says my name. I tell him to go away. He opens the door. I hug myself all tight. I don't want to look at him. I don't want him to shout at me. I know I am bad. I don't know how to make it go away.

"I came to get the box of cars," he says. But he can't have them. They are mine. My special cars. I got them off my Nan and

Graham. I don't let anyone play with them.

"They can't play with them," I say to him. He tells me they can and they will. But I tell him no. They don't be allowed to touch my things. They are mine. Not theirs. They don't get to play with them.

My dad keeps saying it. He tells me to give him the cars. But I say no lots of times. They don't get them. I shout it at him all loud. They don't get the cars. I stand up and then I go to where they are. He doesn't get them they are mine. My dad tells me to move and get out of the way. I don't. I make it all loud and shout very bad. He doesn't get to have them. They are mine.

My dad tells me to stop being so selfish. I don't let anyone touch my things. Maybe he should take Peter home. I tell him he can take Peter home. I don't want him to play here. I don't want him to play with my brother and my Lego.

My dad moves me but I don't let him. He doesn't get to get my cars. "Move," my dad says.

"No," I tell him. "No, no, no."

My dad is very mad. He shouts at me. He shouts the word next to my face. I shout them back. I tell him no very loud. Then he smacks me because I shout. But I don't care. I say bad words to him. I tell him I hate him. I tell him to get out of my room. But he doesn't want to.

If I don't give him the cars then he is going to take them. Then I don't ever get them back. He tells me if I don't let them play with them he is going to be very mad. He pushes me out the way. I shout very loud. But he is bigger than me. He gets my box of cars and then he takes them downstairs. I tell him to stop it. They are mine. He has to bring them back. He shuts the door and then I hear him walk down the stairs. He doesn't come back.

I open my bedroom door. I bang my feet. I shout and make my throat all scratchy. I want my cars back. My mum comes then. She is mad too. She shouts at me. I tell her she is bad. I tell her I don't like her. I wish she goes away. I wish my brother went to heaven and didn't ever come back. I wish they all leave me alone.

My mum stomps up the stairs. She points very hard and tells me to go into my room. I don't be allowed to come out. I don't be allowed to talk to anyone. I shout. But she doesn't say any more words. She just tells me to go in my room. I have to stay there all night long.

I go away. I go in my room again and I sit in the corner. I wish they all got to go away and leave me alone.

I don't move off the floor all evening. I don't go and have any food. I hear my brother and Peter. They are playing downstairs. They get lots of nice things. I hear them laugh and play. Maybe they have a very fun time because I don't be there.

I only get up to turn the light on. I don't like the dark. Maybe the bad man comes then. My mum comes in. She says I have to close the curtains. But I don't talk to her. She doesn't say anything to me too. It is very late. My legs are all invisible. I wish I was invisible too. I hear my dad say it is bedtime.

My dad lets them make a den in the lounge. They make it under the stairs. My mum tells them how to do it. They have lots of pillows and covers. They sleep in a jungle. They get to sleep downstairs and have torches. I wish I get to go away and then I don't be sad about it. I don't want to listen. It makes my tummy hurt inside. I don't keep the crying away. I don't cry lots. It just falls out of my eyes when I lie on the floor.

My mum says night-night to them. She stays up though. I hear her put the television on. My dad doesn't. He has to go to work in the morning. He doesn't ever stay up very late. He says night-night too and tells them to be good. Then I hear him come upstairs again.

He comes into my room and I close my eyes. I pretend to be asleep. I don't want to talk to him. I don't want him to see me. Then he turns the light off, goes out of my room and closes the door. I get up and I put the light back on. I don't like the dark. I don't be able to sleep in the dark. The bad man comes when it is nighttime and all dark. I have been bad too. He comes when I am bad. He makes me be sorry for all my badness.

My dad comes back. He asks me if I am awake. I turn my face then I don't have to see him. I don't want to. He talks to me about being good. It was only a game. I didn't need to get all bad. I tell him to go away.

My dad sits on my bed. He tells me to get up and stop being silly. I don't need to lie on the floor. I shake my head. I don't want to get up.

"You'll get cold," he says.

I tell him good. Maybe I can freeze to death and then I go away because no one likes me. I don't be able to say the words because my crying comes again. My dad tells me to come to him. I don't need to cry about it. But I do. I don't be able to make it go away.

My dad gets off the bed. He comes to me on the floor. He pulls my arm then I have to move. I turn my head away. I don't want to see him. But he is big and he picks me up. He sits me on his knee and puts his arms all around me. He hugs me very tight and all the crying comes out. Then he gets my pyjama top and he makes it unfastened. I don't make him stop. He lifts me up and puts me on the bed too and then he takes my pants down. I don't look at him. The crying goes away.

He lies on me and he puts his thing inside. I squish my face into the bed. Then he doesn't hear when it gets to hurt. He leans on me. His face is all next to my ear while he does the hurt thing. He tells me that I am good. He knows I am really. I just got upset. I nod my head.

My dad makes me slide onto the floor. Then he can get his hand on me too because I am all squished into the bed.

My dad asks me about Peter when we were in the shower. But I don't know what he means. Maybe he knows what I got Peter to do. I feel my tummy turn upside down. I don't want to be in trouble. I don't want to get told off. I had my badness inside. My dad asks me if we had a good time in the shower. I tell him yes. I whisper it so he doesn't know. He squeezes me all tight in his hand and it hurts a little bit. But he isn't mad at me. He doesn't shout.

He asks me if I saw Peter with no clothes on. I don't say it though. I don't want him to know what I did. He asks me again. He whispers it at the side of my ear. I nod my head, but I don't tell him anything.

My dad asks me about it. He wants to know what we did in the shower. He knows what I am like. I like all the sex things. He knows I do. He asks me if me and Peter did things in the shower. I shake my head. I didn't do anything. But he says yes we did. He asks me if I liked it. I don't tell him. I don't want him to know. I am bad inside. I don't want my dad to know that he is right.

My dad does the hurt thing very hard and it makes me

cry. He doesn't ever do it like that before. He makes me squish hard on the edge of the bed. It digs into my tummy. He still has his hands there too. He tells me all about Peter. He says things that I didn't do. I didn't do the hurt thing with Peter. But my dad says we did. I didn't. I just touched him. I didn't make it like my dad does.

My dad asks me if I liked it. Maybe I want to do it lots of times. I shake my head very hard. I cry because he doesn't believe me about it. His hand is there until I make my breath hold in. And then he knows I got to the like it part. He tells me I am a good boy. He takes his hand off me. He wants to finish the hurt part. I close my eyes all tight. Maybe I can go away. Maybe Peter and my brother are all asleep downstairs in their den. I wish I was there. I wish my dad knows that I am sorry I was so bad. I didn't mean to be.

When my dad makes all his noises, he stands up. He presses his hand on my back so that he can get up. It hurts when he does that. I cry about it. It gets me in the middle of my back. It feels like he got to break it into lots of bits. I don't be able to breathe very well. He gets his clothes back on and then he goes out of the room. He turns the light off too. But I don't stand up to make it go back on. I get my pyjamas but it is hard to pull them on. My hands shake and I don't be able to see because I cry and it is dark. I climb on my bed and get in the covers. I wish someone got to take me away. I don't want to be here anymore. I don't like it.

I ask God if he can take me away. Please don't let me wake up in the morning. I say it lots of times. I hug my covers all tight. I lie in the bed and curl up. I don't care that the springs stick out of it and they stick into my leg. I press my leg more. Maybe I can make the blood come out when it cuts me lots of times. I say it lots of times. Please take me away. Don't let me wake. Up. Don't let me wake up. Please.

Eleven

I know I am very bad inside. It made me do the bad thing to Peter. I don't say anything about it at school. I don't say hello to him. I don't talk. Maybe he tells lots of people and then everyone knows I am bad inside. I tell Mr. Ted I am sorry. I didn't mean to do it. My badness came out and then it made me. I didn't mean to.

I do all my schoolwork very hard. I try my best to make it all good. Then I can have goodness inside and not badness. Mr. Ted says if we just don't do lots of things we can be good. I tell him I promise. I don't do any bad things. I read my books at night times. Then I don't get in trouble. I know my dad is very mad at me. He doesn't give me dinner lots of nights.

I just get lunch at school. But I don't sit with Peter. He asks if I am still his friend. I tell him I am. He asks about more sleepovers. But I don't want to do it. I don't want to do the things to Peter. I don't want my dad to get mad. I don't want my dad to do the hurt thing. It is fourteen days and he didn't do it. I don't let him. I don't get in bed and let him read the stories. I don't be bad. My badness doesn't come out. Then my dad doesn't have to do it.

Peter asks if we can have a sleepover tonight. It is Friday again. I shake my head about it. I don't want to. He says please.

But I say no. I don't want to. Kirsty asks if I don't like them anymore. But I do. I like them very much. I am just lots of bad inside. I don't know how to make it go away. I hug myself all tight then I turn away from them. I don't want to say anymore words to them. Maybe they can go away and leave me alone.

I don't want anyone to talk to me. My dad doesn't talk to me either. He is mad at me. I don't want to talk to him too. After school finishes, for the weekend,. I walk to my dad's work. I don't talk to him. I sit in the car and read my library books. Then he doesn't have to talk to me too. I wait until he finishes then we go home. Maybe I get dinner tonight. My Nan comes around to eat dinner on Fridays.

When we get home, my Nan is there. I am very excited about it. I tell Mr. Ted. Look it is my Nan. He is happy too. He misses her very bad. We sit next to her all night long. My Nan asks me if I have been very good. I don't tell her about all my bad things. I tell her about all my books. I show her my story that I write about. I drawed the pictures too. It is about Sheba. She eats a chilli pepper. It is spicy. It makes her head very hot. I draw her with lots of fire. It comes out of her nose and ears. She is like a dragon. My Nan says it is very good. She shows my mum. But my mum doesn't want to see it. She doesn't ever like my stupid stories. But my Nan tells me I have lots of imagination. I hope imagination is good. Maybe I can get lots more of it.

Me and my Nan sit and watch silly television. I like the one with the old ladies that live in the house. They have boyfriends. Old ladies don't get boyfriends. Only girls get boyfriends. I tell my Nan about it. I ask if she ever had a boyfriend before. She says my Gaga was her boyfriend. But I don't believe her. She tells fibs. My Nan doesn't ever have boyfriends.

My dad finishes helping my mum with all the dishes. My brother is sitting by the fire. My dad says it is time for my Nan to go home. He takes her home all the time. I ask my dad if I can go to bed now. He says yes. "We have to be up early," he says. "We are going to the lakes. Don't wake up late."

I promise I don't. My Nan says it is very exciting about the lakes. I like the lakes. Sheba likes to swim in them. I tell my Nan night-night. Then I go to bed. Me and Mr. Ted check all the room. Maybe the bad man gets to hide in there. We do it a special way every night. Then he doesn't get in. We turn on the light and then we jump back. Then the bad man doesn't get to jump out. Then we go in at the wall. Then he can't sneak. We slide and look all around. But he doesn't be there. Then I run to the other side of the room. I get two lights. My dad puts them in. I keep them both on in case the bad man sneaks in and turns one off. Then I still have one and he doesn't get me.

I close my door. I put my dog teddy there. Then it doesn't

close properly. But it doesn't open too and he can't jump in the room like he did when we all lived at my Nan's house. I check in the wardrobe. I check in the box that keeps the wardrobe closed. I check under my bed and I check the curtains. There is no bad man. But maybe I didn't check right. The stupid pictures get in my head. I didn't do it properly. Maybe he hided very good and I didn't see him. I check in the wardrobe again. But he doesn't be there. Then I check the big box and under the bed and behind the curtains. No. No bad man. But I did it two times. Two is nearly a bad number. I don't like bad numbers. They make bad things happen. Four is the baddest number ever. Two and two makes four. I don't be able to just do it two times. I check it all again. Then it is three. I check it very good. I don't want to get to four. Four is too bad. That will make the bad man come.

My brain keeps putting pictures there. I don't like it. I don't want the bad man to come. Maybe he sneaks in and turns the light off. Maybe he gets it broken. I turn the light on and off. It only turns one light off. It isn't broken. I hear the click sound inside my head. I make the noise lots of times. I click the light three times. Then I know they don't get broken.

I am very stupid. I wish my brain didn't have all the pictures. I get my pyjamas on. I didn't get to brush my teeth. Maybe I don't have to. But my mum checks my tooth brush. If it doesn't be wet she makes me come downstairs. Then my dad is mad at me. I get in the way. I am always there when they want lots of quiet time. I make it bad again.

I put my slippers on too and then I go downstairs. I ask my mum if I can use the bathroom. She says yes. But I have to be fast. She wants to get a bath before her programmes start on the television. I run to the bathroom very fast. I go to the toilet. Brush my teeth and wash my face. Then I say night-night to my mum.

I go to bed. Then I look at my bedroom. What if the bad man got in when I was in the bathroom? I have to look in the wardrobe. I have a very stupid brain.

Twelve

We get up very early to go to the lakes. I don't wake up late. I didn't sleep lots. I make myself stay awake. Then the bad man can't sneak in when I am sleeping. I wake up lots of times and look at the time. Then I get up. No one else is awake. They all snore very loud. But I don't make my dad mad and be late.

My mum puts coats in the car. It is cold. It doesn't be summer time anymore. Then we drive to the lakes. It is very far away. It is over an hour. My eyes are tired. They fall to sleep lots of times in the car. I hug Sheba. She doesn't get mad about it. My mum and dad don't talk to me. I don't walk with them. I walk behind them. Then I don't get on their nerves. My dad walks with my brother. He talks lots to him. He tells him all about the boats and all the names of them. They are special names. But he doesn't talk to me.

We go to the fish and chip shop. It smells very nice. I sit outside with Sheba. I don't talk about the food. I don't ask for it. Then my mum and dad don't get mad because I am greedy. Me and Sheba and Andrew play with sticks. I had to leave Mr. Ted at home. He doesn't be allowed to come. I don't want him to get lost. Then I never see him again. I throw the sticks and Sheba goes to get them. She brings them back and I throw them again. But I don't throw them in the water. It is too cold. Maybe Sheba will catch a chill. That is what my Nan says when I don't wear my coat and it is raining. I will catch a chill. I don't want her to get wet too. I don't be allowed on the back seats. I sit with Sheba in the boot. If she is wet, then she makes me very cold and she smells. Wet dogs smell very bad.

My mum says we won't be able to come to the lakes again until it is in the next year. It is wintertime and it is too cold to go there. This will be the last time. My brother is sad about it. There is a big park. It has a slide and a swing. He says he will miss it. He cries about it. I don't look at him when he cries. His stupid mouth gets all upside down. It is just a slide and he is very stupid. But I don't say the words.

My mum gives my brother a big hug. She makes his sad parts go away. She doesn't make my sad parts go away. "Maybe we can buy a slide," my dad says to him. "Then you can have one at home and play on it." My brother smiles very big. He is excited and he jumps up and down. He makes lots of stupid happy noises. I wish he would fall over and go away.

He asks if we can get it now. My dad says yes, if they can find one. But they have to see how big the box is. Maybe it is too big to put on the roof. I don't want him to get a slide. He gets everything. He is spoilt. I tell Andrew that I don't want them to buy a slide. He doesn't want them to either. We ask God not to let them. But he doesn't listen. He knows I am bad. He knows I listen to the bad things from the devil. So he doesn't listen to me.

There is a summer shop at the top of the hill. My brother is all excited. He jumps up and down and he is very happy. He hugs my dad because they have an orange slide. He asks my dad if he can have that one. He says please very long with his stupid voice. My dad says yes.

My dad goes inside the shop to ask the man about it. My brother holds my dad's hand. I hope they don't have any. But they do. It can fit on the roof too. I don't want the stupid slide on the car roof. I try to say something. My dad asks me what. He has a mad face and his angry eyes. He does the stare thing at me. I don't say anything.

My mum asks me if I am jealous. Maybe I should stop being bad all the time. I tell her I am sorry and I go back outside with Sheba. Then I don't have to listen to them talking about it. I don't care. I don't want to know about it.

My dad carries the box. It is big and long. It has to go on top of the car because it is too long. I am glad. I hope it falls in the lake and goes away. Then my stupid brother can cry about it. Maybe if I don't eat food and get a nearly heart attack I get special things too. My dad carries it all the way to the car park. He has things to make it fasten to the roof. My brother sits in the car then he doesn't get cold. But we don't go home yet. We wait for my dad to get the slide fastened. I don't get in the car. Maybe they drive away and then they forget about me.

My dad tells me to climb in the boot. I do. I don't say anything. I sit with Sheba and I fold my arms over. I have a book in the back. I read that. I got it from the library. Then I don't have to talk to anyone and I don't get in trouble. My mum and dad tell my brother to get out of the car. They didn't get ice cream yet. I don't listen to them. I don't hear their words. I don't want to. I have to look after the slide. Then no one steals it.

They don't ask me if I want any ice cream. I don't. I tell them no inside my head and then they can go away. They don't say goodbye and they don't tell me they will be back in a minute. I don't feel the stupid tears when they get out of my eyes. I don't think about them at all. It isn't me crying. It's stupid to cry. I don't care. I don't want the things they have.

They don't come back for a long time. Sheba falls to sleep and I lie on her. She doesn't get mad about it. I read lots of my book. It is nearly dark and it makes it hard to read all the words. My mum and dad come back. My brother is sleeping. My dad has to carry him. My mum opens the back door of the car. I don't look at them. I pretend I don't see them. She says hello to me. But I don't answer. I pretend I can't hear her. I read my words in the book and I don't listen to her stupid words and her stupid voice.

My brother is snoring in the car. He has a bag of things.

My dad puts them inside the boot with me. He tells me not to touch them. I don't answer him. I won't touch his stupid toys. I don't want them anyway. I hope they get broken and then he can cry about it. Maybe I can make them broken. My dad says I break all my toys.

My mum and dad get in the car and then we drive away. My eyes feel tired because the car is moving and I don't know I fall asleep. When I wake up we are stopped and we are outside the house. It is cold and I don't have a coat. I don't be able to stop all the shivering. It makes my teeth bang together.

My dad carries my brother into the house and he takes him upstairs. My mum opens the boot and she tells Sheba to come and she leaves me there. It is dark and cold. I look along the road. Everyone is sleeping. It is after midnight. I can hear the sea at the end of the road. It roars and crashes. I wish I could float away in it.

I get out of the car and I pick the bags up and take them into the house. I put them in the kitchen. My mum has bought some clothes and there is the rubbish too. I put them in the kitchen. But I don't say anything; I know she doesn't want to talk to me.

My dad comes down the stairs and he tells me to come outside. I have to help with the slide in the box. It didn't fall away. It makes me sad that it didn't. I hope it is broken. I go outside with my dad. He tells me to help unfasten it. My hands are all cold and it hurts to pull the rope things away. They have big metal hooks and one of them catches my arm. It makes it bleed. It is good that it bleeds. Maybe it can bleed a lot and then I won't be here anymore.

I wipe it on my pants. Maybe my mum will shout at me for that. I don't care. She gets mad anyway. She shouts at me from inside the house because I didn't put the clothes in the right place. I put them by the bin and now she has to wash them because they got dirty. I walk in the house with my dad. I carry part of the box and I tell my mum I am sorry. I didn't mean to do it. But now she has lots of cleaning to do and it's my fault again. I don't think. I always forget to think. I tell her I won't ever do it again.

She tells me to go to the bathroom to get ready for bed and then I have to go upstairs and she doesn't want to see me again all night. I tell her okay. I don't get any food. My tummy is hungry inside. It growls about it. But I don't ask. I know my mum will say no. I didn't be good enough to get any food so she will shout if I ask.

I do what she says and brush my teeth. I get my clothes changed and I go to my room. It is dark in there. I don't like it. Maybe the bad man hides. I put the light on and jump away very fast and then he doesn't get me in the dark. But he doesn't be there.

I go in my room and sit down. I don't talk to Mr. Ted. I don't want to. He knows I am bad and stupid. I don't get any nice things. My mum and dad don't like me. I am too bad inside. Maybe they wish I could go away too. I hear my mum and dad downstairs. They laugh about things. There is a secret part on the stairs. I open my door quiet and sneak out. I lie on the floor and slide like a worm. Then I get to the top and I can see in the lounge. It is like a spy hole. Me and Mr. Ted hide there sometimes and we watch lots of things. My mum doesn't ever catch me.

My mum is lying on the floor by the fire. My dad is there too. He lies on top of her. I know what he is going to do. They do it lots of times. I try to make myself get away. I don't want to see it. My mum hears me. She shouts my name. I tell her I wanted a drink. I am sorry. I didn't mean to make a noise. My dad tells me to go away. He swears at me all bad. He tells me I don't get a drink. I can go in my bedroom and stay there. He is very mad at me. I didn't do anything wrong. I run back into my room and close the door. Then my dad doesn't shout any more. But I can hear them. He does the thing to her. I hear them make all the noises. I try not to listen but I can't help it. They make lots of noise about it. She sounds like she cries about it. But then she laughs. I wish they would stop it.

Thirteen

I wake up early. Everyone else is still sleeping. I don't sleep lots because I get scared. Maybe the bad man comes when everyone is sleeping. Then they don't hear him and he doesn't stop. Mr. Ted sleeps in the edge of the bed. He lies there and then the bad man can't get me. But maybe he can sneak in and then I don't know about it.

I keep a dog at my door. It doesn't be real. My Nan got it for me. I put it there and the door doesn't get opened easily. Then the bad man can't sneak in with the door quiet. He doesn't get in anywhere.

I get out of bed quiet. I don't make my bed tidy because my mum shouts when I do that. I don't be allowed to because I don't do it properly. But I make my pyjamas all folded up.

I don't make any sounds when I get out of my bedroom. My mum and dad's room is dark. It is dark downstairs too. I go down very slow and then I don't make the steps creak and wake them up. I don't like when I go downstairs. My mum says that Sheba is going to go to heaven soon. She has poorly legs. She doesn't be able to run very fast. She says it is because my dad made her fat. He feeds her lots of bad food and then she gets big and lazy, and fat people die. I don't want her to. My mum says one morning we will come down and then she will have died.

I sneak down the stairs. Sheba is asleep on the sofa. But she doesn't move. I don't see if she is breathing. It makes my tummy turn over. I whisper her name. "Sheba," I say, but it doesn't make her move. Maybe she is gone. I sneak down more and try not to wake my mum and dad. But I wish Sheba would move and then I know she didn't die. I sneak all the way to her. It is very dark. I try not to look all around. The walls and doors are all glass. Maybe the bad man hides too. But Sheba doesn't know about it.

I put my hand on her head and then she lifts her head up and licks it. I feel all phew inside. I sit down and I give her a big hug. I don't ever want Sheba to die. She hugs me too and then she gets off the sofa. Maybe she thinks it is breakfast time. But I have to go to the toilet. I don't be allowed later. I go when my mum and dad are sleeping. But I don't like it. It is at the other side of the house and if the bad man comes then no one can hear me. There are lots of rooms he can hide in.

I sit with Sheba and I stare at the door. It makes my tummy hurt inside. I don't want to go there. But I have to or I don't be allowed to go later. It makes my skin feel all spiky inside. I walk very slowly. I feel my tummy jumping up and down. I look all through the glass. I don't see anyone. Maybe no one is there. I open the door. But I don't be allowed to leave it open. I go through it and then close it very fast and run to the bathroom. I run in and lock the door and no one can come then.

There is no one in the bathroom.

I use the toilet and brush my teeth and wash my face. I make it all clean again because then my mum doesn't have to do it. Maybe the bad man tried to get me and he missed. I can't see in the hall because the blind is down. So maybe he can hide there and he can get me when I don't know about it. I open the door slow and then I look around it. But I don't see him. I run all the way to the lounge again.

I make the click sound in my head. Like the door did. I make my brain hear it. I count them. But I don't say four. Just one, two three and then I make the door click sound. I do it lots of times. It makes my mouth feel funny inside. But I don't be able to make it go away.

The kitchen is all nice and bright. There aren't curtains there and the sun comes in the window. It looks nice. I know there doesn't be anyone hiding there. I can see it all the way. No one can get me. I keep all the doors closed so my mum and dad don't get mad about it. They like to keep all the doors closed. My mum says it makes a draft and then we are just wasting money.

I make some cereal. My mum didn't say no. I make it before she gets out of bed and then she can't say no. I feel hungry inside because I didn't get any dinner. I don't ever get dinner when I am bad. I don't remember when I had any. I haven't been bad. But I don't let my dad do the hurt thing for two whole weeks. I don't talk to him or my mum. They make me feel sad and I get in trouble. I eat it very fast. The milk is cold and the cereal is all crunchy. I don't like it like that. I like to make it all squished in my mouth and then suck the milk out. But my mum says playing with my food is too bad. So I don't ever do it when they are there.

I eat my cereal so fast maybe I will burst. Maybe it all gets stuck. But my mum and dad wake up. I see my dad, he comes down the stairs. Then he goes to Sheba and he strokes her head. She wags her tail all big about it and stamps her feet. She likes my dad. He is nice to her. He comes through the dining room to the kitchen and he opens the back door. She gets to go out and play. Maybe she needs the toilet. He puts his dirty cup on the side and then he fills Sheba's bowl and puts it down. He doesn't say hello to me. Maybe I am invisible.

He doesn't look at the bowl. I hide it under the one that was there. I don't know if I am allowed breakfast. But I eat it before they get out of bed and then they don't be mad. My dad gets a tray and a bowl. He fills it with cereal. My brother has special cereal. I don't be allowed to ever touch it. It is for my brother not me. Sometimes I sneak it and then no one knows about it. But they don't catch me. His cereal is nice. It is funny shapes with sugar on the top. He gets it because he is fat and stupid. Maybe it can make him sick from his tummy.

My dad makes him a nice drink too and he puts the kettle on to make coffee. I don't move. Maybe I don't breathe too. Then my dad doesn't see me there and I don't get shouted at like always. I get out of the way. My dad takes my brother's breakfast and he puts it on the table in the dining room. He shouts for my brother and my mum and tells him that his food is ready.

My mum comes too. My brother sits at the table and she gives him a big hug. She writes in his book about his cereal and his juice. She just has on a big shirt and I don't like it when she bends and gives my brother a hug. I get to see all her underneath and she doesn't wear underwear.

She doesn't talk to me too and I know I have been very bad again. I wish I could make it all go away. I get my hand and I put it in my top. I make my nails all go inside. I don't stop when it hurts all bad. My mum gets the cow cup out. I don't see that for a long time. It makes me feel scared inside. It makes my throat get stuck. She gets the things out of the cupboard. She makes the medicine again. It has been a long time since I had to have the medicine. I don't want it. It makes the sick get out. I don't like to be sick.

I pinch on my skin very hard to make the crying go away and then it doesn't come out of my eyes. I don't be able to look away. I watch the medicine. I don't want it. I don't like it. She makes a glass of milk. She puts the medicine in that. It makes the milk all pink and spotty. It looks like a milkshake. But it doesn't be one. I don't be allowed those.

My mum gives it to me. She doesn't say any words. I don't want to drink it. I don't want to make the sick get out. It makes the tears come out of my eyes. I bite my lip very hard and my nose starts to get runny. I try to make it all stop but it doesn't want to. She gets her cigarette and lights it. Then she stands at the back door. But she does the stare thing like my dad.

I try to drink it all down. But it doesn't taste very nice. It makes my throat do the thing that tries to get the stuff out. I make it all go down. It hurts to do that. I take lots of big gulps. But my tummy gets all upside down inside and the sick tries to come out. It gets in my mouth. But I make it go back down. I make it swallow away. I don't be able to breathe. My eyes water. It is all gone. But it is going to come back out. I run past my mum and go outside. Sheba is there. I make the sick get in the drain so it doesn't make a mess. Lots and lots of sick comes out. It is all pink and has the cereal in it. It tries to come out of my nose too. I bash my knees on the floor because I don't stand up. I hug my tummy until all the sick comes out.

My mum stands at the door. She watches. She smokes her cigarette and blows the smoke out. I look at my feet. I sit at the wall and hug my knees up. I put my head down and then I don't have to see my mum and dad. No more sick wants to come out. But my throat hurts bad. It doesn't taste very nice. It is all burning inside. My mum finishes her cigarette. She throws it on the ground near me. Then she goes inside and closes the door. I don't know why God doesn't let me go away.

Fourteen

My tummy hurts all inside. I try to stand up. My head wants to fall off and roll away. It bangs all inside when I stand. But I don't let it. I go back into the house. My mum is washing the dishes and my brother has finished his breakfast. He sits at the table and drinks his juice. My dad is in the lounge. He has the box open for the slide.

I go into the lounge. I don't sit. Maybe I am not allowed. I don't be allowed to sit on the chairs when we lived in my Nan's house. Only my Nan lets me sit on the chairs. But not my mum and dad. I am too bad. My dad tells me he is making the slide. They are going to keep it inside because it is too cold to play with outside. "You can't go on it," he says. "You are too heavy and fat and it will break. It isn't made for you." I nod my head about it. I know I am too fat like my dad says. But I don't eat any food and the fat goes away. Maybe that is why my mum gave me the medicine to get the sick out. Because I eat the breakfast and I didn't ask and then it makes me fat. But it is all gone. My tummy is empty. But I don't feel hungry because it hurts too bad inside. Maybe it is like fire.

My dad says he is going to the library later. He asks if I want to go. I don't. I don't want to go anywhere. I shake my head and tell him no thank you. "I have some new books," he says to me. "They are about real ghost stories. Do you want to read them?" I like real ghost stories. I read lots of them. They don't make me scared. I like to tell them to Peter. They make him scared because he doesn't like ghosts. I make them scary too when I make the sounds. Peter tells me to shut up. My other friend, Kirsty, thinks it is funny. Sometimes we write the ghost stories together.

I ask my dad if I can go and play outside. He says I have to help with the slide first. But I don't want to make the stupid slide. I don't get to play on it. My brother should make it not me. Maybe it can fall down and then he can hurt himself on it. I hope it doesn't work very well. My dad tells me what to hold and then he puts the screws in. I have to hold it in the right places for him. It doesn't take very long to make. But my tummy still hurts inside. It jumps up and down and makes gurgle noises. It makes me feel dizzy in my head. I wish I could close my eyes and go away. But I don't be allowed to go upstairs. My mum makes all the beds nice and tidy. We aren't allowed to touch them when she does that. If they get into a mess then she gets mad about it and she has to make them again. I don't know why.

The slide gets finished. It is big and orange. It has green stripes down the side and lots of steps. My brother is very excited about it. My mum takes his cup and she puts it in the kitchen. She has on big yellow gloves. They are soapy because she is cleaning. But she stands at the door and she watches my brother.

He smiles very big about his slide. He races up it and then slides down it. My mum smiles big too. She thinks it is very good. She asks him if he likes it and he does. He is very happy. He tries to give her a big hug. But her hands are soapy so she doesn't hug him back.

I don't watch him slide on it. He says my name. He is very excited. He tells me to watch and then he goes down it. But I don't look at it. I don't want to see. I tell my dad I am going out now. I don't wait for him to say no. I don't care if he doesn't want me to. I don't want to be in the house anymore.

I pick up my tennis ball again and I go and play at the front. I hope that I see Faye again. There isn't anyone outside yet.

I just bounce it. I check if anyone comes out. I hope they do. I make the game in my head about it. Lots of different ways to catch the ball. Andrew is there too. I talk to him in my brain. We talk about lots of things. Maybe I am not real. I don't feel like I am really there. Maybe it is all a dream. Andrew doesn't know. It makes me feel like I float in my head.

I don't hear Faye coming over. "Hi," she says from the gate and I smile big because she is there. She asks me if I want to come and play again. I tell her I do. I bring my ball. She says we have to call for everyone else. There are lots of children.

We go to the house at the end of the road. The shop is

there. The boy is called Simon. His mum and dad own the newspaper shop. He must be very lucky because he gets sweets and chocolate all the time. He brings his bat. We are going to play a game like cricket. There are lots of children when we are ready.

There is a boy called Jason. He is younger than me. But he has a mad face. Like my dad's angry eyes. He swears lots when he talks too. He asks me who I am and I tell him. He says I can play. Maybe he is the boss of everyone. He says whose turn it is to be on the bat and whose turn it is to throw the ball.

I don't get to be the on the bat or the ball. I have to stand all the way back. Jason says I am tall so I can catch the ball and get them out. We play the game and my tummy hurts. But I try and play and catch. Sometimes it makes me feel like the sick will come out. But I don't let it. There isn't anything left inside anyway. I try to play very well. I want to catch the ball because then I get to be on the bat. I know I can hit the ball very far and very hard. I do it all the time at school. It takes them a long time to get me out. I want to have a go.

It is Faye's turn on the bat. Simon throws the ball. He throws it up and it is easy to hit. Faye hits it her hardest and it comes to me. Jason tries to run and catch it. But I am bigger than him. I jump up very high and I catch it. It doesn't go on the floor. Jason gets mad at me. He swears at me and calls me a bad name like my dad does. He was supposed to catch it not me. I am stupid. He gets his fist and he punches me very hard in my tummy. It makes me fall on the floor because my tummy is already sore. It makes me cough and I don't be able to breathe. He laughs about it. He laughs when I try to stand up. I don't let him see me cry. I don't want him to know. I swear at him when I can breathe. Then I get up and I run away. I don't want to play with them anymore. They are mean. No one else laughs. But he does and then they all walk away.

I run down the side of my mum and dad's house. It has a driveway and then it goes all the way to the back of the house. My mum and dad have a patio too. It has steps and flowers. I sit on the steps and hug myself all tight. I don't stop the crying. It feels all bad inside. No one ever likes me. They just hit me and tell me to go away. I don't know why I am so bad. I don't mean to be. They just always do bad things to me. I wish I could go away. I wish I don't be here anymore and then people don't hit me and make me cry. I feel it all inside. It makes me cry very hard. I don't be able to get it all out. I can't cry hard enough and it doesn't go away.

Fifteen

Maybe people will always do the bad things to me. I think about Jason. He didn't need to punch me. I just caught the ball like I was supposed to.

I don't know why he is mad about it. It makes me feel mad inside. I wipe the tears away. He doesn't get to hit me. I just did like I was supposed to. He is a bad loser. I don't like him. I don't want them all to think I am a baby.

I stand up and make myself all neat again. I clean my face all on my top. I don't want Jason to know that I cried. I don't cry now. He doesn't get to be mean to me like that. No one ever does. He is just like my dad. They hit me when I don't do anything wrong. They shouldn't do that. I don't know why they do. But Jason doesn't ever get to hit me again.

I run out of the back garden and up the driveway. No one is playing outside. Now they all went away. Jason spoilt our game. It was a good game. But he wanted to win and he didn't like that I caught the ball. He is a baby. Not me. I don't be. I played it better and I won and he didn't like it. I don't know where they are gone. But I am going to find them. I listen when I walk. I walk very fast. Maybe then they don't know I am coming.

Jason and everyone are in a garden. I don't know whose house it is. It is around the corner from my mum and dad's house. I see Jason and I run very fast. I don't stop not at all. I run into the garden and I shout his name and then I punch him very hard in his back. "You don't ever hit me again," I tell him. I shout it bad and I swear at him. I try to punch him again but he lies on the floor and he starts to cry about it. I didn't mean to make him cry. He was meant to be mad about it not sad.

He says he is sorry. He asks me not to hit him. I want to. But he makes my madness go away. I don't like it when people cry. I tell him okay. But he doesn't get to hit me ever again. He says he is sorry. He just got mad about it.

He asks if we want to play games. He asks if I have a bike then we can go down to the beach. There are big ramps there and they like to race on them. I tell him yes. I do have a bike. But it is old and rusty. It is a chopper. My dad got it for me from the rubbish tip. I like it though. We all go to get our bikes and then we meet at the end of the road.

Me and Jason get there first. He has some sweets and he offers me one. I take it. It is very nice. It is a ball of aniseed. I don't get them because my mum says sweets are a waste. Jason says that Simon gives everyone sweets. He gets them from his mum. He is very lucky.

Jason doesn't live with his mum and dad. He lives with

his grandma. But she is mean. He lifts his top and shows me. He has a line there. She hits him with her stick because he is always bad. He laughs about it. He tells me that he doesn't care. She is crazy. When he is big, he is going to move away and then he won't ever see her again. He doesn't know where his mum is. He says I am lucky because I have a mum and dad. I don't tell him about my dad.

The others come and we ride across the tram tracks to the rocks. We look over and it is very high. Maybe if we jumped down we could die. It has lots of rocks. It looks very good for climbing. I ask Jason if he ever climbed on them before. But he says no. "We get told off."

Maybe we can climb them. I want to. I don't be scared about falling off them. I can climb lots of big things. There is a big ramp that goes down between them. I don't ever see one so big before. I bet I can go very fast on it. I wish Mr. Ted got to see it. But I don't take him outside. Andrew sees it. But I don't talk to him when Jason and all the others are there. They don't see him and maybe they think I am strange like my dad does. Maybe they think I should be sent away.

We all get to the top of the ramp. There are five of us. Me, Jason, Faye, Simon and another boy called Chris. We all sit on our bikes. The ramp goes to the promenade and it is very long. Maybe if we can go fast enough we can be faster than cars.

Jason goes first. He stands on his bike and then he goes. He is very fast. I don't be scared. I go next. I don't jump my bike down like he did. I just make mine go on the ramp. It is so fast. I didn't know it would be so fast. It makes my tummy turn over. The wind makes my eyes water and my cheeks get to sting because it is cold. I don't breathe. It is so fast. I feel like maybe I can fly away. The bike rattles under me on the ground. I don't sit on the seat. I stand up on the pedals. Jason is miles and miles away. I go down the ramp but I don't turn the pedals. Maybe I don't want to go any faster. Then when I get to the bottom and it is all smooth it slows down. I start to pedal to catch Jason. I don't believe how fast I just went. He stops and then I catch him up and I stop too. I don't be able to breathe properly and when I get to Jason we just laugh about it. It was so good. I want to do it again.

The others come down after us. They come and stop their bikes next to me and Jason. We are next to the sea. The tide is in. It is windy and sunny all at the same time. Jason asks if we should do it again and I nod my head. But we have to get our bikes all the way up millions and millions of stairs. Maybe we get too tired carrying the bikes up. But we don't care. I like riding my bike with them.

We ride the bikes for a long time. We go all the way along. We go up and down the ramp. But we can't ride up the ramp because it is too stiff and it makes our legs ache. My legs don't even be able to pedal and the bike doesn't move. Jason laughs because I just sit there and not move until it falls sideways.

We go the other way later and pedal all the way to the other end. There are lots of ramps. It makes us all very tired. My legs ache and my fingers are cold. It is dark when I go home. I have to take my bike into the garage at the back. But I don't like to because it is too dark and I don't be able to see. My dad says I have to. I don't be allowed to use the front door either. He tells me now. I have to take my bike into the garage and then lock it all up. Then I run into the house and lock the back door behind me so no one gets me.

I don't get any dinner because it is all gone. They have done all the washing up too. They are in the lounge. My dad is reading and my mum is watching the television. My brother plays with his slide. I wish I got to go out again. But I have school in the morning. Jason said we can meet after school and then we can play out. I don't be able to wait. I like Jason. He is lots of fun.

Sixteen

My brother goes to bed. He has had lots of fun on his slide. I had lots of fun outside with Jason and all my friends. But I don't tell my mum and dad about it. Maybe they don't like me playing on the beach. They don't say anything about it. But it's okay. I tell Mr. Ted later. I tell him lots of things. He doesn't get to play outside. Maybe it makes him sad in his tummy. I give him lots of hugs.

I am hungry because I didn't get any dinner. I don't know if I am allowed to have any food. I ask my dad. "We shared your dinner out," he says. "If you can't be bothered to come home and eat it, then why should we bother to feed you?" I tell my dad I am sorry. I didn't mean to. I was just playing outside with my friends. I don't get dinner lots of times. I didn't know I had dinner. I don't ask for any more.

My dad tells me to come and sit down. I am allowed to stay up for one hour and watch the television with them. He doesn't let me watch television all the time. I try to watch it now. But my tummy flips around and I look at my dad. Maybe he wants me to do something and I don't know about it. I don't want him to do the hurt thing. I don't let him do it for two weeks. He doesn't get mad about it though.

I don't know that he is mad with me. He didn't shout

when I got in the house. But he smacks me across the face. It stings very bad and I didn't know he was there. It makes my brain bash inside my head. He shouts at me very loud. Maybe he is going to smack me again. I wasted the food and I didn't come in. I don't be any good. They buy this food and they cook it. Then I don't come home and eat it. I waste everything.

I don't get the crying out when he hits me. I look at my feet on the floor. Maybe he will stop shouting if I don't look at him. I tell him I am sorry in my brain. But I don't think he gets to hear it. I don't mean to waste food. I just didn't know I had any. They don't make me dinner lots of times.

My dad says I am a burden. I make all the house mad. I make everyone get in lots of fights because I think I can do as I want and I don't care about anyone else. It isn't true. I do care. I try to be good all the time. But I always make it bad. I don't mean to. The badness just happens. I am sorry that I am a burden. I don't mean to do that too.

My dad doesn't hit me again. He tells my mum he is going to bed. He tells me that my brother is in bed asleep and he is going to get in bed with him. My dad says he is a nice little boy. He says that to me when he does the hurt thing. Maybe he is going to do the hurt thing to my brother. I don't want him to. I don't want him to hurt my brother. He doesn't be allowed to. My brother is little and then he will cry about it.

My dad goes on the stairs. But he looks at me when he is walking. He walks slow and I feel scared inside. Maybe he will hurt him. I don't mean to make him do that. My dad goes all the way up the stairs. Then I hear the bedroom door be closed and my dad is in the bedroom.

I ask my mum if I can go to bed now. She says yes. She doesn't shout at me about the food. She doesn't say anything. But I tell her I am sorry. She says I am always sorry. But then I just do it again. I don't mean it.

I know I am bad. I am sorry. I just don't know how to not be bad all the time.

I walk up the stairs. It is dark at the top. I stand outside the doors. Maybe I can just go to bed. But maybe he does the hurt thing. I don't hear anything. I think about going to my room. Maybe I just go to bed. But I don't be able to. I feel it all inside. I knock on the door for my mum and dad's room. My dad says hello and tells me to come in. I get the door opened quietly.

My dad doesn't have his angry face. He smiles at me. He tells me to come and get in bed and then he can read a story. My brother is asleep in the bed next to my dad. I do as I am told. I get in the bed. I get in where my mum sleeps on the other side of the bed. My brother doesn't move.

I lie down and close my eyes. Maybe my dad will read a book. But he gets his hand over to me. I don't tell him no when he makes my pants unfastened and pulls them down. I keep my eyes closed. Maybe he can think I am asleep too. My dad climbs over my brother to my mum's side of the bed. He gets the covers off and takes my pants off. I look at my brother. He is facing me. But he is sleeping. I don't want him to wake up. I don't want him to see that I am bad inside and then I let our dad do the thing to me.

I hold my brother's hand. It is warm. I try not to make it hurt when I squeeze it. My dad puts his thing inside. My brother squeezes my hand back. I keep my eyes closed and then I don't see. My dad does the hurt part. I think about Jason and playing. Maybe tomorrow we can go on the beach again. We can go on the ramp and it can all be fast. My dad does the hurt thing until he makes all the sounds. He doesn't say any words to me. He gets off me and then he goes back to his side of the bed. I let go of my brother's hand. I pull my clothes up and I say goodnight to my dad. I go to my bedroom.

I didn't mean to be bad. I am sorry. I hear my dad get out of bed. I hear him talk to my brother and he puts him in his bed thing. Then my dad goes downstairs. I watch him walk past my door. He goes down to my mum and they watch the television. I get my pyjamas on and climb into my bed. Maybe I can go away in the nighttime.

Seventeen

I ask Mr. Ted about the hurt thing my dad does. Maybe it is bad that I don't let my dad do it. Then he doesn't like me lots more. I don't ever say no. He does it lots of times. I don't talk to Mr. Ted about it anymore. It makes me feel bad inside. Sometimes I go away and then I cry about it. I write it lots of times in my books. My brother doesn't do it. I don't know why I get to be so bad all the time. I wish it goes away.

Mr. Ted says maybe if I play outside with Jason then my dad doesn't get mad. I play with him lots of times. Even when the rain is out. We have adventures on our bikes. I write lots of stories about it. Maybe we can find magic places. But we don't ever.

I ask Santa when it got to Christmas time if I can get some things. I tried to be good all the time. I asked Mr. Ted about it. I tried my hardest. But I didn't get lots. My brother got lots. I asked Santa for a train set. I like trains they go very fast. But I didn't get one. Santa gave it to my brother instead. He got a big one on a board. It was so giant. We have to keep it on the table in the dining room. Then we don't eat at the table anymore. My dad says he will buy some trees and people and things for it. I tell Santa I am sorry. I don't know why he gave the train to my brother. My brother doesn't like it very much. He asks me to play with it lots of times. But I don't like to. It makes me sad in my tummy about it.

My dad tells me off if I play too much with it. "It isn't yours," he says to me. I nod my head about it. Then I hug Mr. Ted. Sometimes it makes me cry about it. I don't know why I cry. It is just a stupid train. Maybe it can get broken.

At the night-time, I go to my mum and dad's bed. My dad gives me a big hug. Then he does the hurt thing. He says he will buy me an engine that I get to use on the train set. I tell him thank you very much. I love my dad. But I don't like the hurt part that he does.

I try to be good all the time. Then my mum and dad don't send me away. It makes me scared in my tummy when we get to the summer time. I ask Mr. Ted about it. Maybe my mum and dad send me to the play place again. I don't want to go there. Everyone is excited at school because we finish for the long summer. But I don't. I don't want to ask my mum and dad. But I don't want them to make me go there again. It makes me think about all the bad things the people do. I don't like all the pictures in my head. I hug Mr. Ted about them. He doesn't like them too.

My mum says we are going out for the day. Because we don't have to go to school. We all go together. I say phew to Mr. Ted about it. Then we don't go to the play place. We don't go together when it is there. Maybe I don't ever go again.

My mum makes us get up lots of early. She is in the kitchen. She is making sandwiches and drinks. She puts them in the box that has the ice thing in them to make them cold all day long. My dad says food has to stay cold or then it makes us get the sick out. I don't like to get the sick out. It makes my mum mad when I make a mess.

I ask my dad where we are going. "Southport," he says. But I don't know where that is. Maybe it is very far away. I don't ever go there before. My dad puts the things in the boot. He puts in the box and a bag. There has to be a bag for all the rubbish. My mum makes us collect it all up. Then we put blankets in too. Maybe they are so we can have a picnic. I like picnics. We don't get them lots of times. I ask my dad if I can sit in the car. I don't want to sit in the boot. He says yes. I can sit next to my brother. I have been good. I ask my dad if Sheba is coming. He says yes. It is a long day. We don't leave her in the house all by herself.

Maybe she gets scared when we don't be at home. I ask her about it. But she doesn't know. Sheba gets in the car. She sits on the floor. It is a hot sunny day. I like to look out the window. I tell Sheba to look. She looks out the window. She likes to stick her head out when the car drives away. Then she sticks her tongue out. I try to do it but I don't be able to breathe.

It is a long time in the car. Maybe it is all day long. But my dad said it is just an hour. Maybe it was a very long hour. But my dad says I am stupid. Hours are all the same. It didn't take very long. My mum tells me to have the window closed. She doesn't like it open. She says it makes her neck cold and then it hurts. But the window doesn't blow on her neck.

My dad parks the car at a place. It is all sandy. There are lots of cars there. Maybe hundreds of them. They all line up on the sand. There are lots of children too. Lots of them are excited. They all run about and chase each other. My brother is excited. He jumps out of the car. But he doesn't be allowed to run off. We have to stay at the car. He is thirsty. My dad gives him a carton of juice. I go to my dad. But he doesn't give me one. I don't ask for it. Maybe he shouts at me. I wish I have Mr. Ted. He has to stay at the house.

My dad has to carry the box with the food in it. My mum carries the bag that has the blankets. My brother walks with them. I don't. I walk behind them. I don't be allowed to run off too. Sheba runs everywhere. She makes me laugh in my tummy about it. Maybe she is excited and wants to play.

We have to pay to go in the place. It sounds very noisy. Lots of people run around and make lots of excited noises. My dad has to buy a band thing. He puts it on my brother's arm. It is like a bracelet made out of paper. He gets a stamp on his hand too. The lady in the box asks if I am having a band too. But my dad says no. She puts stamps on everyone's hands.

There are some gates. The lady says we can go in there. We have to go one at a time. It has the bar thing that spins around. I push it and it lets me get in. Sheba runs under it. She is silly. She doesn't know that she has to push the bar thing.

It is all big inside. I didn't ever see it before. There are big giant blow up things to jump on. There is a house. It is blow up too. It is big and lots to jump about on. There is a big pool too. But it doesn't have wall. It has lots and lots of coloured balls. I went in one a long time ago when my Nan took me to the tower near her house. They are ball ponds. I like them very much. They are fun to jump in. I have lots of fun in them.

We have to sit on the grass. My mum and dad sit next to a table. They put their bags on it. My mum gets the blanket and she lays it flat on the ground. My dad takes my brother to another gate. There is a lady there. She has a big silly hat on, made from balloons. My dad shows the lady my brother's arm with the paper thing and she opens the gates. He goes inside to play. He has to take his shoes off. He leaves them at the side. He runs off very fast to the blow up house. He jumps and then he nearly slides off it. I don't keep the laughing away. Maybe he hurt himself. But he didn't.

I ask my dad if I can go there to play. My dad shakes his head about it. "It isn't for you," he says. I don't know why. I am not too big. There are lots of big people. It says fourteen outside.

I am nine. I don't be too old.

I say please to my dad. I promise to be good.

He laughs. "You don't know how to behave. You'll spoil it for your brother," he says. "We didn't come here for you."

I don't look at my dad. I don't let the stupid crying out. I ask my mum if I can sit on the blanket. She says no. I just get in the way. She tells me to go away. I get my book and I have a personal stereo with a tape in it. I sit at the bench. Then I don't get in the way. I read my book. I don't let the crying get out. It makes a big hole inside. I don't say anything to my mum and dad about it.

I read my book. I don't look at my brother. I don't look at the fun things he does. It is very hot. It makes me all sweaty. My brother comes out to my mum and dad. He is tired. He laughs lots because he has fun. He asks my mum and dad for a drink. I don't look at them too. I read my book. But I just read the same word lots of times. I don't want to hear my mum and dad. But I don't be able to keep them away.

My brother shows me his drink. I don't get one. I don't want to ask about it. I know I am very bad. I don't deserve to get nice drinks. I don't deserve to get to play. I wish I didn't be bad. I wish I knew how to be good like my brother. Then my mum and dad like me. I am sorry inside. I don't mean to be so bad.

My brother gives me his carton. He asks if I want to finish it. But I don't be allowed to. I look at my mum and dad. They lie on the blanket. They have their eyes closed. I tell my brother thank you. I drink some. But I don't drink it all.

My brother runs back to the lady. She lets him in the blow up place again. I hear him shout. He shouts my names and tells me to watch. But I don't want to see. He goes on the big slide that is from the top of the house and it goes to the bouncy part. Then he slides down it. It looks like lots of fun. I try to read my book. I don't look at my brother.

The lady at the gate lets lots of people in. Maybe she can let me in and she doesn't look at my arm. I don't have a paper thing. She doesn't look at lots of people's arms. I go there quiet. Andrew thinks it is a bad idea. Maybe we get in big trouble. But she doesn't look at my arm. I get in the blow up place. I take off my shoes very fast. Then I put them with my brother's. My mum and dad don't get to see. I get to him very fast. He is excited I get to play. I chase him. He screams and runs away. But I am bigger than him and he doesn't be able to get away. He laughs about it. I pick him up and throw him on the bouncy thing.

He tries to run and knock me over. But I jump out of the way and he doesn't get me. Then I run away and he doesn't get me because he is little and I am big. I can run faster than he can. I laugh because he doesn't catch me.

It gets to be time to eat something. But I don't go. There isn't anything for me. I don't want anything. I don't listen to my tummy get hungry and I don't want to go out. Maybe I don't get back in because I don't have a paper thing. My brother goes. He sits with my mum and dad. I see them laugh. They have lots of fun. Maybe because I don't be there. It is always nice when I don't be with them. Then my badness doesn't make all the bad things and they don't fight about everything.

My brother eats all his food. My mum doesn't write it in a book anymore. He eats lots of food. He is very fat. My dad laughs about it because he is heavier than me. I watch a film with Jason about looking for pirate treasure. It has a fat boy in it. They make him shake his fat belly. I get my brother to do that. It is very funny. But my dad shouts when my brother does it. He calls him a stupid fat demic. I don't know what that is. But it makes my brother sad. He doesn't shake any more.

Eighteen

We play in the bouncy thing for a long time. We play until three o'clock. Then it has to close for the day. The lady doesn't catch me and my mum and dad don't catch me too. I am very good at sneaking. My dad says we are going somewhere else.

I help my mum and dad put all the stuff in the bags. Maybe they know I can be good. I ask my mum if she wants me to carry the food box. She says yes. It isn't heavy because it is all empty now. I carry it. Me and Sheba walk together. She runs around because she is having a good day. I don't have Mr. Ted. He is at home. I don't take him lots of places because I am too big and no one knows that he is magic. I don't tell them. He keeps the bad man away. The bad man doesn't ever come at the new house yet. But maybe if Mr. Ted doesn't stop him then he can come back. I hope Mr. Ted doesn't be sad at the house all by himself.

I put the things in the car and we drive to the new place. It isn't very far away. It is big. It has rides like the one near my Nan's house. But the rides look big and it is very noisy. My dad parks the car in the car park. We have to put Sheba on a lead because maybe she gets lost. I don't want her to get lost. So I hold it and she walks with me.

The place is called Pleasure Land. It is a big fun fair. My brother has never been to one. He was too little and didn't go with my Nan. But my mum and dad doesn't let her take him. Maybe she gets him lost. She will try and steal him. But she doesn't. She is very nice. They just don't know about it.

We walk inside. My brother asks if he can go on the ride that looks like big giant ladybirds. My dad says yes. They have to buy a ticket. They buy it at the gate and then the man lets my brother get on. He doesn't know which one to pick. They are lots of different colours. I ask my dad if I can go on it too. It is for babies. But maybe I can sit with my brother. Maybe if I go on the little ones with my brother, I can get to go on the big ones. I like the ones that drop from very high places. They make my breath go away and my tummy jumps up and then I scream. My Nan thinks I am crazy because I like them so much. But they are fun.

My dad says I can't go on the rides. He doesn't say why. I don't want to ask him. I try to be good. I try to keep all the badness away. I stand at the bar and I watch my brother. I smile at him. He waves his hands big at me and he yells about it. I don't get the crying away. They come out of my eyes. But I smile to my brother. I don't let my mum and dad see the crying. Then they will say I deserved it. It is good when I cry. I don't want them to know. I wipe it on my sleeve when no one knows about it and then no one can call me a baby.

My brother doesn't see the crying part. His ride goes all high up in the sky and it spins around. He has lots of fun. I wish I got to be like my brother. Then my mum and dad could like me and I get to go on things.

My dad buys my brother some candyfloss. My mum holds it. She gets an ice cream. I don't ask for any. I don't want them. I don't like stupid candy floss anyway. Maybe the ice cream melts away and falls on her dress then she can be mad about it. My Nan buys me lots of candyfloss when we go to the other place near her house and my brother doesn't get any. I have had more candyfloss than he has ever.

My brother gets off the ride. He tells me all about it. He is very happy. It made his tummy tickle. He asks me if I saw him all up in the sky. I tell him I did. It was very big.

My dad gives him the candyfloss and then my brother asks about the next ride. I don't be allowed.

My brother goes on lots of rides. He doesn't go on the big ones because he gets scared. He doesn't like them because they make his tummy tickle too much. My mum doesn't like them too. But I do. I don't be allowed on them.

I don't get anything. My brother gets lots of sweets and candyfloss. My dad says I have to ask my brother. But he doesn't want to share it. The things are all his. He has a giant cup of coke. It is a special cup with a bendy straw. He gets to keep it and take it home. I ask my brother if I can have some. But he says no. He goes on a ride. He asks me to hold it.

I drink some when he doesn't look. It is cold and icy. It makes my throat freeze inside. My brother sees me drinking it. He shouts very loud about it. I put it down very fast. But my mum and dad are mad at me for it. My mum takes it off me. She shouts at me. I always do what I want. I don't do what others say. I tell her I am sorry. I was thirsty. She says I can have a drink of water. They have fountains at the middle I can go and get some from there. But I want coke. I don't want water. My mum says it is tough. I don't behave so I don't get things. It is my own fault. If I want to have things then I have to be good like my brother does. But he doesn't be good.

We are going to get some dinner. It has been a long day. My brother is tired. He has been on all the rides. He likes them. My mum says we can have chips. I know I don't get any. We walk to the place that makes them. I don't walk with them. My brother talks lots about his fun day. I don't want to hear about it. It makes the tears come out. I don't like when they do that. I don't make them go away. I know my mum doesn't like me and that I am very bad.

My mum and brother sit at a tall thing and wait for my dad to get the fish and chips. I don't sit with them. I know they will shout at me and then they won't buy me any food. I don't want to smell it. Then it makes me hungry. Me and Sheba sit at a different place. But she wants to sit with them. They have food and they give her some. I don't go. I stay at the other table. I play with the lolly stick that is on there and I make lines on the table with it.

My mum shouts at me. I am being a sulky pants she says. I should come and sit with them. But I don't want to. I fold my arms on the table and then I lean on them and she can't see my face and she doesn't see the crying. Then she doesn't laugh at me about it. She laughs because I sulk because I am spoilt.

My dad brings me over some chips in a tray and some fish. He tells me I better eat it or there is trouble. I tell him thank you. I am stupid. I didn't think they would give me food. I pick it up and go to my mum and dad's table. I don't know why I get all silly about it. Maybe if I just be good I can get things. Maybe I have been good and that is why I get the chips and things.

I eat it all up. I don't waste any. I am still hungry after. But there isn't anything else. We are going to walk on the seafront and then we can go to the shops. My mum wants to look at some things. I am tired. I wish we could go home. I know I don't get anything from the shops. My brother will get lots.

We don't have to drive there. It is near the Pleasure Land. We walk outside and my dad gives my brother a piggy back. We go in lots of shops. I walk behind and play on the path. I don't step on the cracks. Me and Sheba jump on them. But she doesn't play it right and she stands on them. She doesn't be very good.

I walk behind my mum and dad. Maybe they forget I am there. Maybe I can go and get lost and they won't know about it. Maybe they will be happy if I go and get lost. But I don't know where I am supposed to go. Maybe it is scary at night outside alone.

Nineteen

I fall to sleep in the car. It is tired inside my head. I try to keep my eyes open. But they don't want to. My brother goes to sleep too. He is asleep very fast. Sheba sleeps on the floor. She keeps my feet warm. Sometimes she moves and then she tickles my leg because I have shorts on. It makes it itchy. She snores very loud. My dad laughs about it.

My brother hogs the whole chair in the car. He gets in my way. He is big and fat and takes lots of space. I push him with my foot. Then he can move out of the way. But he makes a noise like a big baby. My mum tells me off about it. She tells me to stop picking on my brother. But I don't. She doesn't know. She thinks he is good. But he isn't. He is bad lots of times. He smiles about it. I kick him. Maybe it can hurt.

He cries about it. He is a big baby. My mum turns around and slaps my leg. I don't cry. I am not a big baby like my brother. I fold my arms and look at my mum with my mad eyes. She tells me off. Maybe I want to get out of the car and walk home. I don't. I say I am sorry. But I don't mean it.

I lean on my arm on the door. I watch all the lights and the people. It is nighttime. My eyes don't want to stay open. They make my head fall forwards and then it makes me jump. It makes the sick in my tummy when it happens. I don't like it. My neck feels tired too. I try to make my eyes stay awake. But they don't want to. I am very good at making my eyes stay awake. I do it at home when I am in bed. Then I stay awake all night long and read my books. Then I know the bad man doesn't sneak in the room. Me and Mr. Ted have to watch and make sure.

It is cold when we get home. The wind comes from the sea. It makes me shiver. I don't have my coat. My mum says my brother has to have the blanket. She doesn't want him to get sick again. I hope he gets very cold. Then he can freeze. Sometimes I freeze in my room. Sometimes it is so cold and I don't get more blankets. Then I can't move because it is so cold. I don't like it when it is like that. Maybe I freeze to death and no one knows about it.

I help my dad get all the things in the house. Sheba lies by the fire. My mum put it on for my brother. He has to get his pyjamas on and go to bed. He doesn't sleep in my mum and dad's bed. It is very late. We all have to go to bed.

"You sleep in our room tonight," my dad says. I smile very big about it. Then I don't have to sleep in my room. I don't like my room when we don't be in the house all day. Maybe the bad man got in and he can hide. I don't get to find him. It makes me check lots of times. Maybe he is there and I didn't look right. If I sleep in my mum and dad's bed then he doesn't come. He just gets stuck in his hiding place.

Good.

I don't want him to come. Maybe he can freeze to death.

When all the stuff is in the house, we put it away. My mum takes my brother to bed. I have to go and brush my teeth. And I have to use the toilet. There doesn't be another time. I have to wait until the morning time otherwise. I make myself use the toilet. Then I don't need it at nighttime and I don't get shouted at when I ask about it because I wake my mum and dad up. They don't like it when I do that. Then they ask why I didn't go earlier when it was time. But I didn't need it then.

I get my pyjamas on. I don't be allowed to wear underwear inside. My mum says when I sleep in underwear they get smelly. But I don't like when I don't wear them. My clothes get see-through because they are small. I try to make it all hide. But my dad still sees. He looks all the time and I don't like it. Then he puts his finger in his mouth and makes the sucky noise. I don't like that too. I don't want him to do those things. They make me feel all bad inside. I try to make it wash away. But it never does. I try to make it cut away too. But that doesn't work. I don't get anything right.

I go upstairs. But I don't go in my bedroom. It is dark in there. I don't want to. I don't look at the door. It is made from glass. I don't want to see if the bad man hides in there. Maybe he can see me. I tell Mr. Ted in my brain I am sorry. I miss him very much. But it is very scary in there. Maybe the bad man comes out and then he grabs me. My mum and dad are downstairs. They get the doors and windows locked. Then my dad makes some tea so he can take it to bed. My mum goes to the bathroom and then she gets changed too and brushes her teeth.

I don't know if I am allowed to get in bed. I don't want to make the covers messy. My mum makes them flat and tight. Then I don't be able to move them. Sometimes it is very hard to get in my bed. They get too tight. My brother is sleeping. He is all worn out. He didn't wake up very much to go in the house. Then my mum and dad put him in bed when he was warm. They make him a hot water bottle for his bed too. But he has it wrapped in a cover. It makes his hands hurts when he hugs it. I think it smells funny. I don't get one of them.

My mum and dad have a magic blanket. It makes the bed hot. My dad plugged it in when they put my brother in bed.

My mum and dad come upstairs. My mum turns the light off for the stairs. Then she comes up. My dad tells me to get in bed. I get in his side. Then I don't make my mum's side all messy. The bed is nice and warm inside. Maybe it makes me fall to sleep and I don't know about it. My mum and dad lie in bed. My dad drinks his tea. They talk about boring things. I don't listen. I lay still and don't move. I don't have Mr. Ted. I hope he is okay. I hope the bad man doesn't get him and make him bleed to death.

Maybe I was very tired and I didn't know about it. I didn't know I fell to sleep. I didn't know my dad got my pants off. I didn't know he was going to do the hurt thing. It hurts and makes me wake up and cry. My dad tells me to shush. It is ok. He does it nice. But I didn't know about it. Then it makes it hurt more. I didn't know he was going to do it. I was asleep.

My mum has the cover off. My dad doesn't lie on me. He makes me lie on my side. My mum gets to see. I wish I got to sleep in my own bed. Then I didn't get the hurt part when I was asleep. Then my mum doesn't see.

I make my face squish in the pillow. I don't let the crying out. I open my mouth and breathe big. The breath makes my face sweaty. It makes my head sleepy. Then I don't think about my dad's thing inside and I don't think about my mum getting to see.

My dad hugs me very tight. He gets his hand and he does the touching me part. I don't like when he does that. He says it is good. He says that is because I like it. I don't mean to like it. My dad hugs me with his arm on my chest. I hold his arm when it gets to the part that makes my breath go away. My dad makes the hug tighter when it is that part. He tells me it is good. I don't look at my mum. She knows I am bad. I make everything bad.

When he makes the noise too, then he lets me go. He doesn't hug me anymore. I feel all cold inside. I try to hug myself up. It all hurts because I didn't know about it. My mum puts the covers back. I don't get my pyjamas back. I make myself into a ball. Then I can go away. I close my eyes so I don't see. I go to sleep. I keep the tears all inside forever.

Twenty

I wish Jason got to play. But he doesn't. He has a poorly tummy. He gets the sick out. But it's okay. I have a poorly ear too. I tell my brother maybe we can play the Lego. I didn't play with him yet in the summertime. I play outside every day. Then I stay out with my friends. We get up very early in the morning. Then we ride our bikes around and play lots of games. I play outside until it is home time. My mum says I have to be in at nine o'clock. I don't get to be late or it is big trouble. Then I get ready for bed and my dad reads a story. Then he does the hurt thing.

He does the hurt thing every night. If I am very bad, then I get sent to my room and he doesn't want to do it. I tell Mr. Ted I am sorry. I don't mean to be bad lots of times. But sometimes me and Jason get lots of fun. Then I don't know what time it is and I get in too late. My dad waits at the door in the kitchen. Then he smacks me about it and makes me sit in the chair. I don't like the chair. He makes me sit there a long time. I tell him I will be good. I make a big promise inside.

I have to go home early because Jason doesn't feel very good. But then I don't get in trouble because I don't be late. My brother asks me to play Lego when I come back in the house. I don't want to play it. But I did before. I said I would play. Now my ear hurts and I feel cold inside. I don't want to play. Maybe he can play it by himself. I wish I got to go to bed instead. But I am not allowed. It is evening time.

My brother asks me to play. He says please lots of times. But I don't want to. I tell him no. He starts to cry about it like a big stupid baby. My dad comes in. He was in his room reading his book. He asks what is going on. I tell him nothing. But he says I tell lies. He asks my brother. My brother tells him I don't play Lego. He tells him I promised I would.

My dad asks me why I don't want to play. I tell him my ear hurts inside. But my dad says I don't play Lego with my ear. I tell him I want to go to sleep. But he says I will feel better if I don't mope about it. But I don't mope. I don't feel very good. It feels sick in my tummy like Jason. I didn't get any medicine. The sick is just there. Maybe it wants to come out.

My dad smacks me across the leg. He makes it hard and I don't have long pants on. I have shorts on because I don't have any pants left. He smacks me very hard at the top of my leg. My brother doesn't cry anymore. I make him jump when I cry about my leg.

My dad shouts at me. He swears and calls me bad names. I know I am bad. I don't mean to be. He tells me I had better stop crying. I try to make it go away. I try to hold my breath inside and then the crying goes away. But my leg hurts very bad and my ear does too. My dad gets mad about it. He grabs my arm and then he makes me stand up. He pulls me very fast and I nearly fall over. He is going to put me in the dining room.

"I don't want to go in the dining room. It is cold. I am sorry. I didn't mean it. I will play Lego. I promise."

I didn't know it was there. It just comes out and I don't know about it. The sick comes out. It gets all on the floor. I know it is bad to do that too. I didn't mean to. I am just very bad. All inside my badness gets there. The sick keeps coming out. My dad lets go of my arm. He stands and watches me. I know he is mad. I didn't mean to get it on the floor. I tell him I am sorry. But the sick keeps trying to get out when I talk. I cry too. It makes the sick burn inside.

I am disgusting. That is what my dad says. I made a mess and I am disgusting. When the sick stops my dad gets my arm again. He makes me go into the kitchen. I don't want him to pull me. It hurts my arm. Maybe he will pull it off. I wish I had a drink to make the sick taste go away. But I don't. I feel all hot inside. My dad opens the cupboard under the sink and pulls out a bowl. He gives it to me. Then he gives me the bottle of soap stuff my mum uses when she cleans up.

"You better get that cleaned up," my dad says. "I don't want to see it or smell it when you are done. I will be back in ten minutes"

I nod my head and I say I will. I tell him I am very sorry. I didn't mean to do it.

I make the bowl filled with hot water and bubbles. I get the cloth from under the sink. I know we don't use the one on the sink. That is for dishes. My mum gets mad if it goes on anything else. I take the bowl into the dining room and put it on the floor. The sick smells all bad. It makes my tummy turn upside down again. I don't mean to be sick again. I stand up very fast and run to the kitchen. I get the sick in the bin. It doesn't go on the floor. Then my mum and dad don't get mad about it. Lots of sick comes out.

I wish I could go to sleep. My tummy hurts inside. I am very hot. My head wants to go to sleep about it. Maybe I can fall over. Maybe I got on a roundabout and didn't know about it. My head feels funny inside.

I go back in the dining room. I don't let the smell get in my nose. I clean the floor up. I have to change the bowl. I don't put it in the sink. I do it outside. We don't be allowed to use the sink either. It is just for dishes.

My dad said he would be back in ten minutes. But maybe it has been a long time and he doesn't remember. He said he wanted to check it. I can see the clock in the lounge. It has a butterfly on it. It is my mum's. She got it for her birthday. I watch the big hand go all the way around. My dad doesn't come and check. I made the sick all wash away.

Then I see my dad. He comes out of his room. Then he sits on the sofa with my brother. They put cartoons on. My dad doesn't look at me. He doesn't see. I am glad. I run to the bin and I get the sick out again. I am glad it is nighttime and my mum is in the bath. She takes a long time to get a bath. Then she doesn't get mad about all the sick.

I don't know if I am allowed to go and sit down. I don't ask my dad because maybe he gets mad. Maybe he will shout at me. Maybe he will smack me and tell me I am bad. I know I am bad. I stand by the place the sick came out. I wait for my dad to come and check.

My mum finishes her bath. She doesn't come in the dining room too. She sits on the floor by the fire. I wish I got to do that. I am all cold inside. It makes me shake very bad. I look at the clock. The big hand has gone all the way around the clock three times. Maybe it is nearly bedtime. I want to go and lie down and go to sleep. My head hurts very bad inside. The sick doesn't come out any more. Just three times and now maybe it is all gone. I didn't get any more on the floor. I got it all in the bin.

My dad turns the television off. They are finished watching it. He comes into the dining room. My tummy jumps inside. Maybe he will shout at me. Maybe the floor didn't be cleaned enough. My dad stands still. He makes the smelling face like Sheba does when she puts her nose in the air. He asks me if I am okay.

I tell him I don't feel very well. My tummy is poorly.

He asks me why I didn't tell him. "You don't need to stand here in the dining room. You could have gone to bed if you told us you were sick," he says.

I try to say something. But he makes the face that will get mad if I say something wrong. I don't say any words to him. I know I am dumb because I didn't say I was sick. I tell him I am sorry. Then I go to bed. I say goodnight. He says goodnight too.

Twenty One

I know I am very bad. Maybe that is why my tummy was all poorly. The sick came out lots of times. It made me scared in my tummy. Maybe I get it on the floor then I get in trouble. But I get it in the sink in my bedroom. I ask Mr. Ted if that is okay. He says yes.

I don't get poorly again. Jason was poorly too. But he got better. We get to play out for all the summer days. We play at the front. Then my brother can play too. We play lots of ball games. The summertime goes away very fast. Then we all have to go to school again. But we play lots of times at the nighttime after school. Even when it is a very cold day, we play.

I see the nice doctor drive near our house. He drived his car onto our street. But then he turned around again and went away. I tell my mum about it when I go in. She asks lots of questions. But we have to keep it a secret. Then my dad doesn't know about it. I tell her. My mum calls him Batman because he has a fast car. Then it is a secret code. She asks me if I am sure. I nod my head very big. I tell her the numbers off the front of the car.

She folds her arms and has a big smile. "Yes, that is his car," she says. "I bet he's spying on me. He doesn't like me being with anyone else. He is very possessive."

I am glad my mum gets happy about it. She tells me to play out lots of times. I do. I play out for lots of days. Sometimes he doesn't come. But my mum asks and when I say no it makes her sad inside. So I tell her he did. I tell her he drived passed. Sometimes he stops and looks down the road. My mum always asks me lots of things about it. I ask Mr. Ted and he tells me it is very good. We have to make mum happy. Then she doesn't get mad at us. Sometimes Andrew sees the nice doctor Batman come. He tells me about it. Then I tell my mum. I don't tell her Andrew saw him. She doesn't know Andrew. He is a secret.

Lots of days go past. I don't get a birthday again. I don't ever get them. No one got to know about it. It went away. I am ten. No one said happy birthday about it. I try to be good all the time. But maybe I am just very bad. I try to tell my mum lots of times about the nice doctor. But it doesn't make me good.

I don't be bad when my Nan comes. She is coming today. It is Friday. She always comes on Fridays. She comes after she has been to a place called Mind. They look after her there. She isn't very well inside. It makes her sad still that my Gaga has gone to heaven. She misses him. I miss him too. I wish he didn't die. Then he could still be here. Sometimes me and my Nan talk about him. We talk about all the funny things he did. My Nan says that when I was very little, I copied him lots of times and it made him laugh. Then he did silly things to make me do silly things.

My Nan comes when I get back from school. She gets the bus by herself. But then later my dad takes her home. She eats her dinner at our house. And then she watches the television. I like it when my Nan is there. Then I get dinner too. We have big roast chicken. It has lots of potatoes and gravy. My dad puts some white sauce on it. I like that the best. I wish I had just that. I could eat it forever. My brother doesn't eat the chicken though. My mum says he doesn't like it. He gets special dinner. It has chicken fingers and chips. He eats it with mayonnaise and tomato ketchup. He has cheese too. But it is funny cheese. It is floppy and comes in plastic. I don't like it very much. I like the big yellow cheese that maybe hides the mice. That is better. I like it on toast.

I am very hungry in my tummy. I have to wait until my dad comes home from work. He doesn't come home until after seven. Then we get dinner. My brother gets his dinner when he comes home from school. He is very lucky. Then he doesn't get hungry all the time. But he gets dinner every day. I don't because I am bad. I don't know how to be good. I get two dinners in the week. When my Nan is there and the one on Sunday. But I don't always get the Sunday one. If I have been too bad I don't get it.

I didn't get dinner last Sunday. Now it is Friday. I didn't have dinner all week long. My tummy growls like a lion inside it. I don't look at my brother's dinner. It makes me want to steal it. I think about it. But then I know I get in big trouble. Maybe it makes me drool like Sheba does when she wants the food. He eats it. I go and play with Jason then I don't have to look at it. But I am not allowed to play out a long time because it is Friday. We eat the special dinner and I can't be late or I get in big trouble about it.

I come in at six. Then I don't be late. My Nan is outside talking to my mum. They talk in the garden because it is nice outside. My Nan likes the garden and all the flowers. Dinner is cooking. It smells nice in the house. Maybe I can taste it if I close my eyes. I wish I could eat it right now. But I have to wait an hour. Maybe that is a long time away. Maybe time takes too long to get there. I want to eat the dinner now. I am so hungry. Maybe it makes me go crazy. It makes my tummy rumble. I don't do anything else. I wait for dinner. But the time doesn't go fast enough.

Maybe I can get some bread. Sometimes I do that when I don't have dinner. I sneak it in the kitchen when my mum and dad doesn't look. They don't know about it. Then I pinch the bread and I make it in a ball and put it in my pocket. Then I go away and eat it and no one knows about it. It makes my tummy stop hurting.

It is just one piece of bread. It isn't a lot. My mum keeps it all in the breadbin. I open it quickly and I take one out of the packet. I fold the bread up like paper. Then I put it all in my mouth so no one sees. There isn't anyone around.

My tummy is still hungry. Maybe I can have two. I don't have two sometimes. I just get one. But I didn't eat anything all day. I am very hungry. No one knows about it. I look through the glass. I can see all the way to the lounge. No one is there. My mum and Nan can't see because they are on the patio. They don't see me from there. I get another piece of bread. I fold it up again and then I put it in my mouth and squash it. I don't take any more. Then I get too greedy and maybe I get told off.

I go out of the kitchen and in the dining room. I don't know my brother was there. He hides by the window. He makes me jump. I don't say anything. Maybe he didn't see. But he did.

"I'm telling on you," he says. He is going to tell my dad what I did. He makes stupid na na na sound at me. It makes me mad inside. He has a toy in his hand. I take it off him. Then I pull the head off and throw it at him. Then I get to say the na na thing to him because he cries about his stupid doll.

He tries to get the head back on. But it doesn't want to go. He starts to cry about it. He is a big baby. He cries about everything. I tell him to go away. I don't like him. But he doesn't say anything.

My Nan comes in. Lots of time goes past. Then it is time for the food. My dad comes home. He washes his hands. They are black and full of oil. He tells me to make the table. I have to get all the knives and forks and then I put them with mats at the table so we can eat. We all sit there together. I sit with my Nan. I like sitting there. She gives me the skin off her chicken because she doesn't like it. I eat it. It is my favourite bit. I eat all my dinner until I will go pop. I don't leave any. Then my dad says I have to take all the plates in the kitchen. I scrape all the food in the bin. I am not allowed to leave a mess. Sometimes my dad gets mad because my mum doesn't make me wash the dishes. But she says no one does it right. The plates will get broken. It makes my dad mad about it. He says I should do it. But she tells him no.

I go and play with Jason after. But I come home at nine. Then my dad takes my Nan home again. He takes her in the car because it is dark. I wonder why my Nan isn't scared about the bad man. Maybe he doesn't ever come when she is there. She doesn't say about him.

My dad gets chocolate from the shop when he comes back. He always buys lots of it. But I don't get it. I am not allowed. He gives some to my brother and he gives some to my mum. My brother isn't mad at me anymore. We sit and watch the television. He asks me if I want a sweet. I tell him thank you. I eat it very quickly. If my mum and dad see it then I get in trouble for it. So I don't let them see.

Then my mum and dad argue in the kitchen. They shout a

lot and they swear. My mum is mad. I don't know why. Maybe it is because I was bad. But my brother isn't mad about it. Maybe he didn't tell.

My mum gets very mad. She walks very fast from the kitchen to us. I hug myself tight. Maybe she will shout at me. But she doesn't. She goes out of the other door. She bangs it very hard. Maybe the glass will fall out. It shakes very hard. My dad chases after her. But he stops. Then he looks at me. "This is all your fault," he says. I say I am sorry. But he doesn't want to hear it.

My brother doesn't like it when they shout. It makes him cry. I ask him if he wants to read a story. We can read it in my room. He doesn't know how to read properly. But I show him. He gets good at his words. It makes him smile. We turn the television off and go upstairs. Maybe they are happy we go to bed.

We don't listen when they shout. I make all the words loud so my brother doesn't hear them. He is in my bed with me. I make him lie at the side next to Mr. Ted because it makes me too scared. The bad man doesn't get my brother.

Then my dad shouts my name. I get scared inside my tummy.

Twenty Two

I promise that I don't tell lies. I will tell the truth. Please make it all go away.

My dad calls my name. It makes me not breathe inside. I listen. Maybe he didn't shout me. Maybe I just hear things. But he shouts it again and I know I am in big trouble. Maybe my brother told about his toy. Maybe that is why my mum and dad get mad at each other. Maybe he told about the bread too. I look at him. But he is asleep. He didn't say that he told. He always says when he told. Then he can laugh about it.

I get out of bed. I have to do it quiet and then my brother doesn't wake up. I don't want him to be scared. He gets scared when my dad shouts. Then he starts to cry and then I get in big trouble. I make everything bad in the house. I press the button on the radio. Then my brother doesn't hear the shouting. I use it when I don't want to hear the bad man. It makes all the noises go away. But it goes off by itself when it has been an hour and then I don't get in trouble for wasting electricity.

My dad walks backwards from the stairs. He moves so I can get down them. My mum is there too. She stands behind him. They both stare at me. It makes me scared inside. I don't know what I am supposed to say. Maybe I have to say sorry. But I don't know what for. Maybe I should tell them about the bread and the toy. But I don't want to. Maybe they don't know about it and then I tell them and then it is big trouble.

My dad says "Well?" and I don't know what to say. I don't say anything. But he says it again and he shouts it.

I tell my dad about the toy. I tell him I am sorry. I didn't mean it. I got mad. I don't know why I am bad all the time. It just happens and then I don't keep it away. I don't tell him it is because of the bread. I don't tell him that part. Then I know he gets very mad.

He asks me why. But I don't know. I look at my feet. I don't cry about it. I know I am in big trouble. I don't know what to say about it.

My mum asks if there is anything else. I don't like it when she says that. Maybe she knows. But then if I say it and she didn't know I get in trouble. I don't like it when they ask me what I did. Then I don't know if they know about it. Sometimes it is a secret and I tell them by accident.

I tell my mum there isn't anything else. It is just the toy. I am very sorry. I don't mean to. I won't ever do it again.

My dad has big steps. He moves very fast and then he gets to me. He grabs my arm and makes his fingers dig in. I nearly fly when he drags me. I try not to fall over. He walks very fast. I try to tell him to stop. But he doesn't. We get to the kitchen then he pushes me very hard. I don't stop myself and I fall over on the floor. It hurts my side. My dad comes in the kitchen too. He is mad. He has his angry face. He doesn't say any words. But I know it is about the bread.

My mum tells him I stole the bread. I was bad and a thief. Thieves don't ever get trusted. They tell lies and no one likes them. My dad asks me why. But I don't say it. He asks me if I don't get enough food. Do I think they don't look after me right. But I don't say any words. I don't want to be in trouble. He feeds me all the time when I am good. But I am just bad all the time instead.

He tells me that I steal the bread because I am no good. I nod my head. He is right. I know I am no good. I make it all bad. I tell him too. He says yes.

He bends down and grabs my arm. He drags me. I don't get time to stand up. I try to make it. But it doesn't work. My dad is too strong and too fast. He takes me into the dining room. My mum has put the chair by the window. I have to sit on that chair when I am bad. I don't get to move until my mum says so. Sometimes they leave me there a long time. Maybe one day they leave me there forever. My dad tells me to get my pants down. I don't want to. I shake my head.

He shouts it at me. "Take your pants down." I don't want to. It makes it hurt in my tummy. I don't keep the crying away. I try not to cry very bad and talk. But my words don't get out. He shouts it at me lots of times. I do as I am told. Then he tells me to kneel on the chair. I don't want to do that. I know he is going to make it hurt. He shouts it at me in my face. It makes me shake inside. My head hurts. I cry very bad. But I get on the chair like he says.

I hug my head all tight. I don't want him to do the hurt part. He tells me to shut up. I hug my head all tight and make the loud cries be quiet. I hear his belt. It makes my tummy hurt. Maybe I need the toilet on accident. I don't want him to do the hurt thing. He will make it hurt very bad. But he doesn't. He gets the belt and then it smacks across my bottom. It makes me cry very loud. But I don't let it out. I know I will get shouted at. He does it two more times.

I don't keep the crying or the shaking away. He tells me to sit on the chair. But it hurts very bad. He tells me I have to do it now or he will do it again. The crying makes my head feel like it wants to pop. Maybe it does. He doesn't let me pull my pants up.

My mum and dad go away. They go into the lounge. I don't look at them. I don't move at all. I know I get shouted at if I do. I am very cold. I don't keep the shivers away. It is a very long time and my legs get all funny. They get the pins and needles. Then I don't feel them. My mouth hurts because I make it stay closed. Then my teeth don't bash together because I am cold.

It is a long time. My dad comes into the dining room. I try to hug myself all up. Maybe he gets mad. But they are going to bed. I have to go to bed now. He doesn't want to see me anymore. I do all the bad things. He tells me to get to my room now and don't make any sound. I get my pants up and then I try to run. But my bottom hurts from the belt. It makes me cry again. I try to sneak in my room. My brother is asleep. I try to sneak on the bed. I get inside it. I don't let the crying be loud. I don't want my brother to see it. I don't sniff then it doesn't make him wake up. I close my eyes. Maybe I can go to sleep and go away. But my brother hugs me and he holds my hand. But he doesn't wake up.

Twenty Three
(Age Ten)

My brother is a scardy cat. He doesn't like the dark. It makes him not sleep. He doesn't like to go to bed all by himself. He is scared. He says there is a man. He comes in the bedroom when it is dark. He doesn't like him. He makes my dad put a towel on the mirror. My brother says the man stands at the door and then he sees his face. It makes him all scared inside. Then he wets the bed. He wets the bed lots of times. My dad calls him names about it.

He uses swear words. My brother is fat and he wets the bed. He is smelly and a baby. That is what my dad says. But he uses bad words. I don't get to say them. When we had Christmas time, my dad called him lots of names because he got lots of chocolate and he ate it all up. My dad says he doesn't get any Easter eggs. No one gets any. I am too bad and my brother is too fat. But I don't care. I don't ever get them anyway.

My dad doesn't keep the bad man way from me. But the bad man hasn't been for a long time. I just get scared about it. My dad calls me names too because I am scared and I still sleep with Mr. Ted. Then he laughs about it.

When I get very scared sometimes, I don't want to go in my bedroom. My brother goes to sleep in my mum and dad's bed. My dad is there too. He reads him stories. I go in. My dad smiles at me and then he pulls the covers open and lets me climb in. He lets me lay on his arm. He hugs me tight. Then he reads the book. My brother snores very loud all the time.

My dad gets his hand in my pyjama top. He makes his hand go all over while he reads the story. It makes me fall asleep. But then he makes his hand go down and it goes to my pants. Then I get scared. Maybe he will make it hurt. He makes my pants slide down. I pretend that I am asleep. I make my eyes closed and I don't stop him.

He puts his thing inside. And he puts his hand on me. He reads the book. I listen to all his words. I don't cry. I let my dad do it lots of times. Sometimes he does it every night. Because I am scared of the bad man.

When it is all finished I get dressed again. I go to my bedroom. Then I write it all in my notebook. I am bad. I keep letting my dad do the hurt thing. I don't know why I do it. I get in the bed all the time. Maybe I can go away. I ask God all the time to take me away. But he never does. I write it in my notebook too. I write lots of words and I cry. Then I fall to sleep. I promise I don't get in my dad's bed tomorrow. But I always do it. I don't know why. I am just bad like they say. I wish my dad loved me like he does my brother.

My dad does the hurt thing every night. I don't ever say

no.

Sometimes I get allowed to stay up. If I have been good. Then my dad doesn't stay upstairs. He comes back down when my brother goes to sleep. Then he puts on the television and I am allowed to watch it. If it is weekend and I have been very good.

My mum and dad watch lots of things. They have blood and people get killed in them. Sometimes I hide behind the cushion and then I don't look. Maybe it isn't there. I wait until the monster goes away then I get to look again. My mum laughs about it. Sometimes she tells me I can look. But when I do, the scary thing is on the television and she laughs about that too. I don't like it when she does that. Then I get scared in my bed. I ask my mum and dad if I can sleep in their bed. They let me. But then my dad does the hurt thing too and my mum gets to see. I wish I didn't get scared all the time. Then I don't do the bad things and no one gets to know about it.

Sometimes they put on things that have lots of sex in it. I don't like it. The people all do it together. They have no clothes on. Sometimes they do bad things to each other and then the girls cry on it. I don't like to watch it. It makes me cry too. But I don't let my dad see. Then he thinks I am a baby.

My dad puts a film on. It is like Tarzan. But it isn't like the one me and my Nan watch. Tarzan leaves Jane in the house. Then someone knocks on the door. It is lots of boys. They go in the house and they all make her do the hurt thing. She screams about it. I try not to look at it. I look at the side of the television. I ask my dad if I can go to bed. But he says I can't. I have to stay and spend time with my mum and dad. But I don't want to.

My dad lifts me up. He puts me on the sofa. I didn't get my pyjamas on yet. But he takes my clothes off. My mum lies by the fire. She doesn't say anything about it. He makes me lean over the sofa. I don't want to. But he holds my hands then I don't get away.

He watches the television too at the same time. He does the hurt thing. He does it very hard. I try to get away. But I can't. I try to squish into the sofa. But my dad squashes me lots more and I don't get away. He keeps my hands and he holds them very tight.

I don't stop the crying because it hurts too bad inside. He tells me to shush. I tell him it hurts very bad. But then he just does it more. It makes my cries get louder, but he tells me it is okay.

When my dad lets go. I ask him if I can go to the bathroom. I pick my clothes up. I hug them all tight. I feel all the sick in my tummy. It hurts very bad. I don't walk very good. There is blood on my legs. I try to get to the bathroom fast. Then it doesn't get on the floor and my mum doesn't shout.

I lock the door. I make it all cleaned up again. It hurts

very bad. I put my clothes on. Then the blood gets in my pants. It makes me scared. Maybe something bad will happen. I don't like it when there is blood there. But I don't ask my mum and dad about it.

I go to my room. It is very hard to get up the stairs. I get scared inside because my brother is there. He sits at the top of the stairs. I don't say anything to him. I don't want him to get in trouble. He gets my bedroom door open and my light on. I try to sit on my bed. But it hurts very bad.

I don't say anything when my brother gets my pyjamas. He helps me to get them on. Then he makes the bed open for me. I get in it and he gives me Mr. Ted. Then he gets in the bed too. I don't let him see the crying part. I put my face in the pillow. Then I go to sleep.

Twenty Four

Me and Mr. Ted like the summer time the best. We like it when it gets to July and I get to play with all my friends every day. I have one more year at junior school. Then I leave and go to senior school. I get very scared about it. I ask Mr. Ted sometimes. He gives me lots of hugs.

It is nice and sunny all summer. I play with Jason and everyone in the back garden. We play there because the driveway is long and we can ride the skateboards down it. I don't have one. I want one. My brother got one because he is good. It has wings on it. He got it for his birthday. We pretend it is a plane. My brother plays too. We put him on the front and he goes very fast. Sometimes I think about making him fall off. But I know that is bad. Maybe it will make him cry. But he gets lots of things and I don't. It makes me sad inside.

My mum and dad say he has to play with me. He is too little to go out on the road like we do. He is nearly six. I got to play out when I was six. But he doesn't because he is just a big baby. Then we have to play. We make the back garden into a swamp. We ride all the things around the bushes and chase each other. We have a fun time. It makes me hot and sweaty.

My mum comes outside. She has a new skirt on. She got her hair all nice and she has lots of make up on. She told me that it is for the nice doctor. The one that she will get to marry. But she can't because of his stupid wife. But she gets new clothes and new hair and then she has to go and see him. She asks me if I like it. I tell her that she looks very nice. It makes her smile. She asks me what about her legs. But I don't know what she means.

She turns around so I can see. Her skirt is very short. Her legs are all brown. I tell her they look nice. She asks me if I can see the veins in her legs. I look at her legs. I can see them. I say yes. My mum says thank you. Then she goes back in the house. I go back to play with my friends.

I don't know why my dad comes out. He runs out to me and I try to run backwards. But it is very hard. My friends all move out of the way. My dad hits me very hard in the face and I fall over. I tell him I am sorry. But I don't know what I am sorry for. I didn't mean to do anything bad.

My dad asks me why I said mean things to my mum. But I didn't. I said nice things to her. "She is crying because of what you said about her legs," he says. "It's taken me hours to convince her she looks nice and then you tell her she doesn't."

I didn't mean to. I said she looked nice. I said it was all nice. I don't tell my dad. He is mad about it. My dad grabs my arm. Then he drags me inside. I tell him I am sorry. I didn't mean to make her upset. But he tells me it is too late. He makes me get in the house. Then I have to sit on the chair in the dining room. I tell my dad I don't mean it. But he tells me to shut up. I can stay there for a long time. My brother gets to play with all my friends. I am not allowed to move. I wish my brother would go away.

My brother comes in the house lots of times. They are having a water fight. He fills his gun up. He laughs because I don't get to play. He makes funny faces and sticks his tongue out at me. I hate him. I wish he would go away. He does it lots of times.

He is all tired from running around. He is all wet from playing all the games. He comes in to get some dry clothes. He sticks his tongue out at me. He comes very close and I stand up. I push him over very hard. I want him to go away and leave me alone.

I sit back down on the chair. My brother cries very hard. He makes it sound bad. But it isn't. He didn't hurt himself. He makes the crying come out. But it is lies. My mum runs in. She picks him up off the floor. She hugs him very big and tells him it's okay. She asks me what happened. I tell her nothing. But my brother tells her I pushed him over. "How dare you hit my son," she says and then she slaps her hand across my face. She tells me she is going to tell my dad about it. I do nothing but make the day bad. I don't say anything. I wish they would all go away. I don't like them. I wish I could make them disappear.

My mum shouts my dad. He was in the front room with

his books. She tells him he has to sort me out. "I have had enough of his behaviour," she says. She tells him I am really bad and she is sick of it. I don't tell them my brother was being mean. They will tell me he didn't. That he was just playing. I was mean because I pushed him over and I shouldn't do that. I am not allowed to.

My dad asks me why I thought it was okay to push my brother. I shrug my shoulders at him and don't say any words. He shouts at me to tell him. But I tell him I don't know. He asks me if it is okay to bully my brother. He is smaller than me. I tell him I don't know too. My dad asks me if I want to be sent away. I tell him I don't. I tell him I am sorry.

I have to sit there all day long. When they eat dinner I don't get any. My dad says I don't act like part of the family. So then, I shouldn't get to be part of it if I don't want to. I don't look at them when they eat dinner. It makes me hungry inside. It makes my tummy rumble lots of times.

I need to go to the bathroom. My mouth needs a drink too. But I don't ask about it. It is dark now. My mum and dad have finished. My dad is in his room reading his books. My brother is playing and I don't know where my mum is. Maybe she is upstairs or in my dad's front room with him. Sometimes she sits in there and they talk about lots of things. I don't have the light on in the dining room. They made all the table clean and they put everything away. Then they turned the light off and forgot I was there.

My mum comes into the dining room. I ask her if I can go to the bathroom. I need it very bad. She asks me if I deserve to use it after the way I behaved today. I tell her yes. It hurt inside. She asks me why I think I should be allowed. I tell her I have been quiet all day. I didn't do any more bad things. My mum doesn't say anything. She goes into the kitchen.

It hurts very bad inside. I don't be able to hold it any longer. I get up and I walk to the bathroom. I lock the door then I don't get shouted at about it and made to come out. I use the toilet. Then I get water in my hands from the tap and I drink it. I know I don't be allowed a drink later. I drink lots of it. My dad bangs on the bathroom door. It makes the glass rattle. Maybe he will break it if he knocks lots of times. I make my mouth dry so he didn't know I got the water.

He bangs very hard and tells me to open the door. I do. He asks me what I am doing. I tell him I needed the bathroom very bad. He asked if I was allowed to go. But my mum didn't give me an answer. My mum is behind him. She asks if it is her fault that I get up and do what I want. I shake my head. It doesn't be. I just needed to use the toilet.

My mum gets mad about it. She shouts at my dad. He has to sort me out. I am just bad all day. She can't deal with it any more. My dad grabs my arm. He drags me into the lounge. Then he makes me fall on the floor. He hits me lots of times. He shouts at me for being bad. I didn't mean to be bad. I make myself in a ball. Maybe he will stop hitting me soon. But he doesn't stop. He keeps doing it. Maybe I can fall asleep and then I don't feel it.

My dad kneels down on the floor next to me. He puts his head down so that he can see me. I don't want to look at his face. But he makes me. He tells me if I don't behave things will get a lot worse. I don't say anything. I don't move. Maybe I can stay there forever and go away.

Twenty Five

My mum and dad don't speak to me for a long time. I don't speak to them too. I don't go and play with my friends. It hurts. I have lots of marks from my dad. He hit me very bad. It hurts sometimes. I don't do anything bad then they don't get mad at me.

My mum is in the bath. I have to use the bathroom for bedtime. I don't get to go in there alone. Then maybe I do bad things. I don't like going to the toilet when my mum is in there. But she says I have to. She sits in the water. She smiles lots at me. But I don't smile too. I feel bad inside.

My dad is in bed. He has put my brother in his own bed. He read the stories to us. I let my dad do the hurt thing again. He says I am good now. Maybe all the bad parts go away when he does the hurt part. Then he told me to go to the toilet. I knock and my mum tells me to come in.

I wish she wasn't there. Then I can make it hurt in the mirror. But she is. She doesn't go away. She talks to me about the nice doctor. He liked her skirt. He didn't see the bad veins on her legs like I did. I tell her I am sorry. I didn't mean to make her sad about it. It just came out. She didn't have bad veins in her legs. She asks me if I promise and I nod my head big about it. I didn't mean to make her feel sad. She is very pretty.

I try not to let the crying out when I tell her. But she doesn't ask about it. She asks me if I am going to bed. I tell her yes. I tell her my dad read the books. Now I have to use the bathroom and go to bed. She tells me about the nice doctor.

He said very nice things to her. He said her skirt was nice. He liked her shoes. My mum says he was looking at her legs. It means he wants sex. That's all men want she says. When I am big, I will just want that all the time. Men are horrible. She says bad words about the nice doctor and she swears. I tell her I don't think he is bad like that.

My mum asks me if it is true. He doesn't be bad? I tell her no. He doesn't be bad. He is very nice. She asks me if I will write a story about him and his wife. Maybe I can make the wife go away. She looks like a horse my mum says. She has big teeth and a big stupid face.

"If I find you a picture, will you draw a picture and make a story?" she asks. I tell her I will. Because I have all the bad inside. I can make bad things happen. If I make the horse wife go away then she will. It comes true when I write things.

She asks me if I write lots of things. I tell her I do. She asks me what I write. I don't tell her. I write lots of bad things about my mum and dad. I don't mean to. But then it comes out. She asks if I write a diary. I do. But I don't tell her about it. Me and Mr. Ted used to write in it lots of times. But now he doesn't write any more. He doesn't be magic now. I wish he did. Andrew still comes to play. I write about him too. But he knows I am bad. So he doesn't be around a lot.

My mum tells me diaries are bad things. Sometimes people find them and then they read them. It makes me scared inside. I don't want anyone to read mine. Maybe they see all the bad things I say. She tells me I must never write one. She makes me promise. I tell her I will. Maybe I can throw mine away and then no one ever sees it. Maybe I can hide it and then no one knows about it.

She tells me when I write the story I have to write it about Batman doctor. That is what she calls the nice doctor. It is our secret word. He has a fast car and he drives it like Batman. So we call him that when she talks about him. I like Batman and the real doctor. Me and Andrew play games. We pretend the nice doctor is real Batman and he makes the bad people go away.

I say goodnight to my mum and then I go to my bedroom. I don't want to go to sleep. Maybe the bad man comes because I have been bad. I don't sleep lots of times. Mr. Ted sleeps in my bed. He sleeps at the edge then the bad man can't come and get me. He keeps him away. When he was magic, he kept him away lots of times. Maybe he scared him so bad. That is why I don't see him for a long time. I don't know. He still makes me scared. I make the door closed. But I don't be allowed to have the door closed properly. I put my teddy dog there. He makes it so the door doesn't get opened.

I have a big box in front of the wardrobe. Then the bad man can't hide in there. Then I have lots of things on the big box. The bad man can't hide in there too. I make it so the bad man doesn't hide anywhere. But maybe he comes when I don't see and I don't know about it. He is very good. I make myself stay awake lots of times.

I like that my mum wants me to write a story. I write lots of them at nighttime. I get my notebook and I hug in the corner of my bed. I draw the nice doctor. Then I draw a lady. But I make her have a horse head. I laugh about it. But I make the laugh quiet and then I don't wake my dad and my brother. I write the story about how she goes away. She is a horse and she goes in lots of races. But races make her scared. Because she is mean and she wants to win all the time. Then she says it is not fair. She doesn't go in the race and she runs away. I write the story very long. It makes me laugh when I write it. I write it very fast.

The horse lady runs away. She doesn't like the doctor any more. Then the nice lady comes along. I don't say that it is my mum. But it is. The nice doctor likes the nice lady. He thinks she is very special and he loves her lots. I write it. He tells her he is sorry about the horse lady. He didn't mean to marry her.

I hear my mum come up the stairs. She opens my door.

She is going to bed. She says night-night to me. I say night-night back. I don't go to sleep though. Maybe it is very late. I put the radio on. But I make it quiet then it doesn't make everyone wake up in the house. I don't like when my mum and dad are in bed. I hear lots of noises downstairs. I tell Andrew it is Sheba. He gets to watch. He says it is too.

It makes me check my room. I check all the places that maybe the bad man can hide. I do it quiet and then I don't make noise. But the bad man doesn't be there. I check under the bed too. Maybe he fits there. I check everywhere. But maybe he sneaked in when I didn't look. He is good at being sneaky. It makes me scared inside.

I am very tired. I write the story and make the picture. I can give it to my mum in the morning. But I am scared about my room. I run to my mum and dad's room. I whisper my mum's name. Then I don't wake up my dad. I tell her I have tummy ache. She asks me where. I point to my tummy. She asks me if I want medicine. But I don't. Medicine always makes the sick come out. She lets me get in the bed. I lie in the middle. Maybe my dad is sleeping. But it wakes him up. He gets out of bed and goes to get some medicine. He brings it back up and tells me to take it. It is the nice medicine. Not the one my mum gives me. I take it and then I go to sleep.

Twenty Six
(Age Eleven)

When the summer was all done. I went back to school. I got a new teacher. Mrs. Pilkington. She is very nice. I like to see her in the school times. When it was our first day. She told us to write stories. It made me very excited. I wrote mine very fast. I wrote all about playing with Jason and all the adventures we had. She liked it very much. She gave me a big star for it.

It is my birthday today. I am eleven. I don't get birthdays. My mum and dad forget about them. My Nan gives me some things. But she doesn't have lots of money. I am excited because it is my birthday. I tell Andrew about it in my head. He says happy birthday. I know my mum and dad don't buy me things. But maybe I got good enough this time.

There is a present outside my door. It has two cards on it. My mum put it there when I am asleep. It is very early. I don't sleep when it is my birthday. It makes my tummy hurt and I stay awake. I try to wish very hard that my mum and dad be happy and then they give me something. They give my brother lots of things on his birthday. He gets all the big presents. They make him smile about it. But I don't ever get any. I ask lots of times. Like my brother. He makes them a big list. I make one too, but I don't ever get the things on it.

It is dark in the house. I open the present from my Nan. She has got me a game. She writes me a card too. She puts the cat's name in it and draws the paws too. She says Love Nana at the bottom. I put it in my room on the side. Then I get to see it. My brother has made me a card too. Maybe he did it at school. It has lots of things stuck to it. It says happy birthday inside it. I put it with my Nan's card. I don't put them downstairs like my brother does. My mum says my cards make a mess. So I keep them in my bedroom.

I wish my mum and dad wake up. They make my brother a special breakfast on his birthday. He gets mayonnaise on his bacon and the floppy cheese. He gets lots of it and he likes it very much. We all wake up very early then he gets to open his presents. I wish I got that too. But no one is awake. Even Sheba is asleep. I go downstairs and I sit on the sofa with her. I hug her very big and put my head on her. She licks my face because some of the tears fall out. I try not to let them but they do.

I have to get ready for school. It is the last day. Then we have the holidays because it is half term. I get to play with Jason and Faye and all the others in the holidays. We are going to go on an adventure. There is a place where people play golf. But it has lots of trees and things. Maybe we can sneak in there. We can make a den. Jason thinks it will be a good idea.

My dad doesn't get up for a long time. I am late for

school. I don't get told off about it. I don't give the papers to the office lady any more. The mean lady is gone. But I still put them in the toilet and no one knows about it. Sometimes my teacher doesn't give them to me. It is a new teacher. She is very nice. She doesn't get mad when I am late. She tells me to sit down.

I get my breakfast before my dad gets up. I eat it quickly. Then I get all my school things ready and I wait for him. He takes my brother to school first. He can't be late. He gets sad when he is late. I sit in the car at the back and wait for my dad to come back. He takes a long time. I am already late. My bell goes before my brother. We don't go to the same school. His school is a long way away.

When I get to school, my dad stops the car outside the big front part. I walk through the playground. It is empty. All the other gates are all locked up and so is the door. I have to go in the big doors. It is a long way from my classroom.

When I get to my classroom, there are lots of words on the board already. I sit at the back next to Kirsty. She says happy birthday to me.

The teacher says happy birthday too. She says it with a big smile and then she writes my name on the board and writes happy birthday. I like Mrs Pilkington very much. She is my favourite teacher. She is very nice.

She gives me a birthday card. She writes her name in it

and the class. When she goes away, I try to keep the crying away. I don't know why it is there. My eyes fill up and I try not to make them blink because the tears will fall out. My eyes go all fuzzy and I can't see. They are all filled with water.

Mrs Pilkington comes over. She bends down then she is as big as me. She asks me what is wrong. I tell her nothing is wrong. She says that she can see I am crying. But I don't be. The tears don't come out of my eyes. She holds my hand. And then it makes the crying fall out. I tell her I have tummy ache. She asks me if I want to go home. She can call my dad and he can pick me up. But I shake my head about it. I don't want to go home. I like being at school. I get to have fun and I get to be with my friends. No one gets mad at me.

I tell Mrs Pilkington that I am okay. She tells me to say if I want to go home. I tell her I promise. She gives me a tissue and tells me to blow my nose. Then she says happy birthday again and she goes to the board and tells us all to write the work. I try very hard at school. I like to get the A's on all my things. I don't ever want to get B's. Then the teachers like me because I know all the work. I try my hardest all the time. I read lots of books too. I have finished all the books for my class. I have to get library ones. The ones for the class are boring. They are like baby books. I read big books like my dad. I read lots of them. I get them from the other library too.

My dad lets me go there on my bike. I get six books at a time. I read them all in the week. Then I take them back. Sometimes I read one book in a whole night. I don't like to sleep at night time. I don't like if the bad man sneaks up. I sleep when it is light and read when it is dark. I read lots of books like that. But I don't let my mum and dad know I don't sleep at nighttime. I am very good at hiding. I am very good at staying awake.

At the end of the day, Mrs Pilkington gives me a big hug. She says happy birthday to me again and tells me to have a good time. I tell her thank you.

My dad doesn't drive me home. I have to go to his work. I can go to the library first because he has work for some more hours and I get in his way and get bored. He works in the garage. The library is next to my school. I go there and I get my books. I like the monster books the best. I read them lots of times. I put them in my school bag then I walk to my dad's work.

It is down an alleyway. I walk down it. My dad is outside working on cars. He doesn't say hello to me. I sit outside and I read my books while he finishes. Sometimes if I get there too early, he doesn't be at the garage. Sometimes he is still taking my brother home and I got back faster than him.

I ask my dad if I can walk home. I know the way. I am eleven now. It makes me big. He says I can. It is not a long way away. I get to walk past my Nan's house. She isn't at home though. She is at the special place that makes her happy. I wish she was. I look at the house. I don't look at the windows upstairs. I know he hides. I don't want to see if he waves from my old bedroom. Then I know he gets my Nan and she is all by herself.

I like walking home. I get to make stories in my head. Andrew walks with me. We talk about them. But I don't say the words outside my head. Then people know I am crazy. I don't step on any cracks. It is bad to do that. I make the click noises when I walk though. It makes all the bad stuff go away. Maybe if I do it right then I get something nice for my birthday when I get home.

I see Jason when I walk home. He asks if I am coming out to play. I tell him I don't know. Maybe I am not allowed. Maybe I have been good and I get something nice on my birthday. I tell him I might come out later. He says okay. He walks with me. It makes me mad inside because I was talking to Andrew and we made up stories and now I can't because Jason is there. He doesn't know about Andrew. I don't tell him.

He goes away when we get to my street. He sees Simon who lives at the shop and goes to play with him. I tell them both bye and then I go to my house. I walk around the back because I am not allowed to use the front door. I don't even get to knock on it. I have to knock on the back door because I don't get a key. I am not allowed. I let bad people in if I have one.

My mum doesn't have a birthday cake. She doesn't say anything about it. My brother is on the sofa. He sits with his tray and he has his dinner. I am not allowed to eat on the sofa or watch television. But he does because he is good.

No one says happy birthday. I go to my room. I don't be allowed to stay in my uniform. I have to get changed. I make my uniform all nice and in a neat pile. Then I put it on the side like I have to. I don't go out. I get my books and then I sit on the floor because I am not allowed to sit on my bed. I read my books. I like them very much.

I hear my dad's car come. He drives it down the driveway and then he parks it. He comes in and washes his hands. I crawl out of my bedroom then no one hears me. I lie on the top of the stairs and look through the secret hole. No one sees me there. I lie there for a long time. My brother's television programmes finish.

My mum and dad eat their dinner. My brother sits at the table too. He gets pudding. He eats it and says he is all full up. Maybe if I go downstairs I can have some. Maybe because it is my birthday they let me have the cake and custard.

I go downstairs. My mum and dad look at me. They don't say any words. I don't ask about the pudding. Maybe they get mad. Maybe they don't want me to be there. They have sad faces that I come down. I make everything spoilt.

I ask if I can go to the bathroom. My mum says yes. I go and then when I finish, I don't say any words to my mum and dad. I just go to my room. I get my pyjamas on and lie on the floor and read my books. When it gets dark, my dad tells me it is time for bed. He puts my brother in bed too. In his room. I get in my own bed. Then my dad comes in. He asks if I had a good day. I tell him I did. Then he gets in my bed too. I make my eyes get closed and I let him do all the things. He doesn't say happy birthday.

Maybe they all forgot about it. Maybe I am just too bad.

Twenty Seven

I don't know why I cry all the time. But I do. I didn't cry when it was the half term from my birthday. I didn't cry when I went out to play. But I cry lots of other times.

Maybe my mum and dad will go away. They don't like me. The words in my head say maybe my mum and dad go away when I am at school. Then I don't know about it. I come home and the house is empty. My dad doesn't drive me home anymore. He makes me walk. I walked once. I can walk again he says. He makes me walk to school too sometimes. But then I don't be very late.

I don't know why I cry. I go in my classroom. We all sit down. I sit with Kirsty and Peter. We do our work together. But my eyes get all fuzzy inside. Then I don't blink and the tears don't fall down. Mrs. Pilkington asks me what is wrong. I tell her I have tummy ache again. But I don't want to go home. Sometimes I tell Mrs. Pilkington yes. Then she calls my dad and he picks me up. It makes him mad. He has to come out of work to get me because I have stupid tummy ache.

I don't really. I make it pretend. But then my mum is there and then I know they didn't go away. I go and read my books in my room. I draw lots of pictures too. Then I know my mum and dad don't take all their things again. I don't know why the thing in my brain says they are going to sneak away. It just does.

Sometimes they sneak away on the weekends. Not for a long time though. On the morning I ask if I can go and play with Jason. My mum and dad say yes. Then I go and play. We play on the beach or on the golf course. Sometimes the tide is in. We play there, but the coast guard person tells us off. But I can swim. The sea doesn't make me go away. But we aren't allowed over the wires. We sneak there when he is gone.

When it gets to lunchtime, Jason is hungry. He wants to go home for lunch. I say I will go home too. I don't get lunch on the weekends. My brother gets it. He has floppy cheese with ketchup. Sometimes I pinch bites. But he doesn't like it. Sometimes I pinch his floppy cheese from the fridge, and then my mum doesn't know about it. But she is in the kitchen lots of times and it is very hard to steal all the food.

My mum gave me a key for the back door. I am allowed to use it. But I have to keep care of it and then I have to make sure the door is locked. We don't want any burglars in there. I promise her I don't.

I go to the back of the house and I make the gate shut behind me. Sometimes it is locked and I have to climb over it. It is bigger than my dad. But I can do it. I like climbing. I get down at the other side, but I don't catch my mum's washing line. Then she gets mad at me if I do and all her clothes get dirty. Then she has to wash them again and I get in trouble.

There isn't anyone in the house when I go in. I shout my mum and dad. But there doesn't be anyone there. Even Sheba doesn't be in the house. I shout her. She doesn't answer. It makes me scared inside. Maybe the bad man got in and he can hide. I don't know where my mum and dad went.

I don't stay in the house very long. I make a sandwich. But I eat it outside then it doesn't make crumbs and my mum doesn't get mad. Then I go back to see Jason. He waits outside for me. He asks where my mum and dad are. Their car isn't there. I didn't notice it was all gone. I tell him I don't know.

We go and play. But maybe my mum and dad went away. Maybe they don't come back. I try to play the games with Jason. But my brain keeps saying maybe my mum and dad went away for a long time. We ride on our bikes and I ride past the house lots of times. But they don't be there. The car doesn't come back.

It doesn't come back when the sun goes away too. It is a long time. Maybe they died and went to heaven. Maybe they got a new house and they didn't tell me. I don't go inside the house. Jason has to go home. It is late. We all have to be home at nine. But my mum and dad still don't be back.

I don't want to go in the house by myself. Maybe the bad man can get me. It is a big house; he has lots of rooms to hide in.

Maybe he got there while I was outside playing.

It gets dark outside. I know I don't be allowed to sit outside. But I don't want to go in the garden. Maybe the bad man hides in the garage too. And then he can come and get me. But I go through the gate. I close it behind me. It makes me very scared inside my tummy about it. My brain shows me lots of pictures. Maybe he runs to me and then he gets me and no one comes to help.

I run to the back door. It is all around the corner. I don't look in the windows. Maybe I see him and then he waves at me with his big smiley face. I don't like it. I open the door very fast and I lock it. I put lots of lights on. It is cold in the house. The fire isn't on. But I don't turn it on. Maybe I am not allowed.

I have to close the big curtains in the lounge. My mum doesn't like them open when the light is on. She says everyone gets to see in the house and then maybe they want to steal all her things. I close them. They are big and orange. They are fluffy too. My mum says it is called velvet. I don't like when they are closed. Then no one can see if the bad man comes.

I sit on the sofa. I don't move at all. I hug myself all tight. I put the television on. Then I don't hear the bad man in the other rooms. It makes me scared inside. I keep very still. I don't let the shivers come. But I am very cold.

It is a long time when my mum and dad come back.

Maybe they didn't come back. But they did. My brother is tired. He has lots of things. He shows me them. He has toys and videos. I don't have anything. They have been to a place called Morecombe. It is nice there. They have lots of rides and things. They went because it is the end of the year. Then everything is very cheap.

I didn't know they were going out. They didn't tell me about it. But they had lots of fun. My mum tells me to get ready for bed and to go to my room. It feels all bad inside my tummy about it. I don't tell her though. Maybe if I am good I can go next time.

But they don't. They go lots of times to lots of places. I don't like it. I don't like when I don't know. Maybe they don't come back. I don't like when I sit in the house all by myself.

Sometimes I sit at Jason's house. My mum lets me have sleepover's there. Then I don't be scared that they aren't in the house. But then on Sundays they don't be there too. They go away on two days.

Maybe when I am at school they go away too. And they don't tell me about it. Maybe my mum disappears and I don't ever see her again. It makes my tummy sad inside. It makes the crying come outside. I miss her very bad inside when I go to school. It makes me cry.

I try to make it go away. The others in the classroom

think I am a baby. But Mrs. Pilkington asks me lots of times if I am okay. I tell her I am. I don't know why I cry.

It gets all the way to Easter and I still cry all the time at school. I keep it away so no one sees but sometimes they do. Then they say he is crying again. On the Easter holidays, my mum and dad go away lots of times. They take my brother to the funfair when it opens. I don't go because I used to go lots with my Nan. Now it is my brother's turn. I don't know when they go. But they are not home when I get in the house.

Sometimes my brother whispers to my dad. He isn't allowed to tell me. He asks my dad what time they are going to the Pleasure Beach. My dad tells him. My brother looks at me then he knows I don't listen. But I do. I don't say anything about it.

We go back to school after Easter. The crying is still there. Maybe Mrs. Pilkington gets mad about it. She asks me to come with her. It makes my tummy turn upside down. Maybe she is going to shout at me. We go to the library. She tells me to sit down. She sits down too. She asks me why I cry lots of times. I tell her I don't know. It just comes out.

She kneels on the floor and she gives me some tissues. She asks me if some bad things happen at home. I don't mean to cry big about it. Maybe she knows I am very bad. Then she will tell the head teacher and I go away to the boys home. Then I don't see my mum and dad anymore. I don't tell her. I don't want her to know about it. I shake my head all big. But I don't keep the crying away.

She tells me I can tell her if there is something bad. I don't want to tell her about my bad things. I tell her my brother is mean. He makes me cry in the mornings. She asks me if that is true. Is that why I cry. I nod my head all big. I tell her lots of things he does and make him sound very bad. Then she knows it is him and not my badness inside.

She hugs me very big. I don't ever get hugged like that before. She hugs me so big that I fall off the chair and I sit on her knee. She smells very nice. She hugs me and all the tears falls out. I don't mean them to. She tells me if there is anything bad that it is okay to tell her anytime. I nod my head and I promise I will tell her any bad things.

She wipes my face and makes the tears go away. I like Mrs Pilkington very much. She is my favourite teacher. It makes me sad when it gets to summertime. Then I am leaving the school. I have to go to senior school. I won't ever see Mrs. Pilkington again. She is going to have a baby too. When it is the very last day, she gives me a card. It has a big smile inside it. She tells me to smile forever. She gives me a very big hug. She gives me a book too. She has written inside it. It is to write my stories in. It is very special. I promise to keep it forever.

Twenty Eight

I can't wait until I go to senior school. But it isn't the school I want to go to. I want to go to the same one Faye goes to. She is bigger than me. She started senior school already. She is the year above me. Jason is going to go there too. But he doesn't start senior school yet. He is in the year below me. He has to be in junior school for one more year. My mum and dad say I can't go to that school. It has girls there. If there are girls there, then I make them do the sex thing and then maybe they have a baby and my dad isn't going to pay for it. But I don't. He says he knows what I am like. I do the sex thing all the time with people. But I don't. He doesn't believe me. I have to go to a school that just has boys. Then I don't get near any girls.

I tell my mum and dad I don't have any friends at the boys school. But my dad says Peter is there. I don't want to go where Peter goes. We don't be good friends anymore. I say hello to him. But maybe he knows about my bad things I do, then he doesn't like me. So I don't talk to him. Then he can't tell me to go away. He tries to be my friend. But I don't want to.

My mum says it is good that I don't see Peter. She doesn't like his mum. His mum is nosey. She gets in all the business that isn't hers. She makes my mum mad. My mum wishes she would go away. Peter's mum knows about the

Batman doctor too. She thinks my mum should leave it alone. But my mum says she doesn't know anything. She is just stupid.

I play with Kirsty. She is going to go to a school that just has girls in it. She doesn't live at the hotel anymore. Her mum and dad don't live together. She just lives with her mum. They live in a flat. It is very good there. She has a funny bed. It is in the kitchen and it comes down out of the wall. Sometimes I get to sleep over and we sleep in it. It is very strange to sleep in the kitchen.

We are in there. Her mum buys us lots of nice things to eat. We get to play games and things. I ask her if she wants to play a game that boys and girls play. I know it because I did it lots of times at the play place. I had to do lots of things with the girls. I don't tell Kirsty about the play place. I just tell her about the game. We play with the cards and we have to take our clothes off when we lose. She loses lots of times. So do I. Her mum doesn't see because she is in the place next door. She drinks beer with her friends and smokes cigarettes.

I show Kirsty about the touching part. I show her how to do it when she loses the game. But then I lose and I have to do it to her too. She isn't like Peter, but I know what to do. My dad does it to my mum too and I did it lots at the play place. She says it tickles. It makes her laugh about it.

She says boys and girls are supposed to kiss. But I don't

like to. She says I have to. That's what they do when they put their hands there. It makes my mouth feel funny when we do it. Her mouth is all wet and slimy and I don't like it. Maybe she does. I don't do it lots of times.

We do the other thing lots of times. I like to do that. Maybe it is like my dad said. It is like the sex part. Andrew tries to see. But I tell him to go away in my brain and he doesn't stay. But he knows how to do it all too.

In the morning when we wake up, we go to my house. We get to play in the garage. My mum and dad have an old sofa there. Just the cushions. We sit on them and we play games and play cards. We talk about lots of things. Sometimes we do the other things too. But not today. There are lots of papers there. We think about maybe making them into a fire. I like fire. I play with it lots of times when no one knows about it.

My dad keeps his motorbikes in the garage too. He has a bottle that he keeps his petrol in. I show it to Kirsty. Maybe we can use it to make the fire. She says yes. We open it up. I like how it smells. I like how it makes my head feel. It is all fuzzy inside.

Kirsty smells it too. It makes my head feel all wobbly. We laugh about it. We smell it some more. I put my nose right at the bottle and then I sniff it deep. Then I fall back on the cushions and Kirsty laughs about it. She lies down with me too.

Maybe we can go to sleep.

Kirsty doesn't stay all day. Her mum is taking her out. She has to go back home. I say okay and then I say goodbye to her. I feel sad when she goes away. Then I don't have anyone to play with. I don't call for Jason yet. Maybe I can go and get him later. My head feels too funny. It makes me walk funny.

I go into my house. My dad is on the sofa. He tells me to come here. I don't want to. Maybe I am in trouble. My dad was with his friend. But his friend isn't there. Maybe he sent him away because I did bad things. I always make everything bad and spoil things. Maybe I spoilt his friend being there.

My dad doesn't shout. He doesn't have his angry face about it. He puts his hand out and tells me to come over. I take his hand. He pulls me down and makes me sit on his knee. He doesn't do that before. But he doesn't do bad things either. He doesn't smack me and I don't get shouted at. Maybe he knows about the petrol.

My dad hugs me very tight. He puts his big arms around me and it makes me want to go away. It makes me get scared. I tell my dad to let me go. Maybe he is going to shout at me. I try to get up and go away. But he doesn't let me. He hugs me very hard so I don't get away. My head feels all dizzy inside. It hurts too. It feels like someone presses it inside.

My mum comes in. She isn't mad. She has a camera. But

it isn't the picture kind. It is one that makes the videos. I don't like it. My dad tries to make my clothes unfastened. But I don't want him to. I don't want the camera thing making the video. I feel scared inside. I don't want to do the sex thing. I don't want my mum to see.

She puts the camera on the little table. Then she opens the door. My dad's friend comes in. I don't want him to see the sex part. My dad tells me it is okay. He has got all my clothes off. I try to make myself hide away and then no one sees.

The man takes his pants off and my dad holds my hands. My mum tells me that I have to kneel down, but I don't want to. I feel the crying inside, but I don't let it get out. My dad's friend sits down and my mum says I have to go over there to him. But I don't want to. I try to shake my head, but my dad makes me go there. Then he puts my head down and I have to put it in my mouth. I don't like to do it. But he doesn't do it all to the end. The man does the sex part too. My mum says to my dad to hold my hands. He makes me lean on his knees. Then I can't make my arms move and his friend does the sex part. I wish I could go away. I don't want to be here anymore. When it is all finished my dad lets my hands go, then I curl up by the sofa. The man gets dressed again. I hug my knees tight. I don't move. I don't look at anything. I don't look at my mum and dad. They talk about boring things.

My mum tells me to go and get dressed in the bathroom. Then I can go out and play.

Twenty Nine

The bathroom is dark. But I don't turn the light on. I don't care. Maybe the bad man comes. Good. I lock the door. I don't want my mum and dad to come in. I don't want anyone to come in. I want them all to leave me alone. Maybe Sheba and Andrew can go away too. I kneel on the floor and hug myself all tight. I hug myself very hard. I don't stop the crying. It all comes out very big. I cry and I can't breathe. Maybe it will make my head go pop. I hug myself tight to make the crying go away. But it doesn't want to. The crying makes lots of noise. I don't know how to make it all stop and go away.

I don't stand to get in the shower. I push the doors open. Then I crawl inside it. I turn it on. It is cold. It makes me jump. But I don't get out. I stay there. The water makes itself warm. It gets all the way to hot. It gets hotter and hotter. I turn it onto full. I sit in the corner and try to hug all the crying away. But it doesn't want to go. It is inside. It feels very bad. I don't keep the crying sounds away. I can't breathe. It makes my tummy turn upside down. The sick nearly comes out. Maybe my mum and dad will hear. Maybe they call me a baby.

The water washes away. I watch it. It has red in it. I stare at it very hard. Then I see my dad's nail brush. I make it go on my skin. I make it all go away. I brush very hard. It bleeds too.

Then I get red lines on my arm and legs. I make them very hard. I make it all go away. I close my eyes and hug in the corner. I don't know I am there for a long time. I don't know that I fall to sleep. My mum bangs on the door. She tells me to hurry up. It makes me jump. I take too long in the shower and use all the water. I didn't know that water has gone cold. I didn't feel it. It makes me shiver when my mum bangs.

I sniff very hard. My nose is all blocked up. My eyes are big and puffy. They feel like bug eyes. I tell my mum I am coming out. I tell her I am sorry. I didn't mean to take very long. I turn the shower off and get out. My dad's towel is on the side. I use that because I don't have one. I look at the mirror. That is not me. That is someone bad. I hate him. I hate him very bad. He makes everything bad. He makes my mum and dad hate me. I wish he would go away. I get my hand and I smack him very hard in the face. I swear at him and screw my face up. He doesn't cry. I hit him harder. I do it again and again and again. He is so stupid. I wish he would get lost. I want him to go away and never come back.

"I hate you," I say to him. "I hate you. I hate you." I smack him and I tell it to him lots of times. I want him to go away. I make my fingers dig in his face. I make it hurt. I wish I could hit him until he dies.

My mum shouts me again. I make my breathing all hard.

Then I get to feel it inside. I stare with a mean face at the boy in the mirror. I want him to know I hate him very bad. We don't be the same. I make my nails scratch down his neck. Maybe it can hurt.

I hope so.

I get dry and dressed. I don't look at the mirror again. I don't want to see him. I don't ever want to see him again. My mum says I should go out and play. Whilst I still have time. I don't say anything to my mum. I don't look at the door for the lounge. I don't want to see my dad and his friend. I don't look at the mirror when I walk past it in the hallway. I don't want to see that stupid face ever again. My mum lets me go out the front door. She locks it behind me. I don't want to play with my friends. I don't want to play with anyone, ever.

I run very fast out of the driveway. I run fast all the way down the road. I don't care that it hurts bad inside. Maybe it bleeds again too. I get to the promenade where the big ramp is. But I climb over the railing to the big steep rocks we don't be allowed to play on. Maybe we will fall and die. I hope so. Then I can go away. I walk on them very fast. All along the top. I try to make my eyes closed then I don't see where I am going. I hope the stupid boy falls and dies. Maybe his head gets broken open. I hope he falls very bad.

I don't fall down. I get all to the end. I don't know why I

don't fall. I try very hard. I turn around and I walk all the way back. I can see people playing. Maybe it is Jason and Faye and Simon. But I don't shout them. I don't want them to see me. I climb over the fence and get away. It hurts when I climb. It hurts inside from the man. Good. It should hurt very bad.

I don't know where to go. Maybe I can get lost. Maybe I can go away and no one ever finds me. I don't talk to Andrew. I know he is there. I feel him watching me. He doesn't like the boy too. It is good. I go to my mum and dad's house. Maybe the friend has gone. But I don't go in the house. I go into the back garden. Then I go into the garage. It is dark in there. I open it up. I have the key on my keys for the back door. I close it behind me. I don't turn the lights on. Maybe the bad man can get me in there. I don't care.

I sit on the cushions. I look at my dad's bottle of petrol. Maybe I can drink it. It is poison. My dad says it is. He shouts when my brother plays in there. Because there is lots of things and it is poison and can make him die and go to heaven. I look at it lots of times. Maybe I can drink it all down. I think about it inside. Maybe it tastes nice. I like how it smells. Maybe it doesn't taste very bad.

I reach over and get it. I open it. It smells nice. Maybe I can count. Not to four though. Four is very bad. I count to three. One, two, three. Then I can drink it and I can go away and then everyone is happy about it.

One.

Two.

Three.

I lift the bottle up and then I put it at my mouth. I don't tip it yet. I don't keep the crying part away. I don't ever be any good. "Drink it." I say it very bad to myself. "Drink it. Drink it." I make the words all big and growl inside. Then I get to feel the D and the K. They scratch my throat. I say it lots of times. But my stupid hands don't make it tip up.

My head feels funny inside. Maybe it floats away. It makes me feel like I can fly away. Maybe I did go to heaven. I breathe in very deep. Then I put the bottle down. It makes me laugh. Maybe I can go to the rocks and I can jump off them and then I can fly. Maybe I fly very far away.

I smile very big. I like when my head feels all funny. I try to stand up. Maybe I can find Jason and I can play with him. But I don't be able to. My legs are like jelly. They wobble lots and I fall over. I laugh about it. Stupid boy always falls over. I don't get up again. I can't be bothered about it. I lie on the floor. It is dusty there. But it doesn't matter.

There is a spider on the floor. He is dusty too. I watch him. Maybe he is scared. Maybe he thinks I will squish him. I put my hand out very far. Then I press him and the spider runs away. I laugh at him. He is a scardy spider.

Maybe I can take him inside. I try to slide on the floor. But I don't be able to. My eyes close and I don't know they do it. I don't know I am very tired. I don't know that I go to sleep. Maybe it is a long time. My eyes close and then I go. Maybe the bad man comes. I smile about it. Then I fall to sleep. Maybe I can fall to sleep for a long time.

Thirty

I like September. I get to start my new school. I get to be a senior. I am very excited about it. I got a new uniform. It isn't new from the shops. My mum and dad don't have a lot of money. They can't buy me new clothes. My mum got it from the jumble sale at the school. It looks very nice. I have to wear a blazer. It has a badge on the pocket. Then I have a tie and a shirt. I get to wear pants. Not like junior school. I had to wear shorts there. I didn't like the shorts. It made my legs cold. I didn't like it when it rained very hard and then my legs got all sore from it. It was very cold.

The blazer is too big. But they didn't have one in my size. My mum says I will grow into it. Then it can last a long time. I have to look after it. I don't get another one and then I get in trouble about it at school.

I get new shoes. My dad let me buy them. I got them from the shop. They are black and shiny. I have to put special stuff on them to make them stay shiny. My dad says I have to do it in the nighttime. But I am not allowed to do it in the house. My mum says it smells very bad. Then it gives her a headache. I do it outside in the garage. I practise lots of times when I sit out there.

I have a mark on my face. It is like a line. My mum says it is a rash. But now it is joined up. It stings when I smell the petrol and the petrol touches it. Then it feels like fire on my skin. But it isn't burnt. I didn't make it on fire. My mum asks me what it is. But I tell her I don't know. I don't stop smelling the petrol. I like it. It makes me feel happy inside. Then I talk a lot. I talk lots to my mum about the nice doctor. We talk all about it all the time. Maybe the petrol takes my bad parts away. Maybe then she likes me. I tell her when I see his car. I don't see it really. But it makes her smile inside. Sometimes we sit in the bathroom when my mum has to get her bath and I have to get ready for bed. I stay in there a long time and we talk about the doctor. She likes him very much.

I ask Andrew if he likes my new clothes. He thinks they are very nice. I make them look nice. My mum and dad are going to drive me to my new school. I don't know where it is. I didn't go there before. My mum didn't let me go when she had a look around it. She said I am going there anyway. It doesn't matter. My brother says it is big and giant.

I don't know anything. My mum says Peter is there too so it doesn't matter. Peter and my brother walked all around the school when they got to see it. But I didn't listen about it. I didn't want to know. My brother is stupid. He gets it all wrong anyway. I don't see Peter all summer long. I don't want to. I don't want to talk about the touching part. I am bad inside and I make him do bad things too. I don't want him to know I am bad. Then he will tell everyone.

My school is down a big hill. My dad takes me early. I have to be there before my brother has to go to school. Maybe because it is big school. Then I have to be there longer. My mum and dad don't get out of the car. Lots of other mums and dads do. But my dad says I am big. I can do it myself. I don't need them with me. I get out of the car and say goodbye. They don't say it back. Then they drive away.

I am very scared about it. It makes my tummy turn over inside. I don't start new schools for a very long time. Maybe I will go to the wrong place and get lost. I have my bag with my pens and papers. I have my notebook and library book too. Maybe I don't have the right things with me. There is a long driveway to get to the school. I walk along it. There are lots of other people coming in too.

There are signs on the doors. They say first years this way and there is an arrow. I have to go in the big foyer and then I have to go to the big hall. It is so big. Maybe it is a lot bigger than the one at juniors. It has a stage. I didn't ever see a stage in school before.

There are lots of other first years too. They are all sat down on the floor. They sit in lots of groups. But I don't sit with them. I don't know lots of them. I know some. But they are not my friends. They just went to the same junior school. Peter sees me. He waves. He sits by himself too. I go and sit with him. He asks me what I did to my face. I tell him it's a rash.

The head teacher comes and she tells us all where we have to go. Me and Peter are in the same class. I smile big about that. So does Peter then we don't have to be by ourselves. We have a teacher called Mrs. Morris. They all say our names and we have to go with them.

Our classroom is outside. It is like a garage it has two classrooms and a cloak room. We have our own desks. Me and Peter pick the ones at the front. They open and we get to put locks on them. Mrs. Morris says we keep our books in there. We have a timetable too. We have to remember what books we need every day.

We get to eat in the canteen. My dad has given me two pounds. He says that is enough for lunch. I can get a sandwich with that. Me and Peter go to the canteen at lunch time. There are lots of others there. They are all big. They push us out of the way. Me and Peter sit at the back. Then we don't get in their way and get shouted at.

We have all our lessons in our classroom. It is a very good day. Our classroom is at the back gate. Peter says that is the way we have to go. His mum is picking him up. She sits there in her car. She has a big smile when she sees us. She asks us if it is a good day. We both nod our heads very big and then Peter gets in the car. They drive away.

I have to walk home. But I don't know the way. My dad didn't tell me. My mum said I could find my own way home and if I got lost, it was tough. I walk all along the road. Then I get to the one with the hill. It is very big to walk up. It makes my legs all hurt about it. I talk to Andrew in my brain about all the things. We talk about the school and lots of things. Some boys get passed me. They are mean. They laugh at the mark on my face. They say stupid words about it. I don't listen to them. Maybe they can fall over and hurt themselves.

There is another boy. He lives near my house. I have seen him sometimes. But I don't ever play with him. I don't know his name. He has brown skin like my Gaga. He goes to my school. He says hi and I say hi back. He asks me if I just started today and I say yes. His name is Aadi he says. He lives around the corner from my house. He says he has seen me play lots of times.

"Would you like to come around one day?" he asks to me. I say yes.

I don't want to play today. I want to go to the garage. I like to smell the petrol stuff. It makes my head feel funny. Then I don't think about all the things. Then my dad does the sex thing. It doesn't make my badness come out. I talk to my dad lots of times when I smell the petrol. We talk about books. He likes them very much. Then he does the sex part and I go to bed. It makes my head fall to sleep.

Thirty One
(Age Twelve)

I like senior school. I like it a lot. There is a lot of homework to do. But I get it done when I get home. I like to get A's at school. I want to be a doctor. I have to do very good there. I do my homework in the garage. Then I don't get in everyone's way and my mum and dad don't know about the petrol.

I like English the most. I like when we have to write stories. Mine always get too long. I write them very fast when I get home. I like to write lots of stories. The teacher today said we have to write a story about a telephone call. I have lots of ideas. It has to be two pages long. Mine always get bigger. I write lots of pages. I am going to make my story scary. The phone call can be from a murderer.

I read lots of scary stories. My Nan buys me the books from the flea market. But they don't sell fleas there. My Dad pretends they do. Sometimes he is silly. My Nan got me a book called Carrie. My mum shouted at her about it. But I like it. It is about a girl at school and they all pick on her. Then she makes them all die in the school. It is an old book. It falls to bits. But I like it very much. My Nan buys me more books. They are by Stephen King. They are my favourite. I read them all in the night. Then my mum doesn't get mad about it.

Sometimes I read them in the garage. I go in there and smell the petrol. Then I lie on the cushions and read the book. Sometimes I fall to sleep and my mum and dad doesn't wake me up. They lock the door. But I don't know about it. I am asleep.

My mum says the Stephen King books make bad things happen. They make the bad man come. She wants to set them on fire. But I tell her no. I hide them. My Nan sneaks them. Then she doesn't get shouted at about it. I hide them at the bottom of my wardrobe. My mum doesn't go in there. I have a big box in front of it. Then the bad man can't hide.

I can't wait to get home to write my story. I write it all in my head like a film. My dad drives past me. He drives past every day. He doesn't pick me up. He says I can walk. I don't like it when he picks me up. He gets my brother. Then he goes to the shop. He buys my brother a carton of juice and some sweets. I don't get any because I am bad. My brother needs them. He sits in the front. I have to sit in the back. My brother is too fat. So he can't walk home. It makes his legs hurt too bad when he walks and then he can't breathe.

I don't wave at my dad and brother when they drive past. My brother doesn't look at me. He doesn't like me anymore. I don't like him too. He is fat and stupid and spoilt. Maybe he can go away. My brother and dad get to the house before me. They go in the front door. I am not allowed. I have to use the back door. I don't even get to use it when it is open. I go in the house. Then I run to my bedroom. I have to make my uniform folded or I get in trouble. My mum likes it folded a special way. She checks. If it is bad she gets mad about it. Then she tells my dad and he shouts at me. So I make it nice and tidy and then I don't get on her nerves again.

My mum is in the kitchen. She is making dinner. She doesn't make me any. My dad says I can make my own. I was twelve a few weeks ago. Now I am big enough to make it myself. But I have to make it before my mum starts dinner. She doesn't let me after. Then I leave the kitchen in a mess and she has to start again making it clean. I don't get any dinner today. She is making dinner already. I walked home too slow. If I run very fast I can get in the kitchen. But I was thinking about my story. It doesn't matter. I will buy some things later. I have some money. I got it from my dad's pocket. He doesn't notice about it. I hide all the food and they don't know about it. I make the wrappers burn away in the garage. Then they never know.

I go to the garage but my dad is there. He is doing some work on his bike. He has a race on the weekend. He races with all his friends. I don't get to go. He takes my brother lots of times. I don't want to go and watch stupid bike races. I don't like them anyway.

I ask my mum if I can go out. She says yes. I have to be

back at nine. Her cigarettes are on the table in the dining room. I take three of them. I didn't ever smoke before. Maybe they are like the petrol. But I can't get to that. My dad is in the garage. My mum doesn't see me take them. I take my dad's lighter too. It is a special one. I use it lots of times when I make the fires and he doesn't ever see about it.

I go to the promenade. I climb over the railings. I don't fall. I climb there lots of times and I never fall. Not even when I want to. I know how to climb. I am good at it. Sometimes the coast guard comes and tells me to go away. It is too dangerous. But I sneak back lots of times. I like to watch the sea. It is very far down. I put my mum's cigarette in my mouth and then I light it. I see my dad do it lots of times. But the cigarette doesn't light. I look at it. I don't know why it doesn't work. I try it again. I suck it like a straw. But it goes in my throat it makes me cough very bad. It nearly makes me be sick. I cough very bad. My eyes water too.

It tastes very bad in my mouth. But it makes my head all dizzy. Not dizzy like the petrol does. Just a little bit. It makes my eyes want to close. I put the cigarette at my mouth again. I suck it in very slow. Then I let it out of my mouth again like my dad does. I don't smoke the other two. I can smoke them tomorrow.

It is very boring on the rocks. The dizzy thing in my head doesn't last a long time. Maybe I can go to Aadi's house. He doesn't live very far away. I climb back over the railing and I go there. I hope it is okay. His mum is very nice. She lets me in and we play tennis. I stay there until nine then I run home again. I get there very fast.

I have to get changed into my pyjamas. Then I go upstairs and get in my dad's bed.

Thirty Two

I get up very early in the morning. But sometimes it is very cold. When it is winter, maybe I freeze in bed. I get my uniform on when I hide in the bed covers. It is too cold to get out of the bed. My nose and fingers feel frozen. My mum and dad don't get out of bed. They don't have to get up until after eight. Then my dad drives my brother to school. He doesn't ever be late.

I go into my mum and dad's room. I have to for my lunch money. They don't leave it out. My dad gets annoyed that I wake him up. But if I don't wake him up, I don't get any lunch. My mum grabs my hands. She puts them on her face. She smells them. I make them pull away. I don't like it when she does that. "Did you touch yourself?" she asks me. I shake my head a lot. I tell her no I didn't. "You did, didn't you?" she says.

"We know you did," my dad says too. "It's nice to do it."

I don't like the words they say. I wish they would stop it. It makes me feel the bad parts inside. I don't want them to talk about the bad things I do.

"You like sex," my dad says. But I shake my head. I laugh about it. They laugh about it too. I ask my dad if I can have my money. I am going to be late for school. My mum makes my pants opened and she pulls my shirt out. I don't like it. I tell her to stop it. She laughs about it. They call me a baby. But I don't be. "We know you like it," my dad says. He talks about when it feels nice inside. But I don't want him to say the words. He tells my mum about it. He puts his finger in his mouth. I hate when he does that. It makes me feel bad inside. I want to wash it all away.

I get my money off my dad. I don't go to the bathroom. I don't go and get any breakfast. I go out of the house. Then I can go away. But my brain is so stupid. It makes me mad. It says maybe I didn't lock the door. I run back and check it. It is locked. I walk to the driveway again. But my brain won't shut up. The door isn't locked. The door isn't locked. It makes me mad. I hate it. Stupid brain. Stupid pictures. I will be late for school. I run to the door and then I check it again. It is locked. I tell my brain to stop it. It's locked. I check it three times. Then I run away so my brain doesn't do it again.

I see Aadi's mum and dad's car. They take him to school. Sometimes they take me. But I don't like it. I say yes if it is wet. But I like to smoke the cigarette when I go to school. It makes my head all fuzzy inside. I like it. I smoke it and no one gets to see it.

I don't smoke one when I finish school because Aadi walks home with me. But I smoke it when he is gone because his house is first. I walk all around the block so I can smoke it before I get home. Then my mum and dad don't see it.

Aadi calls for me after school. He does lots of times. My mum and dad like him very much. My mum likes his mum too. I know it is Aadi when my mum opens the door all happy. Then she tells him to come in. My mum likes him because he is brown.

My dad is home. He is going to do some work on his motorbike. Aadi asks my dad about it. Aadi likes motorbikes too. He has a big brother who has one. He wants one too when he is bigger. Aadi asks my dad if he can see the bike. My dad says yes. But we are not allowed to touch it. Aadi says he won't.

My dad has a special bike in the garage. He takes it out at the weekends. It has a big back wheel for the racing. I have never been before. My brother has. My dad gets the bike out. It makes Aadi's eyes get all big and excited like bug eyes. He says wow in a really long way. My dad smiles very big about it. "Do you like it?" my dad asks. Aadi nods his head.

My dad tells him all about it. I don't listen. I don't want to. Sheba is outside. I stand at the door and I throw the ball for her. She runs and gets it and brings it back. My dad shows Aadi the pictures for the bike he is making. It is a special one. It is a trike. It will have three seats on it. Aadi likes it very much. My dad says he will take it on the sand dunes and race it.

My mum comes outside too. She comes into the garage. She talks to my dad and Aadi. She smiles very big about it. "Do you like the bike?" she asks him. He tells her he does. He tells her about his brother's bike. I yawn very big. My brother comes outside too. He wants to know what we are all doing. I ask Aadi if he is going home soon. My mum shouts at me. She says my name very loud. I am being rude. I don't say anything about it. I tell her I am waiting to go out and play.

"Well go them," she says. "You don't need to wait for Aadi."

I give my mum a mean look about it. I hate her. I hate all of them. They are all stupid. I don't say the words to them. But I think it. I hope they hear me. I storm out of the garage. I wish I could slam the door. But I can't. I storm all the way up the driveway. I hate them and I wish they all went away.

I don't really need to go out to play. But I don't want to be at the house. I walk all around. I smoke a cigarette in the alleyway and then I hide it. Maybe my mum sees it. I know how to do the smoking and not make the cough now. I know how to smoke properly. I watch my dad do it.

I walk around all the streets. There are some girls. They are playing stupid games. They are trying to play football. Girls are no good at football. They aren't fast enough. They can't get it in the goal. I watch them play it. I laugh about it. One girl kicks the ball very hard. Then the other girl misses it. She has to chase it up the road. I laugh very loud. One of the girls tells me to shut up. Stupid girls. The girl catches the ball. She kicks it very hard back. It goes all the way past to me. I pick it up. I ask them if they want it back. They say yes. I laugh at them and run away.

The girl who shouted at me chases me. She chases me all the way around. She shouts at me to give her the ball. I don't. She tells me I better stop or she is going to beat me up. I laugh about it. She can't beat me up. I run backwards and laugh at her when she runs then I throw the ball at her and stop. I try to throw it at her head. But she catches it. She calls me a bad name. But I don't care.

She doesn't go back to her friends. She asks me why I took the ball. I shrug my shoulders and tell her because they are stupid girls. They can't play football. She has a funny voice. I ask her where she is from. She says London. She is called Rachel. I tell her my name. I tell her she has to learn how to play football. She says she can.

I don't believe her. I saw her play. It isn't very good. We play together with the ball. I kick it to her. Then I get it off her again and make her chase it. She falls for all the tricks all the time. She smacks me hard in the arm about it. We play with the ball until it is home time.

"What are you doing tomorrow after school?" she asks me. I tell her nothing. She asks if I want to meet her. I say yes. Then I go home.

Aadi isn't there at the house. He has gone home. His

mum came to get him. They all talked for a long time. My mum doesn't know what is wrong with me. I am so rude all the time. She taught me to be nice and I don't be. I tell her I don't care. I say, "So."

"So?" she shouts it at me. She says it lots of times. I fold my arms and sigh. I don't care. She points and tells me to get in the dining room right now. I make a big yawn at her. I always have to go in the dining room. I always have to sit on the stupid chair.

She goes and gets my dad. I hear her shouting. She is sick and tired of how I am. My dad comes out with my mum. Now he has to shout at me because she told him too. I tell them why don't they have Aadi as a son instead. My mum says yes. He is better than me. Maybe they should. I tell them good. Everyone is better than me. I know I am bad. I know they don't like me. I don't like them too. I fold my arms over and I don't talk to them anymore.

My dad asks me what my problem is. But I don't answer. He gets mad because I don't talk. He shouts loud at me. He shouts his words all at my face. I don't let the crying part come out. I don't let him see it.

He smacks me hard in the head because I am so bad. I nearly fall off the chair. But I get back up again. He scrunches my face in his hand. I make my eyes get closed then I don't look at him. He tells me I have to get upstairs right now. He doesn't want to talk to me. I am too bad.

I go upstairs. But then he comes too. He follows me to my room. I tell him he said he didn't want to see me. He gets mad at me. He shouts at me for answering him back.

He tells me to sit down on my bed. He asks me why I am being so bad. I make my shoulders shrug about it. I don't know. I don't help it. My dad says he doesn't like to shout at me. But I get bad too much. He stands up. He gets his pants open and then he puts it in my mouth. I close my eyes then I don't have to see. I don't like it. But I don't cry about it. I tell myself inside my head that in an hour I will be asleep in bed. I think about that instead. I don't think about my dad. I try not to be sick when he finishes inside my mouth. He makes me look at him. He watches me swallow it. I don't like it. It makes my tummy turn upside down. It all wants to come back. But I make it go down.

My dad fastens his pants back up. "Go to bed now," he says. Then he goes out of my room and closes the door. I hug myself very tight. I roll over on my bed. I cry very hard until I fall to sleep.

.

Thirty Three

Rachel is my best friend. Better than Peter and Kirsty and Jason. She doesn't ever get mad at me. Not really. I see her every day. After school when I have got my uniform changed. Then I run to her house and call for her. We don't talk to anyone else. Jason doesn't like her. He gets mad at me. He gets mad at me a lot. I see her too much and I don't ever see him. He says I am mean. But he has lots of friends. He doesn't need me too. Rachel says maybe he is jealous about it.

Jason did like Rachel. He thought she was nice. He asked her to be his girlfriend. She said yes. But they aren't now. She didn't want to be anymore. Then he told me I couldn't be friends with him and Rachel. I shrugged about it. Friends don't make friends pick like that. He got mad about that too. He told me I wasn't his friend anymore. He shouted lots of bad names at me and told me to get lost. Everyone shouts bad names at me though. No one likes me. Not really. They say they do, but I know it is just pretend. Everyone gets mad. Then they shout at me and say mean things. Rachel doesn't.

Sometimes Rachel gets grounded. She gets grounded lots of times. We play out too long and then she is late. Her mum gets mad about it. Then she shouts. Sometimes we get things broken. Or Rachel gets mad at her mum and says mean things. Then she gets grounded again. I haven't ever been grounded. I get on my mum and dad's nerves when I am in the house. They want me to go out and play.

Rachel's house is a guesthouse. They have people who stay there for their holidays. She has a bedroom at the side. It is very high. I sit in the alleyway. Then Rachel hangs out of her bedroom window and we play catch. She throws the ball to me. Then I throw it back up to her. Sometimes I miss. Sometimes when Rachel wants to make me mad, she throws it far away and then I have to run and get it. But I don't play when she does that. Sometimes it hurts inside to get the ball.

Her mum gets mad about us playing ball. We are too noisy. The ball bangs on the wall. She tells me to come inside. If we are going to play then I can come in. Because Rachel isn't allowed out. Rachel has a thing to play computer games on. We have to load up the tapes to play them. It makes a bad loud noise. But we don't care. It sounds like a screech. Sometimes it takes forever for the game to load up.

It gets cold in Rachel's bedroom. We lay inside the bed to play the game. We have to take our shoes off. Sometimes I get Rachel to do the touching part. She doesn't say no about it when I put her hand in my pants or when I put my hand in hers.

My mum doesn't like Rachel. She doesn't ever be allowed to come in our house. It makes my mum mad because I don't see Aadi anymore. Sometimes he comes around and talks to my mum and dad. Then I get in trouble because I am rude. I don't want to talk to him. It's all boring things. They want him for a son, not me.

Aadi wants to be a doctor too. My mum says that he will do it because he has passion. "He's very clever," she says. "He gets very high marks at school. Perhaps if you were more like him, you would too."

I tell my mum about all my A's. I have them in everything. She tells my dad then he gets mad about it. He says I have sex with my teachers. That is why I have good scores. But I don't. They don't ever believe me about it. My mum says I copy Aadi when I say I want to be a doctor. I wanted to be it first. But she says I am a liar. Rachel wants to go into the air force. My mum says she won't do anything. "That girl will end up in some backstreet with ten kids by different fathers," my dad says.

Rachel thinks my mum is stupid. We laugh about it. I don't tell Rachel lots of things. I don't tell her my mum is scared about lots of things. She doesn't mean to be mean. She just has things bad inside. Rachel tells me off when she sees the cigarettes. I pinched them from my mum. She doesn't like it when I smoke. She gets real mad and shouts at me. She doesn't call me bad names. But she gets mad and it makes her cry. I don't want to make her mad. So I don't tell her and I don't let her see the smoking. If she finds them in my pockets, that makes her mad too. Then she snaps them all up and puts them in the gutter.

I don't ever tell her about the petrol. Maybe it will make her really, really mad if she knows. I don't think she likes lots of things like that. Her big brother died. It wasn't a long time ago. He took drugs and horrible things. Then he went away. It makes her sad when she talks about him. So we don't. I don't like to make her sad.

I sniff the petrol when I get home. My dad doesn't shout at me. I am home for nine o'clock. Then I can go in the garage and he doesn't care about that. I sit on the cushions and read. My mum doesn't care too. I make the cushions so I can see the kitchen. Then if my mum turns the lights off. I know it is time to go inside. She locks the house up at night time. I don't like it when they lock me out. Then I am far away and they are in the house all the way upstairs and they can't hear me. I get scared of the windows. Maybe the bad man can look in. Maybe he sees I am there. I don't move at nighttimes when I am locked out. I sit in the corner. I don't go to sleep. I am good at not going to sleep. I do it a lot in my bedroom. I go to sleep when it gets light.

The garage doesn't have a good lock and the alley is just over the wall. Maybe the bad man can get over there and I don't see him. I don't ask Andrew. I don't talk to him anymore. But he is there. He watches. I know it is him. Maybe he sees the bad man and then he will make him go away.

Thirty Four

My mum has to go to hospital today. She is having an operation. She has something wrong inside. Not in her head. It is in her stomach. It makes her not be able to eat a lot of things. Food makes her get sick. Maybe it is like my brother. Maybe she will nearly have a heart attack too. The doctor is giving her a new kind of medicine. Not the nice doctor. A different one. He works at the hospital, but he is nice too. He is doing something called keyhole surgery. I don't know what it is. Maybe they make a hole inside. Maybe they use her bellybutton. I don't like that. It makes me think about a long time ago and the church people. They stick things in my belly button. They pushed it in very hard and made it all bleed. They put lots of things inside at the same time. I don't like when I think about it. It makes me hug myself very tight. Sometimes it makes me cry. It gives me lots of bad dreams about it. I don't like to think about all those bad things. It makes me make the click in my throat. Then I can feel it. "Will you stop that?" my dad say. "If you don't stop it, you will end up being sent away to a mental hospital."

I try to make it stop but I can't. It comes back. I make my throat click. Click. Click. Click. My dad looks at me with his mad face.

I have to go to school. I tell him I am sorry. My mum and

dad got up early because she has to be at hospital early. They will take her gallbladder out. She has stones in it. But I don't know what that is too. It has to be small if they are doing it with a key hole. Keyholes don't be very big. My mum is excited about it. She says it will make everything better. Then she can go outside and not be scared. Then no bad things happen. The angel people told her about it.

My mum has angel people. They wear suits. They dress very smart. I have never seen them. But my mum does. She tells me about them. She saw one when she had to be in jail because she hurt my big brother. The angel man came and he brought her a cup of tea. He told her it would be okay. She didn't need to cry about it. He told her that she would marry the nice doctor too. That is why she knows one day she will. But his mean wife won't go away. She doesn't leave him alone and then my mum can't be with him. It makes my mum cry. She loves him very much.

I don't say goodbye to my mum and dad when I go to school. I don't want to get in the way. My dad gives me my money. He doesn't ask me about the sex part. Or if I touch myself. My mum doesn't get my hands to check. But I keep them away so she can't. I don't like when she does that at morning time. I go out of the house before they get mad at me. My brother isn't going to school. He is going to the hospital because he is sad about it. I am not because I'm not bothered. That's what my mum says to me.

My dad isn't home when school is finished. I don't like to be in the house by myself. I get scared about the bad man. I run upstairs. Then I make my door locked. I change my clothes very fast and go out to Rachel's. She isn't home yet. But I sit and wait for her. We are going to play at the golf course. We have a den there. It is in the round trees. We aren't allowed there, but no one sees us and no one tells us off about it. We go there all the time. We have a rope and we tied it to a tree. We run and jump and swing on it.

We also have lots of golf balls. People hit them and lose them. Then we find them and collect them. We keep them in a bag. Rachel says we should sell them. But we don't. There is a pond near the gate. We throw the boring ones in there. We have to climb through trees and brambles to get to the pond. Sometimes the brambles scratch my skin and make it bleed. Sometimes it hurts too bad inside and I pretend the brambles hurt when I have to climb. But it hurts inside from my dad. I don't tell Rachel about that.

Sometimes it hurts too bad inside that I don't ride my bike too. I don't tell Rachel. I tell her I am tired and then we push them instead. She says I am lazy. She laughs when I say I am too tired to ride my bike. She gets hers and rides away. Maybe she can make me do it and come after her. But I don't.

It gets dark. All the stupid rich people have gone away. They don't play golf in the dark. Me and Rachel lie on the grass. She lies with her head on my tummy. We look at the stars and talk about lots of things.

We don't stay there late today. I have to get home early because my mum isn't there. I have to be home for seven. My dad wants to know where I am and he doesn't like it when I am out getting into trouble. He says Rachel makes me do bad things. But she doesn't. I make her do bad things.

My dad has made dinner. I walk in the back door and it smells very nice. It makes me hungry. My stomach growls. Maybe I don't get any. But my dad tells me to come and sit at the table. He has made the table nice. Me and my brother sit there. My dad has made roast chicken. It has lots of sauce and gravy. I like when my dad cooks He makes the best food ever.

"How was school?" my dad says to me. I tell him it is good. "What are you doing?" he asks. I don't like it when he asks about school. Maybe I am not hungry any more. The food feels all big and I don't want to eat it. Maybe I did something bad and he knows about it. I don't like when he tricks me. He makes it all nice then he hits me very hard when I don't know he is going to do it.

I don't want to say bad things and make him shout at me. I don't want him to tell me I am stupid. He thinks I am stupid all the time. I tell him I am doing algebra. He smiles very big about it and he eats his dinner. He doesn't hit me about it. "Do you like it?" he asks.

I do. But it is very hard. I look at my hands. I don't want my dad to say mean things about it.

He doesn't. We finish dinner. Then my dad washes the plates and things. I dry them and my brother puts them away. We don't leave them for my mum. My dad says he can teach me algebra if I want. When my brother has gone to bed. Maybe I want to.

I tell him yes please. My dad doesn't ever teach me school things before.

Thirty Five

My brother sits and watches the television. I don't know what he is watching. Some stupid fighting thing. It's boring. My mum doesn't let him watch it when she is at home. But she isn't. She is in the hospital so my dad says he can watch what he wants. He isn't allowed to watch bad things. Maybe they make him bad like me. I make everything bad. He is all soft inside. My mum says he doesn't understand the bad things. Not like me. I know how to do all the bad things because I don't care. She doesn't let him watch the bad things because then he will get bad because he doesn't know any better.

My brother is stupid and a baby. My mum doesn't know. She thinks he is nice, but he is bad really. He tells lots of lies and she doesn't see it. I tell her about it and then he starts to cry. My mum says that it is me and how dare I say such bad things about her son. Then my dad gets mad and he hits me. I hate them all. They are always mean. I don't know why they are mean. When I am good, they are mean and when I am bad they are mean. Maybe they would like it if I went away.

My dad doesn't ever ask about my homework. Maybe he likes maths. I show my dad my sums. I don't know what they mean. The teacher told us all about it. But I didn't listen. I was writing a story in my book. It didn't want to wait. So I wrote it very fast. We have to do algebra. It is very hard. My dad says it is easy. He gets a pen and paper and he writes a sum down. I don't know what it means. He asks me to try. I stare at it very hard. But I don't know how to do it. Maybe he will shout at me because I am stupid. I don't mean to be. I try very hard. I hug myself tight and say I am sorry. I don't want him to be mad at me. I don't know the sum.

He doesn't get mad about it. He moves up and sits closer. He starts it all again and writes the numbers. He asks me what I am supposed to do next. I tell him and he smiles because I get it right. He tells me well done. He doesn't ever tell me well done before. Maybe I don't hate my dad. He shows me lots of times and I get them all right.

"Maybe you can do some more?" he says. "While I am in the shower?" I nod my head about it. My dad gets some more paper and he writes some sums down and gives them to me. It makes me excited inside. I do them and then my dad knows I am not stupid. Maybe he can like me.

My dad goes to get a shower and I sit on the floor with Sheba. She isn't good at sums. She leans her head on my crossed leg. Maybe she reads the paper. The sums are very hard without my dad there. I try to think about what he said. I do them all. My dad doesn't take a long time in the shower. He comes out and he has got changed. He smells like medicine. My mum makes him use special shampoo. It gets all the oil out of his hair. She doesn't like it when he smells like cars. She says it is bad and disgusting.

My dad looks at my sums. I didn't get them all right. He sits down again and he doesn't get mad. He tells me to come and sit on the chair with him. He tells me which ones I got wrong and he shows me how to do them. But he says I tried very hard and he is happy. I smile about it.

My dad says he is going to put my brother to bed now. It is his bedtime. He has school in the morning. My dad doesn't stay upstairs though. My brother goes to sleep because he is tired. My dad comes back down and asks me if I want to watch some television. I don't know what to say. Maybe he gets mad if I say yes. But then if I say no he might be mad too. Maybe he gets sad if I say no. Because maybe he wants to do the sex thing with me and if I say no, then he doesn't get to and he feels bad about it. I don't know what to say. I don't want him to shout at me because I don't answer.

I nod my head very slow. My dad says I can pick. But I don't know what to watch. I flick the four channels over. They have lots of boring things on. But I don't get to watch lots of television. I watch a police program. My mum doesn't ever let anyone watch the television at nighttime. She likes to watch the soap things. I don't like them. They are boring. But my mum watches them all the time. We don't get to use it.

When the police show finishes, my dad tells me it is bedtime. I have to go to the bathroom and brush my teeth and use the toilet. I don't want to go to bed. Maybe my dad goes too and then there isn't anyone downstairs and then the bad man can come and no one hears him. Maybe the bad man hides in the rooms at the bathroom. It is very dark. I turn the lights on.

I go in the bathroom and brush my teeth very slow. Then it is a long time. But I don't take too long. If I do, my dad gets mad about it and I don't want him to be mad. He will shout. I finish in the bathroom and go back to the lounge. I tell my dad goodnight. Then I go up the stairs. But I don't like it there. There isn't a light at the top. I don't like to open my door. It makes me scared inside about it. Maybe the bad man waits inside. Maybe he got in and he waited all day for me. I don't want to open the door.

My dad is getting everything locked up. I hear him let Sheba out. She has to go to the toilet at bedtime too. Then she doesn't wake us up so she can go outside. My dad finishes everything and then he comes to the stairs. He is going to shout at me. He always does. I take too long and I don't do things like I am supposed to. I don't get in my bedroom yet. I tell my dad I am sorry. I can feel the crying inside. Maybe it comes out if he shouts at me.

"Do you want to sleep in here?" he asks me and I nod my

head about it. I do. I don't want to sleep in my room.

My brother is asleep in the middle of the bed. I get in at my mum's side. My dad closes the door then he gets in at the other side. My dad turns off the big light. But he leaves the little one on. I am glad. I don't like it when it is very dark. Not even when my dad is there. It makes me see the bad man in my mind. Then he might come when my dad is sleeping and no one can stop him.

I face my brother. He is snoring all loud. He doesn't even move when we got into the bed. Maybe he doesn't know and it will be a surprise when he wakes up again. I close my eyes and go to sleep. I like when my mum is at the hospital and I can sleep in the big bed.

I don't open my eyes when my dad moves. He makes the bed dip and I nearly roll into my brother. But my dad lifts my brother up and puts him out of the way. My tummy feels funny inside. I don't get to breathe properly. I know my dad is going to come over to me. I roll away and then maybe he thinks I am asleep.

"Move up," my dad says to me. He has picked my brother up. I have to move to the middle of the bed. But I don't open my eyes properly. I slide over and my dad puts my brother on my mum's side. Where I was just sleeping. He pulls at my pants, but he doesn't take them off. He wants me to do it. I don't say no. I push them down and hug myself tight.

My dad pulls at my top too and I take that off. I pull the covers all on me. It makes me shiver. My dad leans down the side of the bed. He has some rope there. I didn't know about it. My dad gets my hands and then he ties them up above my head to the top of the bed. But he doesn't do it tight. I can still move about. He ties them together.

My dad makes me sit up. My hands slide all the way up and I have to hold them over my head. He takes his clothes off too. I make my eyes close when he kneels over me. I just open my mouth. He doesn't tell me to do it. I do it lots of times now.

He doesn't make the disgusting part in my mouth. I don't like it when he does that. It makes me want to be sick. But he doesn't this time. I open my eyes. My brother is asleep. He isn't facing us. I don't want him to see that I am bad. I don't want him to know about it all.

My dad slides me back down again. Then he rolls me over onto my front. I don't know he has another rope. But he uses it to tie my feet down. My dad lies on top of me. He whispers lots of things to me. He tells me I am good. Then when he starts the sex part he tells me I like it very much. I nod my head. I watch my brother. Then he doesn't wake up. It makes me afraid inside. I don't want him to see. Then he will hate me forever. I don't want him to.

It hurts inside. But I don't cry about it. It doesn't take very long. When my dad finishes, he takes the rope off my feet, but not my hands and I go to sleep.

I like when I sleep in my mum and dad's bed. But I wish I got my hands down. I am very tired though and I go to sleep. I sleep for a long time. I know the bad man can't come and get me. Not when I am in the middle. Then he has to get past my dad or brother. It is dark when I wake up again. I don't know what time it is.

My dad has the covers off. I didn't know about it. He has his hand on me and then he tells me to open my mouth. My dad sees that I like that part. I don't mean for him to see it. But he does. He always likes it too when he puts his hand on me and it makes things happen. I wish he didn't see. He says things about it and it makes me feel bad inside. I know I make him do all the bad things. He likes it when I make the noises because it feels funny inside. Then he does the noises too and it gets in my mouth. I don't get sick with it. I know if I swallow very hard and lots of times I don't get sick. My dad holds my jaw so it is all gone. Then he lets me go back to sleep again.

He wakes me up one more time in the night. I don't know what time it is. It isn't as dark. Maybe it is nearly morning. I don't know. I am too tired to think about it. My dad wakes me up for school. He unties my hands and tells me to go and get a shower.

I go very fast to the shower. My dad and brother stay in bed. I make the door locked behind me. No one can come in. But I watch the door too and then if the bad man is hiding, He can't sneak in and I don't know about it. I scratch all down with my dad's hard brush to make it all wash away. I don't cry. I make it hurt though. I make all the bad parts wash away.

My dad doesn't drive me to school. He isn't allowed to. My mum doesn't let him. But it is okay. I meet Rachel and we walk. I don't know what to say to her. I want to ask her about things. I think about it lots of times. Maybe she can keep secrets and she doesn't tell anyone.

"I have a friend at school. He said his dad is doing bad things to him. Would you tell the teacher?" I ask her.

She asks me what kind of things. I tell her sex things. But I don't say them all. My hands shake very bad about it. She thinks about it a long time.

"I would tell my mum or the teacher," she says.

I nod my head about it and say thank you. I don't tell her anything else. We walk to school.

Thirty Six

There is another boy and girl called Simone and Aaron. They are brother and sister. They live in a flat near my mum and dad's house. Simone likes to hang around with me and Rachel. But she isn't allowed to stay out very late because she isn't twelve yet. She is only nine. But we like her and we let her play. She is lots of fun. Her brother is little. He is like my brother and he is seven. He doesn't know many things. He has something wrong inside his head. It makes him say lots of stupid things and then his mum gets mad about it and tells him to get out of the house. But he comes and plays with us too. My brother doesn't like him. He calls him names. My brother is mean and stupid. I tell him he is fat and he should get lost. Then he cries.

My mum doesn't like Aaron either. She says he has something wrong with his head because his mum drinks lots of alcohol and then she drank it when he was inside. She calls her bad names and says she has sex with lots of men. "Probably doesn't know who the father is." But she does. Simone and Aaron have a dad. He is nice. Both the mum and dad are nice. They let me and Rachel come inside. Then she gives us fizzy drinks and biscuits. I don't get them at home. Just my brother does because he is good and I am bad. Sometimes, Simone's mum makes us a nice dinner. I don't tell my mum about it or she will say I am not allowed to play there anymore. I don't like when I am not allowed to play at people's houses. But I do it and I don't tell my mum about it. Then she doesn't get mad.

Simone's mum and dad ask me and Rachel if we want to babysit. We are allowed to watch a film if we do. We say yes. I don't ask my mum. She has just come out of the hospital and I am not allowed to bother her. My dad says so. I didn't see her at the hospital because my dad says I make her too sad. So I don't go. I stay and play with Rachel. My brother goes, but I am not allowed to. I don't know why I make her sad. I don't do it on purpose. I try my best to be nice. But then it doesn't work and my mum gets mad about it. Except when I talk about the Doctor Batman, then she likes it and it makes her happy. It is okay that I don't get to go. I don't want to anyway. It's boring and they are all stupid.

My mum says the operation didn't work. She cries about it sometimes. But she still can't eat all the nice food. It makes the sick come out. She thinks the doctor made it worse. She says they don't like her then they do it on purpose. I tell my mum maybe it was an accident, but she shouts at me and says I don't know anything. I tell her maybe she can ask Doctor Batman about it. My mum likes that. She smiles about it. She says, "Maybe them up there did it so I have to see him. They do things like that."

Maybe my mum is right. She says them up there all the

time. She means all the ghosts and things like that. Like my Gaga. He is up there and then he can see the bad things and make them into good things. I don't tell him about my bad things or the sex. I don't want him to see that. Maybe he thinks I am bad if he sees that. I don't want him to know I let my dad do the sex thing.

Simone lives near the beach. She lives in a flat. There are lots of other flats there, but I don't ever see the other people. We are going to babysit there. Simone's mum and dad just go to the pub on the promenade. They won't be a long time, they say. Just until ten. But I have to be home at nine. "We will pay you," Simone's dad says and me and Rachel say yes. Maybe I can go home at nine and tell my mum I go in the garage, then I sneak away and she doesn't know. She doesn't come in the garage at nighttime because it is dark and she doesn't like it.

We babysit at their flat and Simone's mum and dad say they have to go to bed. Simone doesn't watch the film with us. We are going to watch Edward Scissorhands. I haven't ever seen it before, but Rachel says it is very good. It looks scary on the cover. The man has lots of scissors on his hands. Rachel says it isn't. She likes it very much. She went to see it with her mum. I tell her maybe he chops people up. But she says he doesn't. My brain says maybe he makes all the scratches like the bad man does. Maybe he hurts people when they are asleep and then no one knows about it. I don't ask Rachel. I can't ever talk about the bad man because he will come.

We lie on the sofa and Rachel lies on top of me. She isn't very heavy. She lies on me lots of times when we play at the golf course. Sometimes it makes me not breathe properly, but I don't tell her about it. She hugs with her head on me and I hug her too. I don't ever get hugs from people. I like to hug Rachel. But maybe then she can smell it from the sex part. I don't hug her sometimes when I can smell that.

We watch the film. It isn't scary. But I get sad when the dad dies and then Edward doesn't have anyone and he cries all by himself. I don't like when I cry all by myself. Maybe someone hears and comes to hug him. The lady takes him home and he lives in her house. He doesn't go to a boy's home. My mum says if my mum and dad go anywhere then me and my brother go to a boy's home. But we go to different ones because I am big and he is little. Then I don't see anyone, not even my Nan.

Rachel leans up and looks at me. She does that lots of times when we lie down and talk about things. She doesn't get off me though. She smiles and maybe she is going to do something to trick me. Maybe she tries to tickle me. But she doesn't. She puts her mouth on mine and I didn't know she was going to do that. I haven't ever kissed a girl before. Not a proper kiss. I did with Kirsty, but we didn't do it properly. Not like my mum showed me how to do it. My mum says I have to open my mouth and then I have to put my tongue on hers. I don't like to do it with my mum. But I do it with Rachel. It is a big kiss and we do it for a long time.

Rachel rolls down at my side. Then she is squashed at the back of the sofa. I don't know why I do it; I get my hand in her pants. She doesn't say no about it. Maybe we can do the sex thing. But I won't make it hurt. Not like the play place. I had to make it hurt there. I didn't like it. The girls cried about it. I tried to say no, but then I got hit and made to do it. I didn't like to make them cry. I didn't like when the boys had to do the sex thing too. Then they make me cry. I don't want to make Rachel cry. But she doesn't and she doesn't take my hand away. We do it for so long I don't see the time, and it gets past nine and I don't know about it.

We don't get to the sex part because Simone's mum and dad come back. They are noisy when they come in. It is good, then we hear them and they don't see and don't know that I am bad. Rachel has her pants open, but she fastens them back up before Simone's mum sees. Maybe they would tell my dad about it. Then he is right. All I like is sex. All the time.

Simone's mum gives us five pounds for babysitting. We tell her thank you very much. Then we go home. We walk in all the alleyways. Rachel thinks it is scary. But I say it isn't. Dark isn't scary outside. Just inside when the bad man comes. I hold Rachel's hand, then she isn't scared about it. Rachel says maybe there is someone scary in the alleyway. But I tell her there isn't and I make spooky noises. She smacks me and tells me to stop it.

We walk to Rachel's house and then I give her a kiss goodbye. I like to kiss her. I wish Simone's mum didn't come back yet. Then we could stay there. Rachel goes in her house and then I walk in the alleyway again. When I can't see Rachel's house, I get the cigarettes out of my pocket. I hide them and then Rachel doesn't find them and screw them up. I light it and smoke it. I like when it is in my throat. When it is all gone then I go home. Then my mum and dad don't know I smoked it.

It is after ten. Maybe my mum locked the house up. Maybe my dad has gone to bed. He goes to bed at ten because he gets very tired. He says it is because of everyone. We make him tired all the time. Then my mum watches the television. I feel scared when I get to the house. I don't want to go in the garage. I don't like to walk all the way at the back of the house. Maybe the bad man is waiting. Maybe he can get me and then my mum doesn't hear. I see it lots of times. I see his face in my brain and he has a stupid smile. I don't like it. Then I feel his nails and it hurts. Maybe he can kill me and I can go away.

I go into the back garden. The kitchen light is on. My mum is in the kitchen. It makes me think phew. Maybe she will be mad at me. Maybe she won't let me in. I have a key. When I sleep in the garage, she puts the key in the other side, then mine doesn't work. I tried it sometimes then I have to run back to the garage. Maybe she has done that.

I feel the thing in my back. It makes me scared and I run very fast to the back door. It feels like the bad man is there. Maybe he hides and watches. I run very fast to the door. My mum didn't put the key in and it opens wide. I go inside very fast and I make my mum jump. She swears at me about it. I tell her I am sorry.

My mum is mad at me because I am late. She shouts at me. She is washing the plates and her hands are soapy. It flicks about when she waves them mad at me. I don't move away. She smacks me if I do that. Then maybe she gets my dad and he makes it very bad. "I saw Batman," I say to my mum when she is quiet. I don't know why I say it. But it comes out and she stops getting mad at me.

"You did? Where? Here?" she asks me lots of things. Her voice is very excited.

I tell her I am very sorry for being late. I didn't mean to. She tells me it is okay. She doesn't mind. I wasn't very late. She asks me about the doctor. She wants to know where I saw him. I tell her that I was babysitting for Simone and then we had to walk on the promenade. I tell her he drove past us in his car.

She asks me if he was by himself. I nod my head. "He looked sad," I tell her.

She asks me if I was sure it was him. I nod my head. She washes some more things and then she doesn't look at me. I don't go away. She didn't tell me to. Then when the plate is clean, she turns around again. She has a very big smile. "Maybe he came here to see me and then he saw your dad's car again," she says. "He is sad because of his bloody wife."

She talks lots about him. I don't say anything about it. I ask her if I can make some cereal. I always get food when she talks about the doctor. It makes her happy about it. She says yes but I am not allowed to make a mess. I tell her I won't. Then I make a big giant bowl of it. I don't move it because then maybe it falls on the floor and she will get mad. I don't want her to be mad. She is happy about the doctor.

I eat my cereal and she asks me lots of things. She asks me if he came near the house. I tell her he turned away first and went down the road where the shop is. My mum says it is because of my dad's car again. Me and my mum talk for a long time. I say all the right words to her and she doesn't get mad at me. It is after midnight and I am very tired. I don't see my dad. He is in bed and then he is sleeping. My mum didn't finish her dishes yet. She talks too much. I tell her I will help her then she can go to bed too. She says no, she will do them herself. She isn't tired.

I tell her goodnight and she doesn't get mad at me. I go

and brush my teeth and things and then I go upstairs. I sneak so my dad doesn't hear me. But maybe he knows I am late. He gets up and he comes to his bedroom door. I stand outside mine for a long time. Maybe the bad man is in there. "What are you doing?" he asks me. It makes me freeze inside. Maybe he will ask about being late. I tell him about helping my mum do the dishes. He says okay and then he goes downstairs.

I open my door before he goes away and then I get the light on. There isn't a bad man in there. I tell my dad goodnight. I turn the other light on. Then I have to check in the wardrobe. Maybe the bad man got in and hides in there. But he doesn't. I check in the big box too. But he isn't in there and he isn't under the bed, or behind the curtains. I check everywhere. I get my clothes and I don't look at the mirror. I don't want to see if the bad man sneaks in through the mirror because he is a bad spirit. My mum says they can get in that way.

My dad comes back upstairs. I didn't get time to get changed yet. My dad opens my door and then he comes in. He pushes me on the bed but he doesn't say any words. I don't say no when he does the sex thing. He doesn't say anything too. Maybe he does it because I am late. But he doesn't make it hurt. My dad puts his hand on me too. Then I make the noises. He tells me I am good. He always says I am good. I don't look at him. I don't say anything when he makes the noises too. He doesn't say anything when he gets off my bed. He goes in his bedroom and then I hear him get in bed. I don't think about it. Maybe it makes the cereal come back out. I don't think about the crying. It just comes out and I don't stop it. I get in bed and hug myself tight. Then I go to sleep in the corner. The bad man doesn't come.

Thirty Seven

I don't talk to Rachel about the kissing part. I don't say anything. She has a boyfriend. He goes to the same school as her. But he doesn't come at her house. I am glad. Then I don't have to see her kiss him. He came a long time ago. Then he came to the den in the golf course. But he didn't want to do anything. We played games on the rope and we made arrows too from the wood. He said it was stupid. I think he is stupid. But I don't tell Rachel. Maybe he can go away.

Rachel says he doesn't like me. He thinks I am bad and I make everything stupid. I don't care about it. I think he is boring. He speaks funny too. He makes his S's sound long and he spits when he talks. He thinks he is clever because he gets lots of A's. I get lots of A's too. Maybe Rachel tells him about the kissing.

I go to Rachel's very early. I don't like my mum and dad's house at the weekend. Then I get in trouble and I have to do lots of things and I don't like it. I like to see Rachel. We stay out all day. Rachel's mum lets me in the house. I have to stay in the kitchen because Rachel has to wash the dishes up from breakfast. She is in trouble. She said bad things to her mum and then she has to wash the dishes, or she gets grounded. She always says bad things to her mum.

I sit on the table when she washes the things. "Do you think that people who run away have a good time?" I ask. I don't know why I ask about it. I thought about it when I had a cigarette before I got to Rachel's house.

She asks what I mean. I tell her about a boy that ran away. He had a fun time when he did it. Then he got money and things because he helped people. He did things like make gardens nice and tidy. He helped lots of people. But he lived all by himself in a secret place. Lots of children came and thought he was very good and they made friends with him and gave him things. He never got in trouble.

I didn't read about it. Me and Mr. Ted made the story a long time ago. We got to read the Huckleberry Finn book and then we made it up. We read it lots of times. It was funny. But then it got sad so me and Mr. Ted made our own book. I don't tell Rachel it is a book. Then maybe she won't run away with me.

She says it sounds like fun. I think so too. I ask her if we should try it. Maybe we can sleep on the golf course at our den. I tell her we can tell our mums that we sleep at other houses, then we sleep outside and no one knows about it. It is nearly summertime. The nighttimes are warm when they don't get wet and freeze. I tell her we can make a bonfire and cook things. I like to make bonfires.

I tell Rachel we can do it on the next weekend. When I have seen my Nan. Then we can go. I don't tell Rachel I am going to run away for a long time. I don't want to go home. I have some money from my dad. I got it out of his pocket. I can get on a train and go far away and then they don't find me. Maybe Rachel can come too. Then I am not on my own. But I will go by myself if she doesn't come. My mum doesn't like me anymore. She gets mad all the time. She didn't miss me when she was in the hospital. My brother is very happy when she came home. He gave her a big hug. But she didn't give me one. I stood at the back. She didn't say hello. My dad doesn't talk to me. I didn't go in their room this morning. Maybe it makes them mad. But I didn't want to. I didn't want to do the morning thing.

When it is Saturday, my mum shouts me. She doesn't shout in a mad voice. She wants me to do the Saturday thing. She tells my dad to stand at the corner. He doesn't have any clothes on. Sometimes he has the underwear thing on that is my mum's. But his thing always sticks out and my mum tells me to get hold of it. Then I have to pull him around the room until she says stop. I don't like to do it. It makes my hand feel dirty. But I laugh about it. My mum watches. Sometimes she takes pictures. She says he is our slave and we have to make him do everything. I pull him all the way to the bed when she tells me to. Then she tells me to push him over so that he does the sex thing with her. I have to sit on the bed too. Sometimes my dad puts his hand in my pants or I have to take them off. I don't look when my mum and dad do the sex thing. I don't like to watch it. But my dad tells me to. He tells me I have to sit on his back like when my brother gets horsey rides.

Sometimes my dad makes me lean over my mum. Like we do the sex thing. But we don't. My dad does it to me instead. But I don't lie down because then I touch my mum and she doesn't have clothes on and I don't like it. Sometimes my dad is too heavy. Then he makes my arms hurt. They get pins and needles in them and feel like they are very fat, but they aren't. When it is all finished, I get to play out with my friends. I go to Rachel's, but I don't let her go near me. I don't like how the sex stuff smells. It smells very bad and I don't want Rachel to know about it all.

I didn't do the sex thing with my mum and dad this morning. I didn't want to. I went to Rachel's house instead. My mum and dad didn't get mad about it. I am happy that she says yes about running away. She thinks it will be fun to sleep outside for one night. But I don't tell Rachel I don't ever go back. It is going to be forever. We write a list of things we need. Maybe I can get my dad's sleeping bag. It is in the attic near my bedroom. I can sneak in when my dad doesn't know. I have some money too. I keep it in my bedroom. I hide it then my dad doesn't know I took it. I take lots of it when he is in the shower. But I don't spend it. I just buy sweets and drinks and I finish them so my mum and dad don't see and then they don't know I stole it.

Andrew knows I stole things. He doesn't like me anymore. He doesn't talk to me. He watches. I see him do it. He has a mean face because I do all the bad things. I try not to be bad. I promise him I don't do the bad things anymore. But I can't help it. Maybe he thinks running away is too bad. Maybe he can come too, then he can look for people at nighttime.

Rachel finishes all the dishes, then we go to the den. We

talk all day long about the running away plan. I am very excited about it. Then when it gets to nearly 9 o'clock, we go home again. I have a cigarette when Rachel goes in her house and she doesn't see. I don't want to go in my house. I want to run away now. When I finish my cigarette, I go in the kitchen. My mum is there. She washes more dishes too. I tell her I am home and I have homework. I do it in the garage. "Did you see Batman today?" she asks me. I shake my head about it. She says okay. She is sad.

I get my homework then I go in the garage. I sit on the cushions and do it. It is easy homework. I do most of it at lunchtime. I don't like the people at school. I don't stay with them. I do my schoolwork instead. There is a boy called Lewis. I don't like him the most. He is mean and stupid and he swears all the time. He asks me lots of times if I want to fight. He says he is going to beat me up. But he doesn't do it. He just says it. I wait lots of times after school and he doesn't come.

Maybe Lewis is a baby. It doesn't matter. When I run away, I don't ever see him again. I can't wait to run away. I write a list of things in my book from school. I steal books at school so I can write stories. My mum doesn't let my buy any. I use one to say what me and Rachel need. Then we don't forget anything. Maybe we can do some work when we run away and then we can get money and we don't ever have to go back again.

I write my list out then I get the petrol from my dad's bike. I put the bottle to my nose and I smell it very deep. It makes me smile. It makes me fuzzy inside and then I don't feel sad. I smell it and then I count. One, two, three. I make it very deep. It makes my head float away. I lie down with my book and my pen. Then I fall to sleep. I didn't know I fell to sleep for a long time. All the way to the morning. My mum locked me out. She won't miss me if I run away. Maybe she thinks I hide in the garage. I smile about it.

Thirty Eight

I wish I could tell my Nan I am running away. I wish she got to come too. Then I don't miss her when I go away. Maybe she will be sad if I tell her about it. Maybe she will get mad and tell my mum and dad. It is Friday again. She has come for dinner. Me and Rachel are going to run away today. My Nan is watching television. She likes the Australian soap things about the beach. They look nice and sunny there. My mum likes the soaps too. But she doesn't watch them with my Nan. She is in a bad mood today. She shouts lots of times at everyone. She calls my Nan mean names too. But my Nan doesn't say anything about it.

I sit with my Nan. Then I can sit with her one more time before I go away. Maybe I can take some paper and then I can write and she can be my pen friend. Maybe she doesn't tell anyone where I live when I run away. I don't get to sit with my Nan for a long time because Aadi knocks on the door. I let him in. I don't want him to be here. But he doesn't go away. I didn't tell him to come and call for me. But he does. My mum smiles big about him. Maybe he comes to see my mum and dad.

I go to my room. I don't tell him to come but he does. He says hello to my Nan when he walks past. She says hello back. I wish he would go away. I have my bag on the table. I have some clothes too. I have my dad's sleeping bag. I got it when no one was in the house. They went away to the park and didn't tell me about it. But then I got it and hid it in my room. My mum and dad don't know I went in the attic. My mum doesn't know I go in there. She doesn't like it if I do. I hide my books in there. I write them all to Mr. Ted. He isn't magic anymore. But I still write them. Maybe his magic can come back. I wish he was a real bear and then he really talks. I don't take him when I run away. He has to stay on my bed then my mum doesn't know. Maybe he can look after my books in the attic and then no one finds them and I don't get in trouble. I write about all the sex things. My mum says I am not allowed. But I write them in there when it makes me cry. I write them at nighttime when I cry very big. It makes the crying go away when I write.

Aadi looks at my sleeping bag then he looks in my bag. "Are you going for a sleepover?" he asks me. I tell him no and then I stuff my things in my bag and hide it down the side of the box so he can't see it. I have food in there too. I got it from the kitchen. I don't want Aadi to say about it to my mum.

"Are you running away?" he asks. But he laughs about it. He makes me mad inside. He is nosey. I wish he would go away.

I tell him no.

He doesn't say anything about it. He sits on my bed and looks at my reading books. I wish he didn't sit on my bed. My mum made it all nice and flat. She gets mad when it gets messy and I don't make it right. She doesn't like all the wrinkles in it. She will shout at me about it because I don't keep it nice and neat. I am bad. Maybe she will be happy when I run away then I don't get on her nerves anymore.

I ask Aadi if he wants to go downstairs to the kitchen. My mum is there. He likes to talk to my mum. She doesn't shout at me when he is there. Just says mean things. She likes him. He says yes and we go downstairs. My Nan sees and then she comes to the kitchen too. My Nan asks Aadi about school. He tells her that he has to choose all his subjects this year. My Nan thinks it is good. He tells her he chose all the right ones then he can go to medical school and be a doctor. My Nan asks which ones he chose and he tells her.

My Nan asks if I will take those ones too. She knows I want to be a doctor. I tell her yes. But I want to be a different doctor. I want to look after children and make them better. My mum sighs about it. She says I won't be able to do it. "What about when you kill a baby?" she asks me. I don't like it when she says that.

"Maybe I make the baby better," I say to her. "Maybe it would die and go to heaven if I don't make it better."

My mum is cooking dinner. She doesn't think I will be a good doctor. She says it lots of times that I won't. My dad says I can't do it because I don't care about anything and I am too stupid. They don't know I get lots of A's in everything. My mum doesn't want to see my school reports. So I don't tell her about it. I like school and then I will go and be a doctor and live away and then my mum and dad can go away.

I leave Aadi in the kitchen. No one notices when I go

away. Aadi talks to them. He can stay there and then leave me alone. I have to get ready. After dinner, I am going to meet Rachel and then we run away. Maybe my mum knows about it. It makes me scared inside. Maybe she knows I am telling lies about sleeping at my friend's house. Maybe they sneak my stuff away from my room when I am not there. I run upstairs to check. But it is there and they don't know.

Aadi goes home. Then I have to set the table for dinner. I do it very quiet. My dad comes home from work. He is full of oil from the cars. He is late. He doesn't get his shower yet. Then I am not allowed to the toilet. I have to go when he gets a shower. He washes his hands in the kitchen sink. Then he sits at the table. I don't walk very close to him. Maybe he knows I am running away and then maybe he will hit me very hard when I don't know it and I can't stop it.

My mum has made roast chicken. She always makes it on Fridays. She did when I was little too. It smells nice. My dad gives me the leg and some skin. It is my favourite part. I like it with the bread sauce. I put some of the bread sauce on the leg. Then I put it at the side and save it to last.

My brother doesn't eat the chicken with us. He had his special food already. He sits and watches the cartoons in the lounge. I see him. He sits on the sofa with his new toys. He always has new toys. New toys and lots of television. He is very fat too. He sits on me and makes me squashed. My dad calls him fat all the time. Fat and stupid. That's what he is. He cries about it sometimes. He should cry. I wish he cried for a long time. I hate him very much. He gets everything. He is bad. I wish he would go away. Maybe he could run away and then they all get sad about it. Maybe he can die and go to heaven.

I tell my brother I am sorry in my head. I don't mean to think about all the mean things. I eat my dinner fast and I don't look at him. He won't care if I runaway. It makes him happy. Then he can have my bedroom and all my things.

When dinner is finished, I put the plates in the kitchen. Then I make the table tidy again. I ask if I can go out and my mum says yes. My dad goes for his shower. He takes his big mug of tea with him. I have to use the toilet before I go out. I ask my dad if I can use it. He says yes and then he comes to the bathroom too. I try to hide so he doesn't see. But he looks and I tell him to stop it. He grins about it and then he takes his clothes off for the shower.

He tells me to get my hands washed. When I do it, he stands behind me and then he makes my pants unfastened. I don't look in the mirror and I don't say no. He does the sex thing. My dad looks in the mirror. I don't want to. I don't want to see the stupid boy there. I hate him so much. He makes everything bad all the time. Sometimes I hit him so hard I wish I could make him die and go away. Then he can stop making everything bad.

My dad tells me I can go out to play now. He makes all his noises and then he gets in the shower. I pull my pants back up. I don't look at my dad. I don't look in the mirror. I go to my room, then I get my bag and go to meet Rachel.

I run away forever.

Thirty Nine

Rachel has her bag ready too. She has a big jumper on to keep her warm and she has a sleeping bag. She got it from her dad. She told her mum she was sleeping at another friend's house and then they are camping on the floor. But we don't.

We don't go to the golf course. We walk to the gates, but it is too dark. We don't want to walk over the big dark field. We go to the promenade instead. It is high there and bright. All the lights are on because it is illuminations time. They are special lights that people come and see.

Me and Rachel have a special place on the rocks. It looks like a castle. It got shaped like that and it is flat on the top. We climb to it lots of times so we decide we can sleep there. It is nice and flat and no one can see it. We have to climb all the way down and no one can get on it. We tried to show Simone once. But she isn't very good at climbing. She slipped and then she fell. I thought she was going to fall all the way down and die. But she didn't. But we don't let her climb there anymore. It is too high and she isn't good because she is a girl.

We hide our bags at the castle. No one can see them because it goes inside the rock a little bit. I ask Rachel if she wants to walk on the promenade. We can walk and see all the lights. She says yes. We have never been to town by ourselves at night before. We are not allowed because Rachel is eleven. Maybe when she is twelve we can. My mum says it isn't safe.

But nothing bad happens. We walk along the wall that is by the sea. We look at all the lights. They are nice and bright.

It is a very long walk to town. It makes me hungry. I ask Rachel if she is hungry. She says yes. We walk to all the fun places. They have lots of rides and stalls. Lots of people play on the machines and things. Me and Rachel go to the stand that sells burgers and chips. We buy some chips. There is a lady there. She is very loud and she laughs. "What are you doing here?" she asks us. I tell her we are getting chips and she laughs with her friends about it. Maybe she is drunk. "Don't you both look cute? Is she your girlfriend?" she asks. But I shake my head and me and Rachel go away. I don't like the silly lady. They laugh like my mum and dad do when they are drunk.

We walk all along the promenade. It is lit up. We don't spend all the money. We have to save it. I don't want to waste it. We buy some drinks. I get real Coke because I am not allowed it at home. It is fizzy and the bubbles go in my nose. We stay out very late. When we walk back to the castle, I look at my watch. It is after 2am. All the lights have got turned off and everyone has gone away. We walk very far and then we get back to the castle. I climb down it in the dark. There are some lights down at the bottom. Where it is near the sea. There are people there fishing. They fish at nighttime. I can hear the waves on the wall. They crash. The tide is in.

Our bags are still there. No one found them and no one took them away. We get our sleeping bags out and then we sit in them. I tell Rachel we can take it in turns to go to sleep. She can sleep first and then I wake her up in an hour and then I can sleep. She says yes and then she lies down. She goes to sleep very fast. I watch the fisherman at the bottom. I can see the sea too. It takes a long time for the hour to go away. My eyes are very tired. I look at my watch then I shake Rachel. I tell her it is my turn. She doesn't want to wake up. But I tell her she has to.

She sits up and then she yawns very big. I give her my watch. She has to wake me up in an hour. Then I can look out. I get my bag and I make it like a pillow. I watch Rachel. But she falls to sleep again. I whisper her to wake up. She can't watch for things if she falls to sleep. She says she is awake but I know she isn't.

I try to close my eyes again. But my mind doesn't want to. It tells me something bad will happen because Rachel goes to sleep again. I say Rachel's name, but she doesn't answer. I take my watch out of her hand and then I sit up.

I can hear noises at the top of the cliffs. There are some steps next to us. But no one can get to the castle if they don't know the special way. I can hear laughing. Maybe it is more drunk people. The sun wants to come out. It is a little bit light. My watch says it is after 4am. It is very early. I have never seen outside at this time, except when I sleep in the garage.

Some people come past us. They don't see us. They don't say anything. Rachel doesn't wake up. They make lots of noise. There are four people. They climb past us on the steps and then they go down to the beach. The sea is gone out a little bit. They go to play on the sand. They laugh and make lots of noise. I don't know why Rachel didn't wake up. They are not very quiet.

I watch them climb over the chain. They are not allowed to go over it. But they do. The chain says danger and keep out. Sometimes me and Rachel climb over the chains when we want to play at the sea. The coast guard comes in his big car and then he gets out and tells us off. He tells us it is very bad to go over there. But we don't stop.

When they are gone, I tell Rachel to wake up. They played at the beach a long time. It is after 5. I am hungry. There is a petrol station near my dad's work. It is open all night long. I tell Rachel we can go there and get something to eat. They have a toilet too. I need the toilet very bad.

My eyes are very tired. I didn't sleep all night long. They feel like they are puffy. Maybe tomorrow Rachel can stay awake and I can go to sleep. She wakes up. But she doesn't say sorry about not being a good lookout. I tell her we can walk to the petrol station for some food. We roll our sleeping bags up then we put everything stuffed in the hole again. We climb down the rocks and walk. My head feels very tired. It isn't very far to the petrol station. I walk there all the time when I went to the school near my dad's. It doesn't take a long time.

We get some crisps and chocolate and I ask Rachel if we should get on the bus somewhere and then we can find another place to run away. It makes me scared inside. Maybe she will want to go home. But she says yes. Maybe we can go to the other side of town. But I want to go very far away. I don't want to be in the town anymore. But I don't tell Rachel about it. I know how to get the bus. I will pay for it and then we can go.

We get near the fence near our things and then we climb over the railing. We climb down to the rocks of the castle. But our bags are gone. Someone came and took them away. I stand up and look around. Maybe they fell down. But I can't see them. They are not anywhere. We climb down to the bottom. My bag has all my running away clothes in. I don't want them to be lost. It makes me scared inside. "Where are our bags?" Rachel asks, but I don't know. They are not anywhere.

I tell Rachel I will climb back to the castle and look. Maybe they just got stuck. But when I turn around there are three men there. They have fishing stuff with them. "Are you looking for these?" one man says. They hold up our bags.

I tell the man to give me my bag back. He shakes his head no. "It isn't yours," I say to him. But he grabs Rachel's arm and another man grabs mine. I shout at him to let go.

Forty

We don't say any words to the men. I look around. Maybe we can run away and then they can't catch us. Maybe we can be faster than them.

"We watched you all night," the man says. "We are going up there and we're going to call the police." I feel the crying inside. I don't want them to call the police. I don't want to go home. I don't want my dad to hit me because I tried to run away. The police will come and he will be mad about it.

The man who has my bag stares at me. "I know who you are," he says. "You are friends with Jason. I am Jason's cousin."

I don't answer him.

"I can find out where you live if you don't tell me or we can go to the police."

I don't want to go to the police. I don't want to go to my mum and dad's house. I want to go away. The man is going to take us home or he will take us to the police station. He tells us if we try to run away, he will catch us. They are bigger than us. Then they make us go all the way to the police station. He says the police will arrest us for running away. I hate the stupid man and his friends. They should mind their own business.

I tell him where my mum and dad live. He tells me if it is lies, then he is going to take us to the police. I promise it is the truth. I walk very slow to my house. I don't want to knock on the door. My dad is going to be mad. Not when the men are there.

When they all go away. Then he will be very mad and he will hit me very hard. I feel it all inside. It makes me feel scared. I make my breath all scratchy in my throat. Then I can feel it. When we get to the house, the man bangs on the door with the letterbox. I hope my dad doesn't hear it. But then Sheba barks very loud. She wakes everyone up. I don't look at Rachel. I don't look at the door. I don't see my dad come. The man has my arm very tight then I can't run away. I wish he would get lost. I wish he didn't find me then I could run away for a long time. I tell him in my head I hate him.

My dad opens the door. He has his dressing gown on. He looks at me and Rachel. He doesn't know why we are there. The man says he is sorry that he has to wake him up. He tells my dad he watches us all night long. We slept on the rocks. He waited until it was light to bring us home. He was sorry about it. I want to tell him good. He should be sorry. He should have left us alone.

My dad asks what's going on. I shrug my shoulders. My dad is nice to the man. The man gives my dad our bags. My dad tells the man thank you and he is sorry. I am always bad. I always do things like this. My dad says he has no idea why I do all these bad things. The man tells my dad it is okay. Then he goes away. I hate the stupid man and his stupid friends. My dad tells me and Rachel to come inside.

My mum is downstairs too. She has her dressing gown on. Me and Rachel have to sit on the sofa. My dad goes to get dressed, then he comes back again. My mum stares at us. "Why?" she asks. But I don't answer her. I don't say anything.

"Were you running away?" my dad says. I don't answer him either. He shouts very loud at me to answer. I nod my head. He asks me why like my mum did. "You have no reason to run away."

I do, but I don't say it. I think about it in my head. I make my mouth shut very tight then I don't say the words. I don't want to say because he has sex with me. But he does and so I run away. They don't love me. They don't like me. I have to do all the bad things. My brother doesn't. I don't know why he doesn't. He is stupid but they love him. They don't love me. They like him better. I don't say it though. I don't tell them. I make my mouth stay closed and then they don't hear it.

"You're lucky to have such a good life here," my dad says. "Some children don't and they would kill for your life."

I don't answer him. He is very mad about it all. He says he is going to take Rachel home. He calls her mum on the telephone first. Her mum isn't mad about it. She doesn't shout. When my dad comes back, he points at the dining room. "You can go and sit in there. If you move, you will have more than sleeping outside alone at night to worry about."

I don't look at him. I don't look at Rachel too. I make my mouth stop it. It tries to shake and the crying wants to start. I feel scared about it. My dad gets Rachel's bag and then he takes her home. My mum goes in the kitchen. She doesn't say anything to me. I don't move from the chair. I know I am in lots of trouble. I wish the stupid man just went away. My dad is going to shout when he comes back. I wait until I hear his car. I am very tired. I wish I could go to sleep. I try to make my legs and arms not shake. I can't help it. They want to. Maybe I will be sick. I feel it inside when everything turns upside down.

My mum comes into the dining room. "I bet it was her fault," she says. "That Rachel is nothing but trouble. I don't know why she needs to run away and why she has to drag you with her. I'm not surprised with a mother like that. She's probably being maltreated at home. But you're not. I don't understand."

I don't answer my mum. My dad comes back. I hear the door be locked. My brother has woken up. He sits on the stairs. He knows I am in trouble too. That's why he doesn't come down. I see my dad through the glass. I try not to cry. I try to make the shaking go away. My dad comes in very fast. He opens the door with a slam and then he runs over to me. I put my hands up. Maybe he will hit me. I say no very loud and I cry. My dad grabs my top and then he drags me off the chair. He does it so fast that I can't walk. I nearly fall. Then my dad throws me in the lounge and I land on the floor. It hurts very bad.

I don't get up. My brother starts to cry very loud. But my dad doesn't hear him. No one tells him to shut up. My dad runs to me again. I put my hands up and then he can't grab me again. But he hits me in the face very hard. He sits on me and I try to put my hands in the way. He hits my arms and then when he hits me, my own hands hit my face. He doesn't stop it. I cry about it because it hurts very bad. I tell him to stop it. My brother cries loud too. He comes down the stairs and then he tries to make my dad stop it. My dad shouts at him to go away.

My dad stands up then he pulls the belt out of his pants. He shouts at me. He tells me I embarrass the family. I have to be dragged home in the early hours of the morning by strangers. Then I make everyone say bad things about us because I make the family look stupid. My dad shouts loud. He tells me to get upstairs right now. I do. I run past my brother. He is crying very hard too. My dad runs up the stairs too. He is shouting lots of bad words at me.

I go in my room. Then my dad comes in too. He bangs the door very hard. I get scared. Maybe all the glass in it smashes on the floor. But it doesn't. "Take your clothes off," my dad shouts at me. But I can't. I shake all over. I stand by the wall. I can't make the crying stop. My nose all runs down my face and at my mouth. I tell my dad I am sorry. I try to say it but I can't because I am crying too much and then the words sound stupid. My dad shouts it again to take my clothes off. But I don't want to. It hurts when he is mad at me. Then he does the sex thing very hard. I don't want him to do it.

My dad comes over. I try to slide away so he doesn't hit me. But he doesn't. He grabs my arms and then he pulls my clothes off very hard. He pulls my top so much then it nearly takes my ears off. They hurt very bad. I try to hold onto my clothes but I can't. My dad is stronger than me.

My dad gets all my clothes off. Then he throws me on the bed. I don't want him to do the sex thing. I try to crawl away and get in the corner. My dad pulls my leg. He shouts at me to stay there. He gets his belt and he hits it across my legs and my bottom. It hurts very bad. It makes me scream very loud. It feels like he makes my skin get cut off. He does it again lots of times. He does it fast. It hurts too bad. I scream loud to make him stop but the words don't come out very well. It makes me wet the bed. I didn't mean to. I am twelve. Babies wet the bed. But I do it. I try to get in a ball. I can't breathe because I cry so much. My dad doesn't listen. He shouts at me. He hates me so much. I always do this to the family. He wishes he didn't ever have me. He wishes he just had my brother. I make everything bad in the house. He says the words right at my face so I hear them. He tells me I should get up and go and play with the moving traffic. He doesn't want to talk to me or look at me. I make him feel disgusted. He stands up. Then he goes away and closes my door. I don't move.

I don't get dressed. I hear my mum and dad shouting downstairs. I made everything bad again. I can't keep the shaking away. I try to cry. But it is too big. I cry loud. It makes me want to be sick. But I can't make the hurt parts inside go away. I hug myself tight. I make my nails dig in my arms and then I let the crying come out until my head hurts too much.

I try to pull the cover on me because I am cold. But I

don't let it touch my legs. They sting from my dad's belt. My hands shake. I can't do it very careful. I don't move from where I wet the bed. I go to sleep. I sleep for a very long time.

It is dark when I open my eyes again. I slept all day long. No one came in my room. The bed is nearly dry too. I get my pyjamas from my pillow and then I pull them on. It makes me cry to move. I don't want to look at my legs. They are very sore. I wish I could get a drink. I wish I could go away. The crying starts again. My dad wishes I went away. I hug my arms around my head and make my hands pull my hair. My dad wants me to go away.

I fall to sleep again.

Forty One

I wake up again. It is very dark. Maybe it is so dark no one can see anything. I don't hear any sounds. I try to, but maybe they all went away. It makes me feel scared to move. I try; I do it very quiet, then the bad man doesn't know I am awake. I don't want him to know. My legs are sore, it makes me hold my breathe. They sting very bad. I don't sit on my legs then they don't make me cry some more. I know I am bad. I know I was bad to run away. I wish I could tell my dad I am sorry. I didn't mean to make him very angry at me. I don't get anything right.

I think my legs made me too hot. They feel like they are on fire. But I am very hot too. My Nan says when I get very hot she can cook eggs on me. She said that lots of times when I was very little. My hair is wet because I am too hot. It sticks to my face and feels funny. My face feels wrinkled from the bed. I didn't move when I was sleeping.

I don't want to put my legs on the floor. I don't know if the bad man is there. Sometimes a long, long time ago when I was little, then he waited and he grabbed my legs. Then I couldn't get away from him and he pulled them very hard. He dug his nails in my legs and made me scream. I don't want to put my legs down in case he hides there and then he can get me. Then no one hears me and no one comes to help me. I just go to the light. Then he isn't there. I see his face in my head. I see his bad smile that he does. I see it very horrible. I count to three. Not four. Then I will run and get the light on. One, two, three, but then I am too scared to move. I wish I didn't fall asleep until it was dark. Then I wouldn't be scared about it. I am stupid.

I think about my drink and some food. I didn't get any because I was asleep for a very long time. If I get my light on then I can go downstairs and I can get a drink. I think about it a lot. It makes me more hungry inside and then my mouth thinks about the drink. I need the toilet too. I didn't go there all day long either. It hurts when I move because I need the toilet very bad.

My tummy shakes inside about it. One, two, three, then I jump off the bed and run to my light. I pull it very hard. It makes me scared in case it goes bang. Or maybe when I turn it on the bad man jumps at me and he scares me. But he doesn't. I get my light on and there is no bad man.

I open my door very quiet. Then I don't get shouted at about it. I look down the stairs. All the lights are off. My mum and dad went to bed and I didn't know. It makes my tummy turn over. I can't stop the crying because I need the toilet and a drink. I can't get any. I can't go downstairs when it is dark. The bad man waits there. He will get me. I don't ever go down there by myself. I feel him hiding.

I look at the clock next to my bed. It is a radio clock. It has bright red numbers. My dad gave it to me then I can go to sleep with the music on. It says it is 3:25am. Everyone has gone to bed. I was asleep and I didn't know. I slept for a very long time.

I don't go to the bathroom. It makes me too scared. I know he is there and then he will jump out. I see it all in my head. It makes my neck feel spikey at the back. I don't like when it does that. It makes me need the toilet lots more because I am scared about it. My mum and dad are sleeping. My dad snores very loud. I wish they would wake up. Then I can go to the toilet. But I don't.

I have a sink in my room. I am not allowed to use it. My mum says she will shout at me if I do. But I need to go to the toilet very bad. I sneak over there. Then my mum and dad don't hear me. I watch the door. Then I see if my mum or dad come when I use the sink for the toilet. The taps don't work. My dad turned them off. My mum and dad don't wake up. They don't come. I run back to my bed in case. Then they don't know. My mum will tell me I am very disgusting. But I had very bad tummy ache about it.

I hug in the corner of my bed. Then the bad man can't get me. I sit up. I make my legs not go on the bed properly. They hurt very bad. They feel like they are shiny and wet where my dad hit me. I don't want to look at them. Maybe it is very bad. I get my book and I try to read it. But my eyes keep looking around. Maybe the bad man can sneak when I am not looking. It makes me read the same words lots of times. I make my mouth say the words very quiet. Then I don't wake anyone. My eyes try to close lots of times. I try to make them stay open. They don't want to. I fall asleep.

When I wake up again, it is day time. I can hear my mum and dad. They are all downstairs. I slept a long time again. I don't ever do that before. I try to move my mouth but it is all dry. It tastes very funny and it makes me cough. My head hurts very bad. I feel hot like maybe I will melt away forever. I try to get out of bed. My head bangs inside. It makes me stop so it goes away. It bangs at the sides like it is my heartbeat. I have to get dressed. I am not allowed downstairs when I am not dressed. I have to get them on very careful, then they don't hurt my legs. My tummy hurts because I didn't get any food yet.

When I am dressed, I go downstairs. My mum and dad are in the kitchen. Maybe they don't see me. My pants make my legs and bottom hurt. It rubs and stings when I walk. I pull my pants away from my legs. I don't ask my mum and dad if I can use the toilet. I go there very quick and they don't see me. I do that lots of times when they are in the kitchen. My dad gets mad when he catches me. I didn't ask to use it. My mum says I treat the house like a hotel. But I don't.

I go in the kitchen after. I ask my mum and dad if I am allowed to breakfast. I didn't get anything to eat all day. I don't say that part. Maybe they forgot about my dinner. I didn't make it myself either because I was asleep. I wish the stupid fisherman didn't bring me home. It is his fault. My mum is right. Nosey people make things bad. I ask my mum and dad very quiet. I don't stand near them. Maybe my dad will hit me again. My brother is sat at the table. He is playing with some toys. My mum and dad don't answer. I don't get my breakfast. I say their names. I say them lots of times. Maybe I am invisible.

I go to the lounge. Then I sit and read a book. My brother comes in. My mum is there too. She has things to put away and then she will go and make my bed nice. I am not allowed to do it myself. My brother asks me if I want to play Lego. My mum coughs very loud and makes him jump. He looks at her and then he shuts up.

I get my book and then I go in the garage. Then I don't make people mad at me all day.

Forty Two

The garage has a toilet and sink inside it. It is dirty. We are not allowed to use it. It is full of spiders and things. But the spiders don't make me scared. I like spiders. I turn the tap on. It has a little bit of water. But it isn't like the taps in the house. They have lots of water that comes out fast. But I put my face in the water and let it go in my mouth. It splashes and makes my face all wet. I drink it all down. It makes me more thirsty. Maybe I will be thirsty all day.

I drink so much water it makes me want to burst inside. I can feel it. I am not hungry anymore too. Maybe I wasn't hungry. Maybe I was just very thirsty. I remember I have running away money. My Dad didn't take it. My dad chucked my bag in my room when my mum went to make the bed tidy. Maybe I can sneak in and then get the money and go to the shop. I go back to the house. I feel excited inside. Maybe I get something to eat. My dad isn't in the kitchen. I don't know where he is. Maybe he is in his front room. He goes in there all day long and doesn't come out. My mum thinks he doesn't like being with her because he is always in there and he never comes out except to eat. He says he goes in there because she watches television all the time and he thinks it's a lot of rubbish. He doesn't like to watch it.

Sometimes my mum puts the films on the television where people have lots of sex. She lies on the floor and she watches them. Then my dad sees when he walks past. But he doesn't come in. He stands in the hallway and watches it through the glass. Sometimes he gets his thing out and makes it move himself. My mum shouts at him when he does that. She gets mad. He isn't allowed to see it.

My mum isn't there too. My brother has his Lego out. "Where is mum?" I ask him.

"Go away," he says. "You're bad. Mum says you're bad. You make her cry again."

My brother gets off the chair very fast and then he runs in my dad's room. He is telling on me because I talked to him. I run upstairs very fast. My mum is in her room. The door is open. I go in my room and I get my runaway bag. My mum got all the clothes and food out. But she didn't take all the things out. My money is there and so are my cigarettes. I get them and then I put them in my pants and my mum and dad don't see it in my pocket. I go out of my room and shut the door very fast. Then I run down the stairs. My dad is coming. I see him come out of the room. He says my name. But I don't hear him. I get outside then I run around the house and get to the front. I run all the way to the alleyway. My dad doesn't chase me. I hide behind the bush and look at the house. My dad doesn't come out. I light a cigarette and then I hide it in case anyone sees it. I walk slow to the big shop near our house.

When I have got some sweets and chocolate, I hide them in my clothes. Then I go back to the house. I sneak to the garage and then my mum and dad don't know I am there. I sit on the cushions and I read my book. I stay there for a long time. No one comes to find me. Maybe my mum and dad are glad I went away again. Maybe that is why my dad hit me. Because the stupid fisherman brought me back and my dad didn't want him to. He should hit the fisherman instead. It's all his fault.

My eyes get tired because I read lots. I nearly read the book all in one day. I lie down and let my eyes get some sleep. Maybe they need some more. But I get made to jump. It makes all my insides jump inside-out. I hear a big noise. It is like a big scream. I don't know what it is. My heart bangs very loud in my chest. I sit up and look out the window. Maybe the bad man came and I didn't know and then he made a noise to make me jump. He likes to make noises to make me jump. I hear the noise again. It isn't the bad man.

I go to the door and stand outside. I hear all the shouting and the screaming. I hear my brother scream very bad. It makes me feel funny inside. It nearly makes me need the toilet. My mum and dad are shouting at each other. They are in the kitchen. I can see them in the window. I put all my things away in the garage and then I get my book and go to the house. My brother is crying very bad. He cries and screams and it makes me want to cry too. I don't like when he cries like that. He nearly gets sick because he cries very hard. My dad is holding a cloth on my brother's hand. My mum is shouting very bad.

My brother grabbed my mum's hot iron. She says he is stupid. He knew it was hot. He could see she was ironing. She doesn't know why he grabbed it in his hand. His hand is all burnt. My dad has to change the cloth and I see it. My brother doesn't stop his crying. My dad gets a bowl and he fills it with water and then some ice from the freezer. He gives it to me and then he picks my brother up and takes him into the lounge. I go too. Then I put the bowl on the coffee table and my dad puts my brother's hand in it.

My dad tells me to stay in the lounge with my brother. I sit on the sofa with him and I get my book. I read it to him. I start it again, but I don't read the boring parts. He sniffs when he cries and then he has the hiccup cries too. I make the story in a stupid voice and then he laughs and cries together. It makes him hiccup It is very funny. We read like that for a long time. Then he starts to cry again. I ask him if his hand hurts. He nods about it and then I tell him I will get a new bowl of water for him. I tell him I won't be long.

My mum and dad are in the kitchen. They shout at each other lots about everything. They shout about all the things from a long time ago. I stand at the door. I don't make any sounds, then they don't know I am there. My dad sees me. He takes the bowl out of my hands and then he fills it with cold water. He gives it back to me and doesn't say anything. I ask him if I am allowed a drink. Maybe my brother wants one too. My dad gets the special cartons of orange from the fridge and gives me two. I didn't ever get to drink one before. I tell him thank you and go away very fast.

I give my brother the bowl and then the orange. I open mine. It is very sweet. It makes me screw my face up and it is cold. My brother laughs about it. I drink it very fast. I wish I got special drinks.

My dad comes in, but he doesn't come to us. He walks past us. He is mad. He slams the door open and then he slams it when he goes out. He goes in his front room and then he slams that door too. It makes me jump. Then my mum comes in. "Is he okay?" she asks me. I tell her yes he is. She thinks maybe we should call the Batman Doctor about it. Maybe he can come at the evening time and check my brother's hand. Then she says she can't because my dad is around. He is going to go to the shop and get some cream to put on my brother's hand. My mum asks if we want some toast. I tell her yes please.

Me and my brother sit at the sofa all day until it is dark. Then we go to bed and my dad reads us a story. I lie in the bed with my brother. I pretend to be asleep. My dad does the sex part. Then I go to bed. I tell him I am sorry for running away.

Forty Three

I am not allowed to be friends with Rachel anymore. My mum says so. She says it with her mad words. She says it lots and lots of times. I get mad about it and tell her I know. But she keeps saying it so I don't forget. My mum tells me if I sneak there, there will be trouble and I will be very sorry. I tell my mum I promise. I don't see her. But I like Rachel. She wasn't bad. It was me. I wanted to run away. I try to tell my mum, but she says no. She says if there wasn't any Rachel, then I wouldn't run away. But I would. I would run away because no one likes me. I make everything bad. My mum doesn't want me. She said so lots of times. "Your father raped me when I was asleep," she says. She says it lots when she is mad. She didn't want me because my dad made it happen. My dad doesn't like me too. He said so when I was a baby. My mum tells me about it lots of times. He looked in my bed and then he was mad and said he didn't want that. My mum should let me run away. Then she can be happy that I go away. It makes everyone happy if I go away. I don't tell her. I just tell her okay.

I see Rachel every day. My mum doesn't know. They don't know it was me who was bad. Not Rachel. It isn't fair if she is in trouble because I made it bad. I tell Rachel we have to sneak. I want to be her friend. My mum and dad are stupid. I ask Rachel if she got in lots of trouble with her mum. But she says no. She just got told off.

Me and Rachel meet each other lots of times. We meet after school at the golf course or the castle in the rocks. Then my mum doesn't know because she doesn't come to those places. We do it every day. My mum thinks I just play out with Jason. I get home every night at the right time. Then I don't get in trouble and my mum doesn't ask. Sometimes I tell her about the doctor. I tell her I saw him. But I didn't. It just comes out of my mouth. Then my mum doesn't ask anything except that. She likes me to say them things. We talk lots about him.

Sometimes I have to hide. My dad takes my Nan home or maybe my brother to the shop. Then my dad comes down the alleyways. So me and Rachel hide and he doesn't catch us. I don't want him to see me. It makes me scared when he is outside. Maybe he is looking for me. My brain says maybe he knows and then he checks to see if he can catch me. When I come home, then I get scared that he knows I have seen Rachel. Maybe he can tell because I am not a good liar.

We are going to the beach. Rachel has some friends to meet. It is a nice day and we can all hang around outside on the promenade. We have been outside all day. The sun is shining. When it gets to the evening, Rachel's friend says she wants to get something to eat. She says we can walk to the shop called Ziggy's. They have the best chips. We have to ask our mums first because it is near town and it is a long way away. Rachel uses the telephone box and she calls her mum. Her mum says yes. I don't ask my mum. She will say no, then I will be in trouble because I asked about it. So I go anyway. Then it doesn't matter.

The chip shop feels like it takes a very long time to get to. I have been there once. I went with my Nan. She likes it there too. They make nice food. Rachel's friend buys some big bags of chips and then some coke. We sit at the window and share it. I don't eat a lot. I don't want to be greedy. I don't want them to know I don't get dinner at home so I eat lots outside. I tell Rachel's friend thank you though. We all walk along the promenade. They live near my dad's work so they don't walk with us all the way. We say goodbye to them and then we walk near Rachel's. We walk along the promenade then we can watch all the illuminations. The road is filled with cars and people. Some people stand at the side and they sell lots of things that light up. My brother got a light up yo-yo from there. But he doesn't have it anymore. I broke it. I made it yo-yo too hard and it smashed on the floor. My stupid brother cried about it. But he is spoilt so I don't care.

We walk through a place that has a waterfall. It isn't a real waterfall. It is like a fountain and then it lights up. Lots of people stand and watch it. They throw money in it too. I stare at the money. It isn't very deep. I could get in there and get the money when no one is looking. The place has a gate. But I can climb over it when it is closed. Maybe I can come back at night when no one is around. But I keep away from stupid fishermen and then I can sneak back home. I can do it when I sleep in the garage. Then my mum and dad don't know I go away.

I walk Rachel to her house. I don't go all the way. But I stand near and then I can watch that she gets inside. I don't want to go home. It is dark. It is past 11. I go to the promenade instead. The lights haven't gone off yet. I want to smoke a cigarette before I go home. Then I can go to the garage and go to sleep. No one will know I haven't been home yet. My mum doesn't check the garage.

It is nice outside. I like when I can smell the sea and I can hear lots of music and talking because lots of people on their holidays come and then they look at the lights. I am not scared outside when it is dark. The bad man doesn't come outside. If he does, then I can run away and he doesn't catch me. I watch the lights while I smoke my cigarette. They have lots that move. I watch the one with the dancing flowers. The music sings Mary, Mary, quite contrary, and then the flowers all light up when she waters it. Lots of them are like that.

My mum and dad take my brother to see the lights. But I don't go with them. I am not allowed. I always spoil things and then it makes everyone sad in the house. My dad likes to take Sheba. She has her walk at the evenings after he has eaten. I don't think she likes the lights. But she likes all the people. They stroke her and she wags her tail very fast.

I sit on the bench and then I smoke another cigarette. I know how to smoke properly now. I make it go deep inside and it doesn't make me cough. I like when it scratches inside my throat. The lights get turned off. Then I go home. I don't like to be on the promenade when the lights are turned off. Maybe I will get in trouble and then I get made to go home and my dad knows I am out.

I walk to my mum and dad's road. It is very bright. There are lots of lights and police cars. There are lots of people too. They look out of their windows and things. It makes me scared about it. Maybe something very bad happened. I walk down to the road and I look at the cars. I can't see the police. Just the cars.

My mum and dad's door is open. It makes me scared. Maybe something bad happened to my mum and dad. I hear the radios. They make crackling noises. A big policeman comes out of my mum and dad's house. I don't like the policeman. They have handcuffs. It makes me think about the mean police at the play place. He used his handcuffs too and he did bad things. He said I was bad. The policeman talks in his radio then he comes to me and asks me my name. I tell it to him.

My mum comes out of the house. She has a mad crying face. She shouts at me. But not a bad shout. It is when she crises and shouts at the same time. "Where have you been?" she asks me. I shrug my shoulders.

The policeman tells me it is midnight and he asks where I have been. I tell him I didn't go anywhere. I was out then I came home. He tells me I made everyone worry. He tells me I can get in trouble for doing things like that. I tell him I am sorry. I didn't mean to.

My dad's out looking for me. My mum says he has been out lots of times and he asks lots of people if they have seen me. He even asked lots of drunk people. But no one did. It makes me scared inside. My dad is going to be mad again. I don't want him to be mad. He makes it hurt very bad when he is mad.

"You have to call your Nan," my mum says. "She is worried. We called her."

I didn't know they would call my Nan. I tell her I will. My mum called her to see if I was there. But I wasn't. I was out. I walked past my Nan's house. But I didn't go inside. I nod my head. My lip shakes lots of times because I feel the crying inside. It wants to come out. My eyes get funny and I can't see because the crying is there.

The policeman says they are going to go now. He tells me again that it was bad what I did. I nod my head and the tears fall out and on my face. I didn't mean to make the police come. He says I shouldn't treat my mum and dad like that. They are good people and they worry about me. He says if I do it again, he will be mad. I tell him I am sorry.

When the policeman goes away, my mum asks if I was with Rachel. I don't say anything. I know I am in trouble. My dad comes back too. If I say I was with Rachel, then it is bigger trouble. "I called her," my mum says. "She didn't care that you were missing. What kind of friend doesn't care? You could have been dead or anything. She doesn't care about you."

I don't listen to my mum. I know Rachel does. She just didn't tell my mum, then I don't get in trouble.

"This is why you can't see her anymore," my mum says. "She just does what she likes and then you are so stupid you go and do it with her."

My mum says lots of bad words about her. I call my Nan. I tell her I am sorry. I tell her I was just late and I didn't mean to be. My Nan says it is okay. She was very worried. I can hear the crying too. She says my mum told her I ran away with Rachel. I don't look at the phone. I look at my feet. I tell my Nan I am very sorry. I don't mean to do the bad things. The crying comes out. My tears fall down onto my feet from high up. My Nan doesn't shout at me. She tells me to stop crying. She doesn't want me to cry. I tell her I promise. She says she loves me. Then it makes me cry lots more. I tell her I am very sorry.

I say goodbye to my Nan. Everyone is gone. I know my dad is going to be very mad. He always is.

Forty Four

My dad shouts at me like always. That's all he does. He shouts and shouts. He shouts loud too, but I don't know what he is saying. Everyone has gone away, and then he locked the door. Now he is shouting. I am hungry. I don't know why. I ate some of the chips. I didn't get any dinner. Maybe that is why. My dad shouts my name.

"You're not listening to me," he says. "What did I just say to you?"

I don't know what he just said. I don't say anything. I don't even shrug my shoulders at him. He makes his arms fly about when he shouts at me. Maybe it's supposed to make me scared. I think he looks stupid. I try not to smile. I can feel it inside. I want to laugh at him. I look at my mum instead. She is by the door. She watches my dad. She has her arms folded. She has that stupid face. Her eyes are very big; she stands by the door that goes to the dining room. I can see the kitchen. The light is on. Maybe I can get something to eat. If my dad shuts up. I sigh about it. I wish he would stop it. Then I can get something to eat and go to the garage.

I could eat some cereal. My brother's special cereal is in the kitchen. I don't get to eat that. Because it's my brother's. I don't know why he gets special cereal. He should have diet cereal he's so fat. My dad calls him fat all the time. Maybe they should not give him dinner too. Then he can be skinny.

My dad grabs my arms. He digs his hands in very hard. "Listen to me," he says. I tell him I am sorry. I'm not sorry. Not really. I just want him to shut up. I want something to eat. I don't know why I do it. I just start to walk away from my mum and dad. I walk to the dining room door and open it.

"Where the hell are you going?" my dad asks me. He says more swear words, calls me lots of names. My mum starts to shout too. Both of them shout and I don't know what they are saying. She makes my ears hurt. I wish they would both shut up. I wish I could tell them to both shut up. But I don't.

After my cereal I am going to get the petrol and go to sleep. I am tired. My head feels like it wants to explode. Maybe it is because of my mum and dad shouting. That's all they do.

My dad makes his shouting louder. But I don't stop. I keep walking. He tells me to come back. He swears at me to get myself back in the 'fucking' lounge right now and only God is going to help me.

My mum tells me to get back in there right now, or there is going to be trouble. There always is trouble. My dad will hit me. He always hits me. My mum shouts at my dad. "Do something," she says. They start to shout at each other. My mum is mad. She walks after me. She shouts that I need to come back and listen.

I don't. I get a bowl out of the cupboard and then a spoon. I get my brother's cereal down and pour it into the bowl. My mum stops at the kitchen door. My dad stands behind her. They shout so loud I think everyone will hear them. My mum folds her arms. She shouts so much that it makes her spit when she says the words.

"Put … the…bowl…down," she shouts at me. But I don't. I hold it in my hand and mix the cereal up. I wait for it to get soggy. "How dare you walk into my kitchen and think you can just please yourself," she says.

My dad storms past my mum. He comes all the way in the kitchen. He shouts to put the bowl down again. But I don't. He swears. I get some cereal and put it in my mouth. I don't look at my dad.

"I'm going to tell you one more time, put the bowl down," he says.

I don't. I look up at my dad. Then I chew my cereal. He calls me names. Swears at me and knocks the bowl right out of my hand. I watch it. It lands on the floor. It doesn't bounce. The cereal goes everywhere and the bowl smashes in a big noise on the tiles.

"Look at what you have done," he says to me. But I didn't do it. I didn't smack the bowl. He did it. I was just eating cereal. I don't tell him that. He is too stupid. He will just shout more about it. I am not going to clean it up. He can do it. I walk over it. I don't say anything to my dad. I am going to the garage. Then maybe I can run away again and they won't care. My dad grabs my arm to stop me. My mum is there. She stomps over too. She smacks me across the face.

My mum doesn't ever hit me. It makes me jump. She hit me when I was little. But she doesn't do it now. She starts to shout. "Why can't you behave?" she says. "Why don't you listen? What's wrong with you? Why do you act like this? Disrespecting your father and me. I wish you were never born," she shouts.

"It isn't my fault you opened your legs," I say back to her. I don't know why I say it. But it comes out. My mum screams at me. She moves very fast and hits me hard in the face. She slaps me lots of times. She shouts that I ruin everything. She says it over and over. She hits my chest and face. I try to get backwards and get out of her way. I walk backwards all the way. She keeps hitting me. She doesn't stop. She hits me and then I get down out of her way. I put my arms up at my head so she can't hit my face anymore. My nose is bleeding very bad. The blood runs down my face. It goes in my mouth then it goes on the floor too.

My mum hits me for a long time. My dad tells her to stop it. He gets hold of her and then he pulls her away. She tells him to stop it. He tells her to leave it now. She has to go upstairs. "Look what you caused," he says to me. "Are you happy?"

My mum is crying very bad. Her nose is snotty, she cries too much and it runs from her nose. I cry too because she kept hitting me. The blood doesn't stop too. I wipe it with my hand. I don't say anything to my mum and dad. I don't say I am sorry about it. The tears come out. I don't stand up. I let my legs flop out and then I sit on the floor. My dad takes my mum out of the kitchen. I watch them. They go up the stairs. Maybe they go to bed.

I sit on the floor for a long time. I get my top and put it at my nose. The bleeding stops. My mum and dad haven't come back. It has been a long time. I look at the cereal on the floor. I get the dustpan and brush. Then I pick up the bowl and food. I wrap it in paper from the big cupboard. I am not allowed to put it in the bin. My mum says that it makes the bag split. Then rubbish goes everywhere.

I wrap it in the newspaper and put it by the bin. I can't put it on the side or it makes the print go on there and that is dirty too. I don't want to walk through the dining room and lounge. It is dark there. My dad turned the lights off. I think about the bad man. I can feel him there. I know he hides. I know he will come because I am bad. Even though he doesn't come for a very long time. Maybe this time he will. I can feel it. I feel when he comes to get me and then he bites and scratches. It makes me scared inside. It makes my neck tingle at the back and then it goes cold because I think about him.

I walk very slow. I listen to everything. I look at the glass walls. It makes me scared to look. What if I see him? I don't want to. Maybe his face is there and he is staring at me. I see his face lots of times in my head. His stupid smile. His dark face and bad eyes. I get to the bottom of the stairs. My heart bangs very fast. If it bangs anymore it might bang itself out. I put my foot on the step. Then I run. I run very fast all the way up the stairs. I can feel it scared in my back. I run to my door, open it and turn on the light. No bad man is there.

I close my door and get my pyjamas on. I know tomorrow I will be in trouble. I go to bed.

Forty Five

My mum and dad don't talk to me a lot now. Maybe I made them hate me too much. I don't talk to them too. I don't want to. They are stupid. My mum just gets mad and then she shouts at me or my dad tells me to go away. He always tells me to go and play in the road. I tell him to shut up. I always say bad things to them when I talk. I don't know why. It just comes out and then I walk off before my dad gets mad. I like it when they get mad though. My mum wishes I would go away. She says that lots of times. She tells me to get lost. She uses swear words too. I just go in the garage and smell the petrol. Then I don't have to talk to them. One day I can smell it too much and go away.

I have the rash under my nose from it. It burns sometimes. My mum says it looks stupid. I tell her then it looks like her. She swears at me. I don't go to the garage tonight though. It is Friday. I don't go on Fridays because my Nan comes around still. She sits in the lounge watching the television. It is late. Nearly time for her to go home. We have eaten all the dinner and cleaned it all away. My mum watches the television too. She lies on the floor by the fire. I don't know why she has my Nan in the house. She says she doesn't like her. She called her bad names today. My Nan brought some perfume for my mum. My mum told her off about it. She told my Nan it was a waste of money. My mum is just mean to my Nan. It is nice that she got a present. I wish I could tell her to shut up.

I sit at the table in the dining room. I have lots of homework to do. I write my stories too. I like to do them better than my homework. I wish I could go in the garage instead. But I can't. I can tomorrow. When I have seen Rachel and my mum doesn't know about it. That's how stupid she is. I see Rachel all the time and my mum doesn't know.

The phone rings behind me. I look at my mum in the lounge. She doesn't get up to answer it. My dad is in the shower. I don't want to go in there and get him. I had to go in there when I needed the toilet. Then he did all the stuff to me. He always does the sex things in there when I go to the toilet. I don't want to go in; in case he does it again. My stupid fat brother is on the sofa. He is playing his new game thing. My dad bought it for him and they bought him a little television to play it on. He is so spoilt. I wish he would go away. Sometimes I want to hit him in the face and make him cry. He is such a baby. Maybe his thing can break and then he can cry.

I answer the phone because no one else does. I am not allowed to answer it really. My mum likes to answer it first. No one else gets to do it. It is a man's voice on the phone. He asks to speak to my mum. But he doesn't say her first name. He calls her Mrs. I ask who it is calling. He says his name is Craig.

I don't say anything to him. It makes me feel funny inside. I know who Craig is. He is my big brother. He got taken away when he was a baby. He cried too much when he was six weeks old. My mum threw him at the fireplace. She made his skull cracked and the bone in his shoulder too. He didn't die though. But my mum got in trouble and the social worker took him away. Then he had to go and live with another mum and dad. My mum says they did it on purpose. They steal babies from people that do nothing wrong. It was a long time ago though. He is four years older than me. I tell him I will get my mum.

I go to the lounge and say mum. She doesn't answer. She doesn't look at me or anything. I say it again. I am not allowed to talk when she watches her soaps. She can't get any peace. That's what she says all the time. So I am not allowed to say anything. Even if I am dying I have to wait.

"What do you want? I'm watching my soaps," she says. She doesn't get up. I tell her there is someone on the phone for her. "Tell them to call back," she says. She never talks to anyone when it is soap time. Not ever.

My Nan looks at me. "Who is on the phone?" she asks.

I look at my mum again. "He says he is Craig," I tell them both.

My mum sits up very fast. She looks at my Nan and then me. "Craig?" I nod my head. My mum starts to cry. She says oh god lots of times. I didn't mean to make her cry. I close the dining room door. I pick up the phone and say hello to Craig again. He says hello back. I tell him she will come in a minute. She is just shocked.

Craig went away for a long time. She has missed him very bad. She tells me all the time. They took him away. It was all their fault at the social services. They wanted to steal him because it makes them lots of money to take babies away. They tried to steal me too. But she didn't let them. The doctor came every day and then he checked on me and made sure I was okay. I was and then he told the social worker woman and so she left us alone and didn't take me away. When I feel very mean with my mum, I tell her that Craig was lucky and everyone should be taken away. It makes her sad when I say that.

Craig has another mum and dad. I don't know who they are. They live in Liverpool. They adopted him. Craig talks with a Liverpool accent. I like it. My mum gets up. I see her through the glass. But she doesn't come in the dining room for the phone. She goes to get my dad. She knocks on the bathroom door and shouts my dad. She opens it and then I hear her tell him about Craig on the phone.

They come in the dining room after. My mum takes the phone. "Hello," she says and then she starts to cry.

They all talk for a very long time. My mum talks when my dad takes my Nan home and she is still talking when he comes back. I talk to Craig too. It makes me very excited. I wished he had been my big brother all the time.

He calls lots of days in the weeks. I don't talk to him all the time. It is a month later and he calls. I answer the phone. He sounds like he is mad. He asks to speak to my dad. I get him. Craig has fallen out with his other mum and dad and they don't want him there anymore. He asks my dad if he can stay. My mum and dad didn't meet him yet. My dad asks my mum and they are very nice to him. They tell him of course he can come. They have missed him so much. He tells them they are very nice.

He is going to come in the morning. He will catch the train and then my dad will pick him up. I can't wait. He is going to sleep in one of the other bedrooms. I go to the garage and sit on the cushions. I smell the petrol and lie down. It makes me close my eyes. I think about Craig coming. Maybe he can live with us. I hope he does. Then my mum and dad can be happy. They missed him a lot. I close my eyes and go to sleep. I sleep for a long time. It is light when I open my eyes.

Forty Six

Craig is so tall. He is taller than my dad. But not as big. My dad rides motorbikes; it makes him very big and strong. Craig is skinny but tall. He has dark hair though. Like my mum. He looks like my brother. Just very much bigger. He has been here a few days. My dad picked him up from the train station. There was lots of crying and hugs and things. I didn't. I just stood at the back and watched them. I like the way he talks. I like the Liverpool accent. He sleeps in the spare bedroom that is next to the bathroom. I like that he is in there. Then I can go to the toilet at night time.

He is funny and nice. He talks to my mum a lot. She cried when he came. She hugged him and cried and said she was sorry. She missed him a lot. But the social services took him away. Craig cried too. He likes to watch television. He watches it and then my brother can't. My brother is fat and stupid. He cries because he is bored. I laugh at him and tell him to shut up. He has lots of toys and things. He can go and play with them. Maybe he could go outside. But he doesn't have any friends. They all think he is stupid too. He had one friend called Thomas. But he doesn't play anymore. He doesn't like my brother. They are both spoilt and then they fell out.

Craig is there when I come home from school. It is nice and sunny and he is outside with my mum. I have to go upstairs and change out of my uniform. Then I can make something to eat. I have to do it quickly before my mum needs the kitchen. Craig follows me into the house. I go upstairs but he follows me there too.

"Go away," I say to him. I want to get changed and I don't want to be slow or I miss making some food. He asks me if he can have some money to buy cigarettes. I tell him I don't have any. He opens the tin that is on my desk. It doesn't have lots of money in it. Just some coins. I put them in there when I get home. I save them. I sell cigarettes at school. Then I buy some more and sell them too. Then I save the money I get from it in the tin. Then I don't have to steal off my dad. I save my lunch money too. I can steal the food from the shops. No one sees me. I am very good at it.

The tin only has about two pounds in it. But he can't have it. It is mine. I tell him no. "Why not?" he says. "I'll give it back to you."

But I don't want to give him the money to buy cigarettes. It is my money not his. I got it. He should ask my mum and dad. They love him so much. They will give him the money for it.

"If you don't lend me the money, I'll tell mum you smoke," he says to me. Then he grabs my bag. I try to take it away, but he is bigger. He gets my arms and he twists it around until I let go. I punch him in the side and tell him to stop it and get lost. He opens my bag and gets my cigarettes out. It makes me scared because maybe he finds the money that is notes. But he doesn't. I didn't know that he knew I smoked. Maybe he saw me do it. Maybe he smells it. He takes my cigarettes. I try to get them out of his hands, but he says he will squash them if I do. Then he laughs about it and goes downstairs.

I hate him. He is so stupid. I get changed and put my bag back. Then I get the money and hide it so he can't find it. It is mine and he can't have it. He made me late too. Now it is nearly four and I missed the time in the kitchen. I can't make any dinner. I wish he would go back to his other mum and dad.

I go out to play with Rachel. We meet at the golf course. She is late so I play on the rope. We have a rope that we tied to a tree. It goes over some nettles. I fell one time when I had shorts on. I slipped and landed in the nettles. It hurt very bad because I had nettle stings all on my leg. My dad thought it was funny. Now I don't slip. I swing and wait for Rachel.

When she comes, I tell her about Craig and that he is stupid. I don't tell her he pinched my cigarettes. She will say that is good. I am not allowed to stay out late because Craig is there. My mum doesn't want him thinking she lets me stay out until all hours and she wants to lock the house up for the night instead of waiting for me. I am not allowed to stay in the garage.

I play with Rachel until seven. Then I have to go. Craig is inside watching television. He watches Robocop. He has watched it every day. My brother sits next to him. I don't know why he does. He is a baby and he gets scared. I am not allowed to watch films when my brother is there. I don't know why Craig is allowed. It isn't fair. I sit on the floor out of the way and watch it too. Then I am not in the way.

"Go and make me a coffee," Craig says to me. I don't look at him. I don't answer. He can make his own stupid coffee. "Oi," he says because I don't answer. Then he calls me names. I tell him to shut up. "You better go and make me a coffee or I'll…" he doesn't say the words. But I know he will tell my mum I smoke. He smiles about it like my mum does when she is being mean. He has the mean smile too. I don't like it. He is going to do something bad.

I look at the kitchen. My mum is in there. She is washing the dishes from dinner. They ate it already. I didn't get any dinner. My mum told Craig I never want any and I just throw it away. But I do not. I just didn't get to make it because stupid Craig was annoying and then he came in my room and made the time go away.

He tells me I better go and get the coffee right now. I know I am going to be in trouble if I go in the kitchen. But if he tells my mum I smoke, then it will be bigger trouble. Then my mum will ask where I get them from and if I tell her, then my mum and dad won't give me lunch money. Then I won't have lunch and dinner.

"Why don't you go back home?" I say to him.

"You want me to go home?" he asks me, he makes his eyebrows lift up. I look at my brother. He is watching. Then I look at Craig.

"Yes, I do," I say to him. I want him to go away.

Craig gets off the sofa. Then he gets my arm and he twists it behind my back. He pushes it very hard and it hurts. Maybe he will break it. I tell him to stop it. I swear at him and tell him to get off. He laughs about it. "Say you're sorry," he says to me. He makes me get down on the floor because he twists my arm so much and it hurts.

I tell him no. I shout at him that I am not sorry. He makes my arm hurt more. Then I have to say I am sorry or it will make me cry. I don't want him to see me cry. No one ever gets to see it. I say I am sorry. He lets go and then tells me I better go and make his coffee right now.

I get off the floor and go to the kitchen. I walk slow and then my mum doesn't shout at me because I make too much noise and because I am not allowed in the kitchen. I stand at the door, but I don't say anything. I wait until she sees I am there. Then she asks me, "What do you want?" She is mad because I disturb her. I tell her that Craig wants a coffee and he asked me to make it. She smiles very big about that. She looks past me at the lounge. "Well make him one then."

I do. I wish I could have one too. But I know I am not allowed. I don't ask. I wish I could spit in his coffee. I think about doing it. But I don't do that either. He will tell my mum and dad and then they will be mad because I did it on purpose. I just make the coffee and give it to him. He laughs at me when he says thank you. I hope he drops it and burns himself.

I want to go into the garage. Then I can sit there and read

and I can smell the petrol. My head is very tired inside. I wish I could go away. But Craig will come if I go there. Then he will spoil it and it won't be my secret place anymore. Maybe I can go to the one under the house. I play under the house sometimes. It isn't very big. I have to bend when I am in there. But it looks like all the rooms in the house. It is the same shape and then I get to hide in there. Sometimes me and my brother play houses in there.

I sit on the floor again and we watch all of Robocop. My dad comes in. He was in his room reading after dinner. He tells my brother it is bedtime. Craig says it's my bedtime too. I tell him to shut up. My dad tells me to watch how I speak to people. I fold my arms and stare at my dad and Craig. Maybe they can both go away and get lost.

My dad tells my brother to go and get his pyjamas on. Then he tells me it is bedtime too. I don't want to. I tell him I am not tired. I don't go to bed at 9. Craig stands up. He is very much bigger than me. He comes over and he pulls my arms to make me stand up. I make myself all dead. Then it is hard for him to pick me up. But he pulls me. I kick him my hardest and shout at him. I tell him to stop it. I am not going to bed yet.

Craig says I am. My dad says it too. They both laugh about it. My dad says I better start behaving. I shout at him and Craig. I swear at them both. My mum hears. She comes in the lounge too. My mum sighs. "He is always like this," she says. "We don't know why he can't behave."

I swear at her too. I hate them. I hate them all very bad.

Craig stands me up and then he carries me to the stairs. My dad points. "Upstairs right now," he says.

I don't say anything else to them. They are all stupid. I wish they would get lost and leave me alone. I hate them all so much. I hate them.

I hate them.

I want to tell them that I do.

I storm upstairs. My dad comes up too. I don't go to my room because he opens his door and then he pushes me in there. I don't say no. I don't even have my pyjamas on yet. But I get in bed with my brother. I cross my arms and then I don't look at my brother. My dad gets in the bed too.

My brother goes to sleep very quickly. Then my dad starts with his hand over to me. I don't stop him. I never stop him because I am so stupid. I close my eyes and then pretend I am asleep. I let him do the sex stuff. Then I pretend to wake up and I pull my pants up and go in my room.

I don't look in the mirror. I hate the boy in there. He makes it all bad. I wish he would die. I want to make him cry. I get my knife. I pull his sleeve up. Then I write I hate you in his arm. I write it lots of times until it starts to bleed a lot. Then it makes him cry. Good. He should cry.

I get in bed and go to sleep. I hate them all. Maybe they can go away tomorrow forever.

Forty Seven

Maybe Craig just likes to be bad. He is bad all the time. My mum and dad told him to go away because he pinched some scissors. It made me sad that he went away. He was mean but I liked him when he was nice. He can't be mean anymore. Maybe he just liked to be mean. I make everyone mean to me all the time. Maybe it is me that is bad.

He asked me for money lots of times. When I was playing outside with my ball, he shouted for me and told me I was in trouble. It made me very scared inside. Maybe my dad was going to hit me because I was bad. I told him I wasn't going inside, but he got my arm and he made it twist again. I didn't like when he did that. It hurt very bad. It made me swear at him.

I asked my mum what she wanted. But I didn't go in the house because maybe they wanted to hit me. But she didn't want me. She shouted at me because I was making a noise and in the way. Craig lied. He wanted to get some money for cigarettes. I told him I didn't have any. But he said I was a liar. He told me maybe my mum would like to talk to about all the money. Then she could ask Rachel about it too. It made me scared inside. Maybe he knew I met Rachel all the time when my mum said no about it.

I told Craig to go away. I said bad words to him. I told him I wish he got lost and went away forever. He said he was telling on me. I gave Craig some money for cigarettes. Then he went away. I wished he went away forever. But I didn't mean it. Now he has. It makes me sad.

He might not have anywhere to live. I think that maybe he is sad my mum and dad told him to get out. Maybe he sleeps outside. I look at the people when I walk past them. Maybe one will be him and I can say I am sorry. I look all the time, but I don't ever see him. It has been a month since he went away. We haven't seen him at all. He hasn't called. When the phone rings, it makes me listen, then maybe it is him. But it isn't ever Craig. My mum is sad about it. But she says it is his other mum and dad's fault. If social services didn't steal him away, then they wouldn't have had him and made him bad.

It is nearly bedtime. I have to go to bed because I have school in the morning. I can't wait. I like school. Me and my brother sit on the floor and we play Lego. My mum lets us make a big Lego town and then we play it with the cars and they drive through the Lego town. My mum said we can play because my brother is bored. He doesn't have any friends because he is fat and stupid. So she tells him to play with me. I made a big pirate ship.

Someone knocks at the door at the front. It is dark. My mum comes out of the kitchen. Then my dad answers the door. My dad shouts my mum. It is Craig at the door. Me and my brother sit and be quiet then we can listen to what they are saying. But my mum tells us we have to go upstairs. I take my brother upstairs. But he goes in my room. I sit on the top of the stairs and look through my sneaking hole and then my mum and dad don't see.

My mum didn't shut the door properly. Then Sheba opened it because she went to see who was at the door too. Craig says he is sorry. He didn't steal the scissors. He just doesn't know where he put them. He asks if he can come and stay. He doesn't have anywhere to go. My dad is mad about it. He tells him he talked to his other mum and dad and they said he is bad too. Maybe Craig is bad like me. Maybe he has it inside like I do. My dad says he can't come in. They don't want a thief and a liar in the house. It makes me think about the money. Because I am a liar and a thief. I tell my mum and dad lots of lies and I steal lots of money out of my dad's pocket. Maybe if they know about it, then I have to sleep outside too.

Craig is sad. It makes me sad inside. He is very sorry for everything. He didn't mean to make it all bad. My mum says if he gives the scissors back, maybe he can come back. But he says he doesn't know. They talk for a long time. It is maybe two hours. It is past my bedtime. They tell him to go away. My dad says if he doesn't, he might break his legs.

My mum and dad come inside the house. They say lots of things about it. It makes my mum shout. She is mad because he came to the house. He didn't have any right to come to the house like that. His other mum and dad spoilt him. Now he is damaged goods. That's what she calls him. My brother has fallen asleep on my bed. He didn't want to listen. It was boring. He better not pee on my bed or I will be mad at him. He pees the bed every night. Sometimes he does it lots of times. It makes my mum mad. She has to clean the sheets every day. My dad calls him the pissy fat kid. It makes him cry.

I sneak down the stairs so my mum and dad don't shout at me. I ask my mum if Craig has gone away now. My dad goes to make some tea. My mum sits down on the sofa. I don't because I am not allowed and she didn't tell me to. I stand in the place I am allowed that is next to Sheba's water. My mum is very sad. She tells me Craig doesn't have anywhere to stay. She tells me all about what they said. "We told him to go back home to his mother and father," she says, then she cries again.

"I don't know why it went wrong," she says. "Did I make him bad? You are bad too. Maybe it is me that makes you all like that."

I tell her no. She didn't make us bad. We were bad already. It is inside. That is why the bad man comes But I don't tell her about the bad man part. I tell her she is a nice mum. She is the best mum in the world. We are just very bad. Maybe it is because he has a mean mum and dad. My mum nods. Then she blows her nose. "It's because they spoilt him," she says. "They give him whatever he wants and now he thinks he can take whatever he wants."

I nod about it and tell her she is right. "Spoilt people are always mean," I say to her. It isn't her fault. I sit with my mum for a long time. We talk about Craig and the social worker. She talks about lots of things. She is sad because they made Craig bad. Then she asks me if I can smell smoking. I sniff up. I can. I try to see where it is coming from. But it is in the room. My mum sniffs more too. She shouts my dad. He has gone to bed. She stands at the bottom of the stairs and shouts him. He gets up and comes down because she shouts him lots of times. He tells her to shut up yelling.

My mum tells him about the smoke. He sighs about it and then smells it himself. He can smell it too. We walk around the house. It is from the bathroom. But there isn't anyone in there. I don't smoke in the house. My mum and dad smoke at the back door. But it is smoke like they are smoking now. Not old smoke.

I crouch down and tell my mum it is coming from the bathroom floor. My mum says maybe it is a ghost. They make lots of smells when they want people to know they are there. I think Craig is under the house. She asks if he can get under there and I say yes. I have lots of things in there. It looks like the rooms inside the house. It has lots of walls and things. I hide cushions from the old sofa there and me and Jason used to play under there. But it isn't very high. We have to bend down and Craig is very tall. Maybe he crawled.

My dad goes to get his pants on. Then he goes in the back garden to the hole to get under the house. My mum goes too. I stand at the corner and hide. Then I don't get shouted at. I don't like the garden when it is dark. I can see all the hiding places. It makes me think about the church people. Sometimes we went to places with lots of trees and flowers. They made me run through them. Then they chased me. I don't like it. It makes me think about the cat the man killed. Maybe he was going to get me too. He came out of the trees. I ran away. I don't like to think about it. But my brain is stupid. It makes me look. Maybe he is there. Maybe he can come. Like the bad man.

My mum shouts Craig's name in the hole. She tells him to come out. But he doesn't answer. My dad gets up and then he goes to the garage. He sees me at the corner. "Get back in the house," he says. I say okay. But I want to stay. I hide so my dad doesn't see me when he comes back with wood from the garage.

He puts it over the hole and then he gets the nails and he hammers the wood so the hole is covered up. He puts lots of wood until the hole is all gone. Then he puts more wood over that and then Craig can't get out. I have to run back in the house before my mum and dad see that I didn't go inside. I run all the way to the stairs then they think I went to bed. My mum and dad are shouting about lots of things. The door bangs.

I don't sleep all night. I think about Craig under the house. I wake up lots of times about it. Maybe he is scared in there. There is no light and it is very dark. Maybe the bad man can get him and then when it is morning, he will be dead and broken. Maybe the bad man bites him lots of times because he couldn't get away.

I make my stupid head think about other things. I don't want to think about the dark. It makes me think about the bad man. If I think about him, then he comes to get me. He knows when I think about him. My mum says I make him come. I don't want to. He makes me too scared.

I am very tired when it is morning. But I have to go to school. I ask my mum and dad for my lunch money. They are still in bed. My mum grabs my hands and then she smells them. She asks me about the touching myself part again. I don't like it. I go out of the house very fast. I don't get time to ask about Craig. I hope he is okay.

I think about Craig all day at school. I don't tell anyone about it. When it is hometime, I run very fast. Maybe my mum let him out from under the house.

My mum says that he tried to bash the wood away so she called the police. Then the police came and they were going to send the dogs in there to get him. So he came out and then the police took him away. Now he doesn't come back. Not ever.

"Hopefully we won't see him again," my mum says. I feel sad about it.

Forty Eight

I love chemistry very much. It is my favourite class. I like to sit at the front. I like the teacher too. Mr. Royal is very nice. He lets me talk to him. I told him about Craig. I didn't tell him he got locked under the house. But I told him that he had to go away because he stole my mum's scissors. Mr. Royal said that wasn't very nice of him to do. Maybe my mum and dad won't be mad at him for a long time.

I think they will. They are always mad. It makes me sad. I don't get to see Craig again. I wish he didn't have to go away.

I don't like that I have to sit next to Lewis in chemistry. He is stupid. I don't tell anyone else about Craig. I sit there very quiet and Lewis says I look like a baby because I am sad. Maybe I am going to cry. Then others laugh about it. I tell Lewis to shut his face. I have to sit next to Lewis because his last name starts with the same letter as mine and Mr. Royal puts us all in alphabetical order. Then Lewis doesn't sit with his best friend, Chris. Chris has to sit at the back because his last name has a different letter.

I sit at the front anyway. I sit there in all the classes. I try to get there first. I like the front. Lots of people says it makes me a teacher's pet. But I don't care. I like to be there. Then I can get lots of A's so I can be a doctor. They are just stupid because they mess about. Then they don't do their homework and they don't get good marks.

Chris throws things to Lewis when we are in chemistry. Then sometimes they hit me instead and he laughs about it. It makes him do it again. I ignore him. He throws a ball of paper at Lewis. But it hits me at the back of my head. I pick it up.

"Give me the paper," Lewis says to me. But I don't. I open it. I don't read it. I pull a bit of the paper off. Lewis starts to shout at me for it. He tries to take it out of my hand. But I move and then he can't get it. I rip it in half. He tells me to stop it because it is important. I laugh at him. It is tough. He doesn't get to have it back. I don't care. He can cry about it. I throw the bits of paper at Lewis so they go in his face. He tells me I better stop right now. I don't. I pick them all up off the table, then I blow them at him. He gets very mad about it. He swears at me and pushes me off the stool. Mr. Royal isn't in the classroom yet. I don't behave bad when he is there. I am always good. Lewis calls me teacher's pet again. Someone else says maybe I have sex with Mr. Royal. It makes me feel scared inside because maybe they know I have sex with my dad. I tell them to shut up. Sometimes they say it outside and I hit them for it. I don't like when they say bad things to me. I don't let them try and bully me. I am bigger. I can beat them in lots of fights.

I fall off my stool and then Lewis comes too. I don't fall on the floor though. I land on my feet. Lewis calls me names. He tells me that Mr. Royal isn't there to save me. But he can hug me later when we are alone and I want to cry about lots of things. I tell Lewis whatever. He is stupid. He doesn't know. Me and Mr.

Royal talk about science things. He knows I want to be a doctor. He asks me about it. Sometimes he gives me the books that he doesn't want anymore. I like them. They are all chemistry books. I read them at home. Lewis starts to say about the sex again. I punch him in the stomach. It makes people laugh, then they shout fight about it. Mr. Royal walks in. We are in trouble.

Me and Lewis stop it. We look at Mr. Royal. He stares at us. I feel very bad inside. I didn't mean to do something bad. He asks what's going on. I tell him nothing. He asks for the paper I have. I give it to him. He puts it on his desk and then he tells us to pick all the bits up. Lewis says I did it. He isn't picking any up. Mr. Royal tells him he has to. But I tell Mr. Royal that I made the mess. I am sorry. I will clean it all up. It makes my eyes feel like they want to cry. It makes it feel bad inside. I don't mean to do bad things. I just do them. Mr. Royal will tell me to go away now. When I am bad, everyone tells me to go away. No one really likes me. It's always pretend. Then they just go away like my mum and dad do. That's why I don't have lots of friends. Just Aadi. But he doesn't stay with me at school. He has better friends than me in his class.

I don't do anything bad all lesson. I don't look at Lewis. He tries to make me. He nudges my arm. He does it hard with his elbow. But I move mine out of the way. Then he can't. Mr. Royal says we have a detention at lunchtime. Just for 15 minutes. We have to write about what we learnt in class. If we don't do it, then we get detention all week. I didn't mean to make Mr. Royal sad about what I do. I know he is. He doesn't talk to me much in the class. Not like he does on other days. Maybe he isn't talking to me.

When chemistry is finished, Mr. Royal tells me and Lewis that we have to sit and talk about the lesson. Then we have to write about it. He says he will be back in a moment. He has to go and get some papers. But he can hear us. We better not fight. I promise I won't. He says he expected more from me. I don't look at him. I am very sorry.

I don't talk to Lewis when Mr. Royal goes away. I write about the lesson on the paper. I write fast. I write lots of words. Lewis asks me what I am writing. I tell him I am writing about the class. He asks if he can look. Maybe he can copy. I tell him yes. He isn't very good at writing things. He says I am clever. I always write the good things.

He copies it all down. Mr. Royal doesn't come back yet when we finish. We sit and wait. We talk about lots of things because Lewis gets bored. He is nice. I didn't know he was nice. Maybe he is just mean to make people go away.

Lewis has two brothers. They are little. He has a mum and a dad. But they don't live at the same house. He likes music like me. He likes Iron Maiden. I tell him I like ACDC. My dad listens to it. He asks me if I want to come out on the weekend. He says it is a really good place they all go. There are lots of people there. I think about Rachel. Maybe she will be sad if I go.

Lewis has a girlfriend. He tells me about her too. He tells

me he has sex with her. He asks if I ever do it. I don't answer. Then he says he bets I don't ever have sex. He smokes too. He asks if we should go for a cigarette. Then when Mr. Royal comes back, we can sneak there. I don't smoke at school. I don't want them to see and then they tell my mum and she tells my dad. Then I get told off for it. Lewis says him and Chris have a good place to smoke. "Do you want to come?" I nod and Mr. Royal comes back.

Chris is waiting outside. He gives me a stupid look. I don't say anything to him. Lewis tells Chris that I am coming to the smoking place. It is behind the tennis courts. We have to sneak through the bushes. Then we jump over the ditch. No one can see us. I look out. I didn't know about this place. I like it. It is like the den at the golf course. Chris tells me I have to give them cigarettes because they showed me their secret place. I do. We smoke them.

When the bell rings we wait for everyone to go away. When they are gone, then we can come out and no one can see us. It makes us late. We run very fast to our lesson. Lewis and Chris sit next to me at the front. Maybe they are my friends.

Forty Nine

I hang around with Lewis and Chris every day. We meet in the morning at the ditch behind the trees and then we smoke cigarettes. We go to class after. They are in a different form than me but we have the same subjects after. We meet at lunchtimes too. I like them. I like Lewis. I don't think Chris likes me a lot. He snaps and swears. But I don't care. He's stupid sometimes, that's all. Lewis is nice. He just likes to laugh about lots of things. I don't have lots of nice friends.

I have been to Lewis's house too. We didn't tell Chris about it. Chris doesn't like the music we like. He thinks it sounds bad. He likes all the pop dance stuff. I go to Lewis's house and we listen to music and play football. His mum is nice too. She lets me stay for dinner. Then she gives me a ride home and I don't get in trouble for being late. My mum and dad don't like her very much. They say she is just looking for a man for his money and no wonder her husband left her. I don't say anything about it. I let my mum say all the bad words. I don't think his mum is bad.

I haven't seen Rachel a lot. It makes me sad about it. Maybe she is sad too that I don't see her. But she doesn't want to come when I go and see Lewis. She doesn't like him very much. He smokes and she thinks it is bad. But I like Lewis. I can smoke and we do lots of things that Rachel doesn't like to do.

I walk to school by myself. Rachel doesn't meet me

anymore. But it's okay. I put my music on. I make tapes with lots of it on. My mum lets me. She has a big stereo that has two tape places and she lets me make tapes and then I listen to them on my stereo. I show them to Lewis. He likes them too. Chris gets mad and then he goes away. He says we are both idiots. Lewis laughs about it.

I walk to school today. I can't wait to show Lewis the new music I have. It is good. I got it from Jason. He likes music too. It has swearing in it. I don't let my mum hear it. She gets mad. She says that it makes me bad to listen to that stuff. But it doesn't. I have to walk all the way around the school to get to the tennis courts. The teachers don't let us walk in the car park when it is morning because of the cars. It is stupid. We are not babies. We don't get run over.

There is something white on the ground. It looks like an envelope. I stop and then I kick it. It jangles like money. No one is around. No one can see. I look about and then I pick it up. Someone must have dropped it. But I don't know who it is. I open it. It has a paper inside. It is for a trip. It says the person's name. But I don't know who they are. There is fifteen pounds inside it.

I can give it to the teachers in the office. Then they will know who it is and give it back to them. Fifteen pounds is lots of money. Maybe they don't know that it is lost. I look at the path. No one sees me. Maybe I can keep the money. I put it in my pocket fast and then I put the paper back in the envelope and put it on the ground again. I run away very fast and go to the ditch.

Lewis and Chris are there. Lewis asks me why I am out of breath. I tell him I was running. He gives me a cigarette and I light it up. He asks if I am coming out at the weekend. I tell him yes. We are going into town. Then I pull the money out of my pocket and show him. "Where did you get that?" he asks me. I tell him that I found it. We can split it into three. Then we get five pounds each.

I give Chris and Lewis their money. Lewis says we can meet at his friend's house. Then we can get some drinks. Chris thinks I haven't ever drunk beer before. But I have. I don't tell him it was my dad's. But I say I drank it lots of times. He laughs and says I am a liar. Lewis says we can buy some cider with it.

When I am in class, I check my pocket lots of times. I don't want the money to fall out and get lost. So I check it is there and it didn't go away. I sit in history at the front and I check it is there. Then the classroom door opens and the lady from the office asks if she can speak to me. My history teacher says yes. I have to go to the office. My form teacher, Mrs. Morris, is there and so is the head teacher. She asks me if I found some money today. I don't say anything. Maybe I can lie and they don't know.

Mrs. Morris says I have to tell her. Chris said I found some money that belonged to someone else. She has the envelope too. Maybe she went to get it. I don't know why he told. He is stupid. I want to go and shout at him about it. Mrs.

Morris asks me if I have the money left. I nod my head. But I don't do it big. I don't want her to see. She says I have to give it back. It isn't mine. I get the five pounds and give it to Mrs. Morris. She asks me where the rest is. The paper says fifteen pounds. She has the money off Chris and me. I tell her that Lewis has it too. I feel very bad. Now Lewis gets in trouble. Maybe he hates me.

They ask me what I think they should do now. But I don't know. I don't want them to tell my mum and dad. I will get in very big trouble about it. Maybe they will make me go away like Craig. He was a thief and he wasn't allowed there anymore. I try not to cry. I don't let it fall out. I tell them I am very sorry. I didn't mean to do it. I feel very scared inside.

Mrs. Morris says that because I don't do lots of bad things, this time it is a detention. But anything else, then she will tell my mum and dad all about it. I don't stop the crying when she says that. She gives me a tissue. I tell her thank you. When the crying stops, she tells me to go back to class.

Fifty

(Age Thirteen)

We are going to the doctor's today. My mum says I have to go because I get lots of headaches. I get them all the time. Sometimes they are so bad that they make me crawl on the floor. They feel like my head bangs like my heartbeat. Sometimes they make me feel sick. I don't like the light when I get them very bad, but it makes me afraid to turn the light off. What if the bad man comes? What if I can't see him and he gets me? My mum says the doctor can look at the bit under my nose. But I don't want him to look. Maybe he will know that it is because of the petrol. He might tell my mum and then I will be in trouble again.

The petrol makes my mouth sore. It makes it crack at the side too. But I like the smell of it. I like when my head gets very fuzzy and then I go to sleep. I don't get scared when I smell the petrol. I don't tell anyone about it though. Except Lewis. I told him. He didn't get mad about it. He thought it was cool and asked if he could try it.

I let him, but I had to sneak him in when my mum and dad wasn't in. They go out at the weekends. They always go and don't tell me. I waited for them to go away and then I sneaked him in the garage and we sat and sniffed the petrol. He sniffed it very deep inside. It made him cough, but he liked it. He said it made him feel a little bit sick though. We didn't tell Chris. I don't want him to know things. If he knew about the petrol, then he would tell someone and get me in trouble so I keep it a secret. I told Lewis not to tell Chris too.

Lewis doesn't get the marks on his face though. He doesn't do it like I do. Just when he sneaks at my house. It is not a lot. Sometimes at school, though, he gets the correction fluid and then he puts it inside his jumper and smells it. I try it too. It is like petrol. It makes my head funny too. But I don't like to do it at school because then I can't listen in the class and then I get bad marks.

My mum takes a long time to get ready to see the doctor. It takes her hours and hours. She makes her hair and clothes nice. Then she comes out to the lounge and she spins around. "Well?" she asks me. I say she looks nice. I don't like the clothes though. Her skirt is too short and it looks stupid. I can see her bottom under it. But I don't tell her. I don't want her to tell my dad I said mean things to her. Then I will be in trouble and he makes me sit on the chair in the dining room.

I hate the chair in the dining room. I sit there a lot of times. I have to sit there even when my legs go numb. I don't like it when it's like that. My dad makes me walk but my leg and foot tingles and then it feels fat.

My mum always goes to the doctors. She goes every week. She takes my brother lots of times because he is a baby and has to see the doctor for little things like sneezes. When I go with her, she laughs at lots of things the doctor says. I tell her to shut up in my head. She is so stupid. She makes herself look stupid too. It is a pretend laugh. She laughs when he says things that aren't a joke.

She has a picture of him in her purse. My dad doesn't know. She got it out of the newspaper. She showed it to me when she talked to me. She has a big picture too. She has it in a frame and keeps it in the drawer at the bottom of her bureau then my dad can't see it. When the doctors got a new surgery, there was a picture of all the doctors so she ordered a copy of the picture. She was very happy when she got that too. My brother saw it once. He asked me why she has a picture of the doctor. I smacked him and told him to stop looking in my mum's drawers.

Sometimes, though, I tell my mum I don't feel well. She likes it when we don't feel well, then she makes us stay off school and then she calls the doctor. Sometimes when I go and get my lunch money, I cough, then she asks me if I feel okay. I tell her no and that I have a sore throat. She tells me to go back to bed then.

I like going to see the doctor, he is nice. I listen to the things he says. Then after, when we walk home, I can tell my mum. She asks about everything he said. She wants to know if he said it happy or sad. Sometimes I look at him and remember what he is wearing. Then, when I tell my mum I see him near the house, I can say what clothes he has on. I don't mean to lie to my mum. But it happens. Then she is nice to me because he makes her happy. So I say them. Then I feel bad.

When we go to the doctor's, we have to go last. We have

to sit in the waiting room a long time. It makes me bored. I take my book to read. My mum says he does it on purpose. He does it because then he has lots of time to be with my mum and no one is rushing. I like to talk to him. He asks me lots of questions about things in the body. He tells me lots of doctor things. He tells me what subjects I have to take to be a doctor. I write them in a list and then I don't forget. He tells me I have to do my best at school. I tell him I try very hard.

I know it is bad to pretend I don't feel well. But I can't help it. She took my brother to the doctor's about his hand. The doctor was very nice to him. I went too. But I stayed at the door. My mum said I had to go then they know it wasn't on purpose. "Those people just want to steal children," she says. Because they stole Craig away. So I go too and then she isn't afraid and I can tell them it is because my brother is stupid and he grabbed the iron.

We are going to the doctor's today when I get home from school. I am excited. I made my mum a painting too. She might like it because she is seeing the doctor and it makes her happy. I took ages to do it. I did it in my art class. It is two otters on a log. My teacher put it on her wall. Now she says I can take it home. We made a frame for it too. I am going to give it to my mum. Then she knows she is the best mum.

I get home and my mum is getting ready. She is in the bathroom. I run upstairs and get changed. Then I wait for her. I give her the picture. She smiles about it. She says it is very nice.

I tell her I worked a lot on it. She says she is going to put it away. Then we can go to the doctor's. She takes it upstairs and then we go.

We go to the doctor's and we are last again. But he says maybe I have migraines. He gives me medicine for it. I don't like medicine. Medicine makes me sick. But I have to take it. My mum asks if we should come back. The doctor says yes. He wants to see if the medicine works.

I am not going to take it. I will pretend. Then I won't tell my mum I have a headache. Then she won't know I didn't take it. I don't want to be sick.

Fifty One

One of my favourite things at school is English class. I like it when we have to write essays. I write long ones all the time. I like to make them different. Our teacher says we have to write a story about the word escape. I don't want to do an escape story. Everyone does those. They will be boring. I draw a computer. I am going to write about and little boy's escape key that comes to life and talks to him.

I am very excited to write it. I like to write stories so much I write pages and pages. I am excited when we get them back from the teacher. I hope she likes it. She reads lots of my stories out to the class. I like it when she reads them out, but it makes me feel funny inside and I don't want to look at anyone. She brings all the escape stories back. She has a very big pile. She takes two off the top and says she is going to read them. I hope she reads mine. I cross my fingers and say please lots of times in my head.

Please read my story.

She stands at the front of the class with two stories. One of them is mine. I can't keep the smile away. But it makes me nervous inside about it. What if she thinks it is bad? She starts to read it and I know when the funny parts are. I have to keep from laughing or I will spoil it. I like it when the class starts to laugh. Especially when the escape key scares Mr. Royal. The teacher laughs too when she reads it. She has a big smile on her face. She tells me well done when she gives it me back. I have an A on it.

I keep thinking about it when I walk home from school. It makes me smile when I walk. I try not to laugh, then people think I am strange. I laugh about it when I get home too. My mum sees. "What are you laughing at?" she asks me. I make my smile go away. I don't want to tell her. But I tell her there was a funny story. My mum doesn't listen anyway. She doesn't ever. She asks me if I can go and get the rest of the clothes in the ironing pile from her wardrobe. She is ironing in the kitchen. I tell her yes. I run upstairs as fast as I can. Then I get dressed quickly. If I get down fast enough, I can make some dinner too.

I go in my mum's room. She keeps the ironing in her wardrobe. It is a special one. It is in the wall and has a sliding door. I open it. I get the washing out. Then I see my picture. The one with the otters on it. She has put it in the pile where she puts the things my Nan gives her that she doesn't like. They are in a box at the bottom. I pick it up and look at it. Maybe she threw it in. The glass has a crack. I stare at it a long time. It makes me feel bad inside. I try not to cry. She could say she didn't like it then I would give it my Nan. I know my mum doesn't like lots of my drawings. She says they are scary. But the otters weren't. They were babies and it was all nice and blue.

I wipe my eyes and then I put the picture back and take the ironing to my mum. I don't say anything about it. I make my dinner. I am having stew. It is from tins. I can make it very fast. I pour it in the pan very careful. Then I don't spill any and my mum doesn't get mad at me and make me throw it away.

She doesn't like when I do the food wrong. She gets mad and then I have to throw it away. I cut an onion for my mum. I cut it wrong. She told me I was being all stupid with it. I was showing her what we learnt at school. But she made me throw it away. Now I do everything like my mum says so she can't be mad about it.

I don't think about the picture while I am making my dinner. I don't want to. It will make me cry and then my mum will see. I try and think about my story instead. I see it like a picture in my head. Then it makes me laugh again. I look at my mum. I don't want to laugh. But she heard. "What are you laughing about? Did I do something funny?" she asks. I tell her nothing I was thinking about school.

My dad comes in. He has been in the back garden. Now he wants his cup of tea. It is a giant cup. My mum tells him I keep laughing. He asks me why. I tell him it was from a funny story at school that I wrote and the teacher read it out.

"It must have been a good story?" my dad asks and I tell him yes. My mum asks me about it. She asks me what it was about. I don't want to say. It makes me feel shy inside. But she tells me to. I tell her the boy's name and that he got a new computer for Christmas, then it came to life.

"Isn't that a stupid name?" she asks me when I tell her what he is called. I don't answer. But then she tells me about things in the story. She has read it. Maybe she sneaked in my room and saw it. It was on my desk. She laughs about the story with my dad. They say the names and the things in the story in a bad voice. They are mean and stupid. I hate them. I wish I didn't tell them about the story. I wish she didn't read it.

I don't say anything. I stir my food and when it is done, I put it in a bowl and ignore them. My dad makes the stupid voice and says things about my story. I hate him. I wish he would just shut up. He doesn't know anything. I think about throwing my dinner at him. I liked my story. Now he makes it feel bad. I want to say swear words at him, but I don't. Then he will hit me. He always hits me because I'm not his super special spoilt son like my brother. I wish they all went away and didn't come back.

I get my bowl and go to the dining room and eat my stew. I don't say anything to them. They stay in the kitchen and they laugh because they made me get in a mood. They are just stupid and I wish they would go away. They keep saying bad things. They don't ever like me. It makes me feel bad inside. I think about the picture too. I try to eat my stew but my mouth wants to cry and then my food tastes bad. I wish they didn't say any bad things.

My dad goes out of the kitchen and into the back garden again. My mum goes too. I don't look at them. I finish my stew and put the bowl in the kitchen. But I don't put it in the sink. I am not allowed to do that. If I do, then she has to wash the whole sink. I look out of the window. My dad is sat in his chair. He has his tea and his book. He tries to read but my mum talks lots to him. Sheba lies on the floor with them. I look at my mum's iron. My brother got spoilt because he burnt his hand. I could just put my hand on it. Maybe it doesn't hurt very bad. My brother is a baby so he cries at everything anyway.

I pick the iron up. It is still turned on. I put my hand near it. But I don't put my hand on it. Maybe it really is too hot and then I cry. I look at my mum outside. I see her stupid face and she talks to my dad. Maybe they can be nice if I make my hand burn. Maybe I get nice things too. My brother gets lots of nice things.

I close my eyes and count.

One.

Two.

Three.

Not four, never four. I put my hand on the iron. It is very hot. It makes my hand hurt so much. It feels like the skin comes off. I don't scream about it but it makes me cry. It makes my stomach turn over and maybe I will be sick with the stew. It feels like someone cut my hand to pieces. It hurts so bad. I can't breathe. My nose runs and I cry.

I see my mum. She is going to come back in the kitchen. She will know I am very stupid. She will tell me I am bad. Maybe I will get in trouble because I touched the iron. I put it back. She comes in and I don't say anything to her. I make my mouth stay closed. Then I don't cry and she doesn't see it. I don't like when she sees me cry. She laughs when I do. She makes me cry more. I tell my mum I am going to read. She says okay.

I go to my room and close the door. I cry very much about my hand. I get my clothes and put them on my face and then my mum can't hear me cry loud about my hand. It hurts so much. I hug it to me but it doesn't stop. It feels like it set on fire. I crawl on the floor and the crying doesn't stop too. I try to make the crying stay quiet. But it wants to be loud.

I lie there for a long time. I make my feet hook together and then I make myself rock. I can do that still. I do it a lot of times when the bad man has been. It makes it go away. It makes me go to sleep. I try to rock myself to sleep on the floor.

I don't know I went to sleep. When I open my eyes it is dark. My hand hurts. I need the toilet too. I can put some cold water on it. I get off the floor and don't hug my hand. I don't want my dad to see. Then he asks why. I put it at the side, but it is very sharp.

My dad is on the sofa when I go downstairs. He is reading. My mum is lying on the floor. My brother has his cartoons on. I ask my mum and dad if I can use the toilet. My dad says yes. I tell him thank you. My brother tells me to come over. He wants to show me something. I want to say no, but my dad looks at me. I go to my brother. He shows me his new videos. My dad sees my hand. He gets it at the wrist and makes me turn it over. "What is this?" he says and I tell him nothing. He tries to touch it but I move it away. Then my mum gets it. She presses it very hard with her fingers. I cry loud about it. I can't help it. It just comes out. I tell her to get off. She presses it again very hard. I wet my pants. I didn't mean to. But she won't let go of my hand. My mum looks at my pants. She swears at me. She tells me I am a dirty little shit. "Are you stupid or something?" she says to me. "Go to the bathroom and get cleaned up."

I nod. I know I am stupid. I know that is why they don't like me. I tell her I am sorry. I go to the bathroom and put cold water on my hand. I look in the mirror. I hate his stupid face. I wish I could make him go away and die. "I hate you," I say to him. I hate his stupid face. I wish I could make him go away. He is a dirty little shit like my mum says.

Fifty Two

When I come out of the bathroom, my brother has gone to bed. I don't know I was a long time in the bathroom. I don't know its bedtime. "Is your hand better?" my mum asks me. I don't say anything about it. I don't want her to say it is my fault again. I hug it to me. "Go and get a flannel and wet it," she says.

She keeps them in the bedroom. I rush up there but I stay quiet, then I don't wake my brother up. I get a flannel and go and make it wet with cold water. It feels a little bit better when it is cold and wet. It makes the fire go away. I go back to the lounge.

My mum says I can sit on the sofa and watch the television with her. I say thank you. I don't get allowed to sit and watch television lots of times. Usually it is my brother. Not me. Maybe it is because I burnt my hand. My mum is watching some hospital programme. I have seen it with my Nan sometimes. I like it. But there is always a big thing that makes the hospital run around.

My dad has gone to the kitchen to get his tea, but he comes back. He sits next to me. I think about the last time he did that, then he hit me because I was bad. Maybe he is going to hit me for burning my hand. I know I am stupid to do it. My mum gets up. She says she is going for a bath. I watch the hospital programme. I hug my hand very tight because it hurts a lot. I try not to think about it.

My mum comes back after her bath. She just has a t-shirt

on. I don't like it when she does that. She doesn't wear any underwear with it and then she sits down and we can see everything. I don't look. My mum puts a tape in the video player and presses play. I know what she is going to watch. Lots of porn films. They always watch them. They are stupid. They have stupid music too.

The woman is doing something, then the man comes and he ties her up. I don't look at it. I look at the floor instead. I want to go to bed. I don't ask my dad though. He got mad last time and then he hurt me very bad. I hug my hand tight. Maybe he won't because my hand hurts and I burnt it like my brother.

My dad unfastens his pants. I don't look, but I hear the noise the zip makes. Maybe he can forget I am there. I feel the sofa shake. I know what he is doing. He makes noises too. I pretend to watch the film. But I look at my mum's ornaments at the side. Then they think I am looking but I don't really. My dad breathes very hard. I wish I could go away.

My mum gets up. I don't look at her too. But I see her at the side. I hug myself tight. My hand hurts when I move it. I look at it and not them. My mum sits at the other side of my dad. I don't know what she is doing. I turn and look. But it is an accident. I didn't mean to. My mum is just sat there. She doesn't do anything. But my dad sees it. He touches himself.

My dad grabs my arm. He pulls me so I have to turn around. I slide off the sofa. I have to kneel down. He doesn't say anything. I know what he is going to do. It makes my tummy turn over inside. Maybe I will be sick because I am scared. I don't want him to put it in my mouth. I don't like it when he does that to me. I don't like how it tastes. It makes me want to be sick.

My dad pulls my head so then his thing goes in my mouth. I close my eyes. I don't want to see. I count lots of times. I know tomorrow I won't be here. I will be doing something else. I will be alive and it will all be gone. I tell myself lots of times. I say it when I go to the dentist so I don't get scared about it. I hear my mum make noises. When I look, my dad has his hand between her legs. I close my eyes tight. I don't want to see.

My dad finishes. He makes it bad in my mouth. He holds my chin like always. He looks at me and then I have to swallow. I don't like to do it. It makes my mouth and throat feel bad. He smiles at me and tells me I am good. He says I need to lick my lips. But I don't want to. He says it again. I do it. Then he tells me to go to the bathroom and get my teeth brushed and my face washed. He looks at my hand and tells me to get a new wet cloth too. I nod about it and go to the bathroom.

I brush my teeth hard. The taste doesn't go away. It doesn't ever go away. I can smell it too. It's there all the time. I hate it. Sometimes it comes when I haven't done anything to my dad. Then I remember and it makes me want to be sick. I even brush my tongue. That nearly makes me sick. I look at the mirror. I can't stop all the crying. I don't know why they do it. I don't know why I am so bad. I wish they loved me like my brother but I have to do the bad things all the time. He doesn't. Just me. I wish they didn't do it. I wish they were nice. My brother gets everything and I don't. I try very hard to be good.

I wash my face and all the tears away. I make myself stop crying. I get the flannel wet and cold again. Maybe I can go to bed now. I go back to the lounge and ask. But I am not allowed. My dad tells me I have to come and sit down. I have to watch the rest of the film, but I don't want to. It makes me feel bad inside.

My dad tells me to take my clothes off. He says I have to stand up and do it. I do stand up. I look at my mum. She tells me to do it too. Her voice is mad about it. Maybe she will hit me. Maybe I made her mad. I turn around. I don't want them to see. I take my top and pants off.

"Turn around," my mum says. "And take off the rest." I don't want to.

I think about Rachel. I haven't seen her for a long time. I keep hanging out with Lewis. Maybe I can go and see her. Maybe she misses me. We could go to the golf course or something. My mum tells me to get on the sofa. I have to watch more of the film but I don't. I think about lots of things. Maybe Rachel will be mad she didn't see me for a long time. I hope she isn't.

My mum shouts my name. She is mad. She has shouted it lots of times and I didn't answer. But I didn't hear her. "You're not listening," she says. But I can't help it. My mind wants to think about lots of other things.

My dad grabs my arm. It hurts. It makes my hand hurt too. He pulls me hard. He digs his fingers in my arm and then he pushes me over. He starts with the sex. He does that fast too. I try to move but he doesn't let me.

I don't think about it. Maybe I can see Lewis instead of Rachel tomorrow. If Rachel is too busy. I can go early in the morning. My dad does it so hard it makes me cry. Maybe I can just go and smell the petrol tomorrow.

My mum makes all the noises, then my dad does. Then my dad tells me to go to bed. I do. I hug my burnt hand tight and go away.

Fifty Three

I like some Saturdays when I go to my Nan's house. I ride my bike there because it isn't very far. She lives near my dad's work. I have to knock on the door in a special way so that she knows it is me. I knock three times, then three and then another three. Then she answers the door. She lives by herself. She doesn't like to answer the door in case it is someone bad.

I put my bike in her hallway. I am allowed to use the front door at her house. I look up the stairs when I go in. I don't like it up there. It feels like the bad man is there all the time. I think about him hiding. I don't ever go upstairs. I use the toilet outside instead. I wonder if the bad man walks around when my Nan is asleep. I would be scared in the big house all by myself. He would come and then no one comes to help.

We go into the backroom and I close the door. Then the bad man can't come in. He doesn't ever come in the backroom. Maybe he comes down the stairs, but he doesn't come in. My Nan's cat hides. It really is a scardy cat. She doesn't like lots of people and then she hides under the chair, but she comes out later. My Nan is trying to clean up. She does her cleaning on Saturdays because she is at the place that helps her be happy so she doesn't get sad about my granddad. She has the hoover out. I ask her if she wants me to do it. She says yes.

Sometimes on Saturdays, if it is a nice day, we walk to town. It isn't very far. Just a very long road and then we are there. I used to walk with my mum, but she doesn't like to walk there anymore. It makes her scared to go into town. She thinks something bad will happen and then she can't get home. Lots of people laugh she says. They know things and laugh at her because they want to do bad things.

I like to go to town with my Nan. She lets me look at things and then I don't get on her nerves and get shouted at. My mum doesn't like me to go shopping. I am not allowed when they go to the supermarket because I ask for things. Then they take my brother for his dinner at a café. I am not allowed there either. When they go to the supermarket, I have to go to my Nan's because my mum says I will cause trouble in the house; I don't know how to behave.

Sometimes my dad picks me up when they are on their way home. They don't take my bike though. I have to get that myself on the next day. They don't pick me up today though. They have friends coming around and they don't have time. I have to be home by six, though, otherwise I don't get time to make my own dinner. I have to help get the shopping in the house from the car. My brother doesn't help. He is lazy. They always let him be lazy. Maybe it is because he is too fat and stupid.

I put my bike in the garage when I get home. Then I go into the kitchen. My mum and dad and their friends are in the lounge. I don't have to do the shopping today; they did it already. I ask my dad if I can make some dinner. He says yes. Sometimes he says no if I am too bad. Then he doesn't let me. Sometimes when I know I am too bad, I don't ask at all. He is happy today. He has his whiskey and his friends. They are drinking the wine he makes. He makes it in the attic in big buckets. Sometimes I sneak it. I like it a lot. My mum and dad and their friends are laughing.

My brother is at the table in the dining room. But he comes in the kitchen because he is bored. I don't make him any dinner. He had it already at the café. My mum and dad always take him there. But he is bored that's why he comes. He doesn't want to be in the front room and listen to all the boring things.

I make my dinner and eat it in the kitchen. Then I don't get in more trouble because my mum has cleaned the dining table and then I would make it a mess again. My brother is playing with handcuffs. He got them in a police set he got from the supermarket. He puts them on my wrists while I eat, but they are not very good. I get them open and take them off. He says I broke them. But I didn't.

I put my plate on the side and all my rubbish away. I am not allowed to leave anything out. I have to put my plate in a special place. Then I get the handcuffs and I put them on him. He can't get them opened though. I laugh at him, then I open them with the key. The key is little and plastic. I put the handcuffs on his legs and he tries to walk up and down, but he falls over and then we both laugh a lot about it. He gets up and does it again, but he falls over too hard and the handcuffs break. It makes him cry.

I say to him maybe we can use rope instead. He thinks it is a good idea too. He has some. He has my mum's old washing line that he uses to tie on his go-kart and pull it about. We use it when we play and I pull him very fast. He goes to get it. Then he comes back and I tie it around his hands. He tries to get them unfastened, but he can't.

He tries to get his arms all the way around so they are at the front, but he can't do it. He can't get his feet through the gap. He falls over again and then we laugh because he rolls around on the floor. I let him get out. Then he wants to do it to me, he ties my hands behind my back but he isn't very good at tying knots and I get my hands out of it. He says I am a cheater. He has to do it again.

I have an idea. I get a scarf and then I tie it around his eyes. I tie his hands too and then I spin him all about. I tell him he has to walk all the way along the kitchen and he isn't allowed to bang into anything. He can't, he is dizzy and it makes him wobble. He bangs into the table and things. He can't walk because he laughs too much about it. He shakes his head to make the blindfold fall off, I tell him he is cheating too.

When I untie his hands, he puts the blindfold on me. He makes it tight. I tell him because he pulls my hair and it squashes my eyes. It makes them hurt. I can't see. He says he is going to tie my hands behind my back. But he still can't do it and I get out of it very easy. He gets mad about it. He tells me to stop it, but I laugh. I can get out of them all the time.

He makes me walk into the lounge. He asks my mum if she can tie them so I can't get out. She says yes. My dad says he will get some more drinks while she does that. He asks what we are doing; my brother tells him we are playing a game. My mum ties the rope around my hands; she puts it around them many times. I try to get my hands out. I pull very hard, but they are stuck. My brother laughs about it, and then my dad shouts him from the kitchen.

My mum laughs because I can't get my hands out. Then she gets my pants and she pulls them down with my underpants too. I hear my dad's friends laugh about it. I try to get them back up so they stop it, but I can't and that makes them laugh more. I wish she didn't do it. I try to say bad words to her. I try to tell her to stop it, but she just laughs some more at me.

I can't get my pants back up and I can't see them. It makes me fall over when I try because my pants have fallen to my ankles. My mum pulls them off instead of helping me. I get scared inside because maybe something bad is going to happen. I don't want her to take them off. My dad comes back. He makes me kneel; he is behind me. I don't want him to have sex with me when his friends are there. I don't want them to see.

He whispers in my ear. He tells me I am good. He makes the sound I hate and it makes me fall back. He does the sucking sound with his mouth. I don't like it. His belt opens, I hear it. It makes my tummy get cold inside. My dad kneels behind me too.

He puts his arm around my chest, and then he puts his hand under my chin and holds it so my head goes back. "Open your mouth," he whispers. I do and someone puts his thing in my mouth. I try to move my head away, but my dad holds my jaw and his fingers dig in. it is not my dad's thing. Someone else grabs my head and I can't move out of the way. My dad puts his other hand down on me so that he touches me too. He whispers that I am good. I can't breathe. I try to, but I don't move away. Someone has his thing in my mouth. My dad starts to have sex with me too. I can't see any of them.

Fifty Four

My Nan has bought me a new book. She buys me lots of them. She buys the scary ones. But I like to read them. I read them at night when my mum and dad are downstairs. They don't make me scared. This one is called IT. It's about a clown.

My dad's friend gets to the bad part. I hate it. I hate how it feels when it all goes in my mouth. I hate how it tastes. It makes me gag and I try not to be sick. I think about the clown. He lives in the drains. He comes up and steals the children. I don't look at the gutters.

My dad puts his hand on my throat, he makes my head go back and he tells me to swallow. His hand is still on me too. He keeps it there until it feels funny inside and then I make all the noises. I try not to cry because they all got to see that I am bad too. I am dirty. I feel it all over. I try to think about my book again, but it keeps going away. My dad doesn't stop with the sex until he gets to the end and makes all his noises too. Then he lets me go.

I can't see because I still have the blindfold on, but I don't want to look. I don't want them to see me. I can't move because my hands are still tied. I try to lie down instead, but it is hard. I get my head to the floor, but I am on my knees.

Someone unties my hands. I don't move fast. My mum and dad and their friends all talk about things. I don't know what they are talking about. I don't hear their words. Maybe I am dreaming. Maybe I am not really here. Someone tells me to go to the bathroom, but I don't know who said it. I just hear the words. I pull the blindfold off and I look at the floor. My head feels heavy inside; everything is heavy. I pick my pants up and go to the bathroom.

I feel very tired. Maybe I can go to bed and sleep until Monday, and then it is school. I have some homework to do. Maybe I can do that tomorrow. I did most of it already, but I didn't finish it yet. My tummy turns over inside, then the sick wants to come out. I get it in the toilet and it doesn't go on the floor. My hands shake badly when I try to wash my face in the sink. I don't look in the mirror. I just leave the bathroom and go upstairs.

It is cold in my bedroom. I don't put my pyjamas on. I don't do anything, I just sit on the floor. I like to write stories. Sometimes I write them inside my head and then no one sees them. I like when I do that, then I can close my eyes. It is like watching television in my head and no one else sees it. I do it lots of times. When I have a favourite part, I make it play lots of times.

I try to remember them to write them down, but they go away. I sit on the floor for a long time. It gets dark and I don't know about it. My mum shouts my name. It is very far away. Maybe she isn't real too. I stare at the big box in my room. I don't know what's in it; I don't remember. Maybe it was an old game. My mum shouts again. I hear her run up the stairs, but I can't make myself move. She opens my door and says my name again. I say "What," I say it slowly, but I am far away too.

"You need to go and get a shower," she says to me. "I want a bath and you need to hurry up." I tell her okay, but I don't move. She shouts my name again. "What's wrong with you?" she asks because I don't say anything at all. I don't move to talk. I think the words, but they don't come out of my mouth. I don't want to say anything. I don't know why she can't hear the words inside my head and then she knows. She shouts my name lots of times. "Shower now," she says. She comes in and then she grabs my arm. Her nails dig in and she pulls me so I look at her, but it is all slow. Maybe my eyes want to daydream.

I don't look at my dad when I walk past. I don't look at anyone at all. I don't know where my brother is. Maybe he went to bed already. I didn't see him. I walk to the bathroom again. I don't turn the light on, I don't care. I take my clothes off and turn the shower on and get in it. It is cold, but I don't do anything about it. I don't care. I can't make my arms move to change it. I stand under the water. I think about getting the shampoo down, but my arms don't want to do that either. I don't move for a long time. Not even when the water gets too hot, I don't turn it off; I just stare at it as it goes down the drain.

I don't even know that I stand under it for a long time. My mum knocks on the door. "You've used all the water up." I didn't even notice. The water has gone cold. I tell her I am sorry. "You never think of anyone else," she says. "Now I have to wait for it to fill again to get my bath. Just self, self, self."

I know I don't. I know I am bad. I try not to, but it happens. I don't know how to make it stop. I don't say anything to her. I just think the words in my head, but I don't say them with my mouth. I turn the shower off, get out and put my pyjamas on. I forget to get dry, but it doesn't matter. Maybe I can catch a chill and die.

My mum and dad say something to me when I walk past them to go to bed again. I don't know what it is, though. I hear their voices, but I don't hear the words. I walk to the stairs and to my bedroom. I don't want to say anything to anyone. There is no point in saying words. I can't be bothered to talk. I don't even turn the light on in my room. I don't care if the bad man comes. Maybe he can do all the scratching and biting so bad that I die. Everyone will be glad when he does that.

I get in my bed. I don't care that it hurts my leg. My bed is old. It is the one my granddad died on. It is broken and the springs stick out of the fabric in the middle where my legs go. Sometimes when I wake up in the morning my leg is cut from it. I have a scar by my knee where it went all the way in one night, but I am not allowed a new bed. My dad says it is fine the one I have.

I feel the sharp springs dig into my leg. I slide my leg down so it hurts. I press my leg more and I do it again. I do it many times until my stupid face starts to cry. I should cry. I'm so stupid. Stupid little shit my dad says. He is right. I say it to myself when the spring is in my leg. It's what I deserve for being so bad. The crying gets loud and the spring doesn't hurt enough. I do it faster to make it hurt; I want to dig right in and make everything go away.

I can see the mirror at the other side of my room. I have it there so that the bad man can't sneak in. It is dark, but I can see a little bit. I didn't close my curtains yet. I stare at the stupid face crying. I hope he dies. I hope someone does something bad to him and makes him suffer. He deserves it. I wish his dad and his friends do lots of bad things to him for a long time. Maybe the bad man can come and keep him forever.

I stare at him a lot and then I cry again. I watch his stupid face cry. He cries very bad. I don't want to make him stop. I don't want to make it get better. I hate him. I want him to cry. I make the springs hurt until he cries too bad. I want to go to the mirror and break it and make him hurt. I hope he knows that I hate him. One day I will get him and make him sorry.

My mum and dad come up the stairs. I hear them. My mum opens my door. I turn my face to the pillow and then I don't talk to her. I know I am bad. She doesn't say anything to me, though. She comes in and closes my curtains and then she goes away. It is dark now. I can't see the stupid boy in the mirror. He has gone away because it is dark. I hope he never comes back. I hear my mum and dad go to bed. I hear the springs make a noise. I hear them start to have sex. I stare at the dark.

Fifty Five

I like the new year at school. I got so excited when we were told that Mr. Royal was going to be our form tutor. He is my favourite teacher. Our form room is the chemistry room. I sit in the same seat at the front. He lets me sit in there when it is lunchtime. Sometimes he helps me with my other schoolwork. He is very clever. I have to get my best marks this year. Then I can choose all the subjects I want to, like Aadi did.

I get many merits. We get those when we have done very well in our work. We have to get A's, but then it is a merit because it is better than an A. I get a lot of these too. We get stickers and they go on the front of our books. We have to get them from our form tutor when we get the merit sign from the teachers. I always take lots to Mr. Royal. My English and Maths books have so many at the front they are nearly covered. He says I do it on purpose because I am trying to steal all the merits he has. Sometimes when it is Friday, he asks me how many and then he has a silly smile on his face.

Lewis gets them too. He doesn't have as many as me. But I started first. Now he tries to beat me. If he gets ones and I don't, then he shows me and laughs about it. But I still beat him. We aren't in the same form, though. He and Chris are in a different one. Peter is in mine, but I don't talk to him anymore. He has lots of new friends.

After form, I meet Chris and Lewis before we go to the lessons. Chris doesn't stay with us very much. He doesn't like me, but I don't like him too. I don't care; he is an idiot. He thinks it is good to not do his work. He calls me names because I do a lot of it and get good marks. I don't care. I want to go to medical school. I have to get all the right subjects. I have a list. I got it from my mum's doctor. He helped me to choose them. He told me what I needed. My mum said he was being really nice.

"See, he likes me," she said to me. "That's why he wants to help you. So he can get me. All men want is sex." Then, suddenly, she is in a bad mood.

I sit at my seat at the front. Mr. Royal comes in. He smiles at me. He always smiles at me anyway, but today it is a big smile. He reads the register out. Then he tells us all the things we have to know. He does that every morning. Then he says he has some big news. He comes over to me and gives me an envelope. I open it. It is an invite. There is a presentation night for some awards. I have one for maths.

"Ninety-nine percent," he says to me. "That's what you got in your maths exam this year."

"Ninety-nine percent ? It is so big. I didn't know I did everything right in the exam. It makes me feel very excited. I didn't ever get nearly one hundred percent before.

"You have the highest mark in the whole year," he says. I smile so big about it. I can't help it. My dad helped me with my maths. He is good at the maths parts. He doesn't get mad at me when I ask him for help. He likes to do it.

My dad lets me sit in his room when I have maths homework. Then he helps me with it. He writes more sums and things. He is nice to me when we do maths. Maybe because my brother is thick. My dad tells him that all the time. "He's lucky if he can add two and two together," he says. I laugh about it. But it makes my brother sad. He goes away and cries. But he is spoilt. I don't know why he cries. I wish I was him sometimes. He gets all the nice things and my mum and dad love him very much. Not me. I am bad. They hate me very much.

The invite says that the presentation is in the evening. It will be at school. My mum and dad can come too. But I won't ask them about it. I know they say no. They don't ever come to things. My dad says that I don't deserve the things. I only get good things because I have sex with everyone and that's how I get these special things. I don't, but my dad doesn't believe me. He says I couldn't possibly get high marks and awards any other way. He says I have sex with everyone.

My mum asked me a few weeks ago if I have sex with my dad. I don't know why she asks me that. She asks me lots of times. Maybe she forgets. "Is your dad doing anything he shouldn't to you?" she asked me when I was in the kitchen. I looked at my dad, but he didn't say anything. I said no to her. But I don't know why she asks about it. She is there sometimes when he does it. I tell her no and then I go away.

Mr. Royal thinks my mum and dad will be happy about

my maths. I nod, but I don't tell him they won't. I don't tell him about what they say. They only want to know if I am bad. Then they can make me sit on the chair in the dining room. I don't tell them I have good marks in anything.

I have to tell my mum I was invited to the evening. She has to sign the letter to say I can. It is at night. I don't tell her she can come, though. Mr Royal says I have to wear something nice, but I don't have anything. I only have school shirts and pants. I don't have other things. He doesn't say anything about it.

When it is the presentation evening, my dad says I can't have a ride to the school. I have to walk. I walk to school anyway so it doesn't matter. He would take my precious stupid brother, but he doesn't take me. Like always. I have to walk all the time, even when it rains and snows or is very windy. But not my brother. He can't walk anywhere. I hate him.

The presentation finishes at 10pm. I have to walk home. It will be dark but I am not scared of it. I walk in the dark lots of times.

I finish school and run home very fast. I have a paper round now. I have to do it before I can go out back to school for the presentation. I get my bike and then I rush to the newspaper shop to get my papers and go to all the houses. If I do them fast, I can go home and get some dinner too and then I can go to school. But I don't go to school on my bike. I asked my mum, but she says no. She says it will get stolen or I will lose it because I don't look after things.

When I finish my paper round, my mum is in the kitchen cooking dinner. I am too late. It makes me sigh, but I don't let her hear it. No, I am too late and I can't cook. Maybe I can make dinner when she has finished. Sometimes she lets me. If she is in a good mood and I don't make a mess.

My mum finishes dinner and then my dad serves it up. I have to set the table for them. I don't eat any. My brother already had his special dinner so he doesn't have any too. He gets special dinners because he is their special super boy. Maybe he can choke on it. He gets his dinner served on a tray with pudding and a drink and then he watches the television with it.

I stand in the kitchen and look in the cupboard. I don't know what I want to make for my dinner. My mum and dad are in the dining room. "Do you think you should be looking in there?" my dad says to me. "You're fat enough aren't you?"

He says I am fat all the time. He shows his friends too. He shows them how fat I am. I am not fat. He says my brother is fat. But he is too. He doesn't show my brother to his friends. Sometimes my mum lifts my top up and pulls my pants all the way down and then shows them how fat I am. My mum pinches my skin on my stomach. She pulls it hard and laughs about it because I am so fat. I close the cupboard. I don't want anything to eat. It doesn't matter. I am not hungry anymore.

I walk in the dining room. "What happened to making dinner?" my mum says to me. I tell her I changed my mind. I don't feel hungry anymore. "What have you eaten today?" she asks me. I tell her I had a sandwich and some crisps at lunch time. I didn't. But I don't tell her. I used my money to buy cigarettes and then I sell them to get more money for more cigarettes. I have lots of money from it. I didn't get breakfast either. I don't ever get it because I don't like to go in the kitchen when everyone is asleep. Maybe the bad man will come. No one can hear me in the kitchen. Then he will be there. I see his face sometimes. I see his stupid bad smile at the corner of my eyes. But when I look, he isn't there. I am just seeing things. Or maybe he is very fast. It feels like he is there.

I go in the lounge. I will go to school soon for my presentation. But I have to wait for my mum and dad to finish their dinner. So I stand in there and wait. Then I can clear the table things away and go out. My dad comes in. He hasn't finished. I know he is mad at me. He says my name like it is a shout, but it isn't loud. "What is wrong with the food in this house?" he asks me. I tell him nothing. I am just not hungry anymore. He starts to shout at me. "Me and your mother spend a lot of time and money to feed you ungrateful kids in this house," he says. He shouts his words at me.

"You better get into that kitchen and eat what your mother has made for you," he says. "If you want to make it to next week."

I don't say anything to him. I go in the kitchen like he tells me to do. I stand there in the middle of the kitchen. There is no food. Maybe it is invisible. I don't say it, though. But I wait for my dad. My mum has finished her dinner. She comes in the kitchen. I ask my mum if there is some dinner for me. She looks at me. She has big eyes. She does that when she is angry. Maybe she thinks I want her to cook for me.

"It's in the freezer. If you want it you can get off your lazy backside and get it yourself, I am not your servant," she says to me.

My dad comes in the kitchen too. I tell him, "See? There isn't any dinner. My mum didn't make me any as usual."

My mum stares at me even more. "What exactly are you trying to say, you little shit?" she asks me. I tell her nothing. "It doesn't sound like nothing," she says. "It sounds as though you are implying I am a bad mother."

I don't say anything about it. There isn't a point. She just gets mad whatever I say. Then it gets into a big fight. My dad gets mad at me. He shouts lots of bad things at me. He says he does everything for the family and all I do is give them crap and make it bad. I make them argue. I always cause rifts in the family. "What exactly is your problem?" he shouts it in my face. I don't answer him either. I try not to look at him, but he grabs my face and makes me.

I don't know why I do it. He makes me mad inside. I wish I could hit him. I want to smash his face in. I want to punch him lots of times. I shout too. I shout loud and call him names. I shout at him that I hate him. I tell him he loves my brother more. He is a bad dad. I hate him. I want to say lots of things so it makes him cry. I want him to cry and be sorry. I tell him I wish he wasn't my dad.

I hate them all. They are shit parents. I hate them so much. I say it lots of times so I can feel the H and the T. I want to make it all scratch inside so I can feel the letters. I get my hands in my hair and I pull it a lot to make all the words go away from my head so I don't say them.

"You think we are shit parents?" my dad asks me.

I nod. I am crying too. My nose is running. I hate them. "You don't come to anything. You don't care. You don't think I do anything good," I tell him. "You always say my brother does good things, but you never say I do. It's always him, him, him." I stop all the words before I say more bad things.

"What have you done that is so special?" he asks me. I tell him why I got the award. I tell him about the maths and that I got ninety-nine percent. My mum starts to shout. "You are just jealous," she says. "That's why you act this way. We would come, but you don't tell us about it."

"Are you coming tonight?" I ask her. I know she will say no; they always say no. She says they can't. It is too short notice. I tell her she wouldn't have come anyway. "You could come by yourself if you really wanted to come," I say to her.

She tells me I don't know what I am talking about, but I do. I tell her to shut up when she makes excuses. I tell her they never do anything for me. They never say they are happy at things I do at school. I swear at her.

I swear at them both and tell them I am going. "You can both fuck off," I say and then I walk into the dining room.

My dad chases after me. He catches me at the dining room door before I get in the lounge. "What did you say?" I scream at him to let me go. I scream it over and over. My mum shouts at me from the kitchen. My dad yells at me too about being so bad. We all shout at the same time. I can't hear what they are saying.

He drags me back into the dining room. I shout at him. I know what he is going to do. My mum goes back in the kitchen. My dad slams me onto the coffee table. I swear at him to get off me. He is bigger than me. He holds me down. He gets my pants open. He opens his too. He has sex with me very hard. It makes me want to be sick it hurts too bad. I stop the shouting. My dad presses my head down. He doesn't say any words, but he makes growl-like sounds at me because he is mad. Then my dad gets off me. He pulls his pants up and goes away. I don't shout anymore.

Fifty Six

I try to move but my hands are shaking. My body is shaking all over. It makes my head feel fuzzy. I scrunch my eyes up to try to make it all go away. I try to move, but it hurts too bad and makes me hold my breath. I try to breathe, but it makes me want to be sick. I have to move very slowly. I can't be sick on the table. If I am then my mum will get mad because she has to clean it all up. Then she starts to break things and cry, because she is busy and has to do all the house work all the damn time. I try to reach down for my pants, but even that makes me cry. I try to keep the crying quiet so I don't make my mum and dad come in and shout at me for it.

I can't pull my pants all the way up. It hurts too much. I pull them up so they cover me up, but I don't fasten them. I feel bad all over. I made him do it. I always do. I don't know why I can't keep my stupid mouth shut and then it wouldn't happen. But I make him mad. I am so stupid. I have to go to the bathroom to wash it all away. I feel all the bad parts all inside. It's all over me and I want to make it go away. I wish I could scratch my skin off.

I don't ask to go for a shower. I just go to the bathroom. But no one says anything anyway. I lock the door. I don't want to see my mum or dad. I know I am bad. I turn the shower on and take my clothes off, but that hurts too. I stare at my pants for a long time. There is blood in them. I try not to cry about it and try to make everything stop shaking, but I feel cold inside and it makes me shiver. My head feels so bad it wants to explode. I don't like it when there is blood. It makes me worry that when I am at school, it comes through my pants and they see it and call me a girl.

I get in the shower. I don't turn it down. It is hot. I get my dad's nail brush and rub it all over my skin until it hurts and is red and bleeding. I brush it down my arms until they are all scratched. I haven't shut the shower door. I can see the stupid face in the mirror. I want him to cry for what he did. He deserves that too.

I get out of the shower and my arms and legs have many scratches on them. Good. They should have. They look like I scratched them with sandpaper. I hate the boy in the mirror. No wonder everyone does bad things to him. He is so bad and ugly. I hate him so much. He just does everything wrong and makes my dad mad at me. I wish he would die. "Do you hear me?" I say to him. "I want you to die." I get my nails and dig them into both sides of his neck and pull down so red lines appear. I do it again until I can see the blood starting. His eyes fill with tears and I laugh at him. I hate him so much. I wish he was never born. My mum is right. He is bad and evil.

He is hungry. His stomach rumbles because he didn't eat. But I laugh at him. He can starve. He deserves that too. "You aren't good enough to eat," I tell him. I can't get my words out hard enough so he knows how much I hate him. I wish I could reach in and punch him in the face over and over.

I don't look at him anymore. I don't want to see his stupid, ugly face. I get dressed. I have to do it slowly because everything hurts. It's his fault it hurts so bad. I wish my dad would kill him. I go to my room when I am dressed and don't look at him again. I go to my room and don't look at my mum or dad either. I don't want to see them. I sit on my bedroom floor and put my arms around my legs. I try to hug myself tight, but it hurts inside. I make myself rock. I count when I rock. One, two, three, then I stop so it doesn't get to four. It makes me cry when I rock because it hurts, but I don't care. It should hurt. I do it for a long time and don't go to school for the presentation. I don't deserve that either. I ruin everything.

When it is late, my dad comes up the stairs. It's my brother's bedtime. I am still on my floor, but I am lying down. He knocks on the door lightly. Maybe he thinks I am asleep. I don't tell him to come in but he does. He turns my light on. I don't move. I don't look at him. I don't want to say anything. I don't want him to see me.

"You didn't go to school," he says to me. I move my head away so he can't see my stupid face. He comes into my room and stands near me. "What was the award for?" he asks. I don't tell him. I don't want to talk. The words stay in my mouth but I don't open it to let them out. "It was this evening, right?"

He says my name because I don't say anything to him. "I can go on Monday," I say to him. Mr. Royal will get it for me. I tell my dad it doesn't matter. I am not bothered. I can pick it up late.

"I'm sorry I couldn't come," my dad says. "We didn't have anyone to look after your brother and you know your mother, she wouldn't be able to go alone. You just have to learn to do things without us. It isn't fair if I came and then your mother stayed with him. Think about how she would feel if I did that."

I don't have anything to say. I tell him I know and that it's okay. He stands there for a minute and looks at me. But I don't look at him. Then he says goodnight and goes out of my room and closes the door behind him.

I stay in my room all weekend, except when I have to get a shower and make dinner when I am allowed. I read my library books. I don't want to see anyone. I am just bad. Everyone probably wishes I would go away so I do. It doesn't matter. I am nothing.

When I go to school on Monday morning, I feel sad inside. I don't know what I will say to Mr. Royal about the award. I was supposed to help him too. He wanted me to get there early so I could set up the chairs and things like that. I don't know why he wanted my help. He should have asked someone better than me. I will tell him I am sorry.

I sit at my table in my form room. I don't talk to anyone when they come in and sit down too. Mr. Royal comes in after. He looks at me, but he doesn't smile. I look down at the table. I know he is mad at me. I didn't mean to make him mad.

He reads the register out and then tells us all the important things and then he says we can go to our classes. He doesn't talk to me. I walk past him slowly, maybe he will say hello, but he doesn't. I walk out last. When I get to the door, he says my name. I go to him. But I don't stand very close. I don't want him to hit me. I know I have been bad and I know he is mad at me. He sits at his desk and puts his glasses on. Then he takes a deep breath and looks at me. "What happened to you on Friday evening?" he asks me. "You didn't come back."

I don't look at him. I look at my feet. I know I am bad. I don't know what to say about it. I am sorry but I don't tell him I am sorry. I look at him. "I hung around with my friends instead," I say to him. "I didn't want to come back to school."

"You didn't think to call the office and let me know?"

I look back at my feet again. I say I am sorry I didn't call. I didn't think about it. I want him to let me go to my class so I don't look at him. Maybe he will know I am lying, then he will know I am really bad because I made my dad mad again. I am sorry. I spoil everything. I don't cry about it, though. Babies cry. Stupid, fat babies like my brother. I feel bad inside that Mr. Royal isn't happy with me. I don't say anything else, though. I just wait. He sighs and tells me to go. He doesn't say anything else, either.

At lunchtime, I go to my form room and sit at my table like I always do. I don't want to be with Lewis today. I smoked my cigarette before he came and then went to my form room. Mr Royal is there. He sits at his desk. I get scared he will tell me to get lost, but he doesn't. He doesn't say anything. Not even hello. He doesn't talk to me like he does normally at lunchtime.

I get my books out and open them. I don't look up at Mr. Royal. I keep my head down so he doesn't see me. I try to keep the crying away but the tears keep getting out and then they fall onto my book. I wipe them off from where they run down the side of my nose. I try not to sniff so he can't hear me. I promise Mr. Royal in my head that I won't ever be bad like that again.

I feel the words in my mouth. They want to come out and tell him why I didn't come to school. I want to tell him my dad had sex with me because I was too bad. Maybe he will say it's okay. I write it on some paper.

To Mr. Royal, I'm sorry. I didn't mean to not come. I wasn't really with my friends. I made my dad mad and then he had to do things to make me stop. He always has to do them because I can't behave. My dad has sex with me. He does it all the time. I don't like it. It makes me feel bad. I try to wash it away. But it takes too long. I'm sorry. I'm sorry I am so bad. I didn't mean it.

I scribble all over it. I don't want him to know. I just want to tell him. But he will know I am disgusting.

I get off my stool and then I stand next to him. I say his

name but he doesn't answer me at first. He tells me one minute. I stand next to him and wait. If I just say it maybe he can keep me at school and then my dad doesn't have sex with me again. Maybe then he knows my mum and dad don't love me. Maybe he likes me and he can look after me instead. I feel my eyes fill up. Then I can't see properly. I bite my lip so it doesn't shake. I am scared inside. I don't want him to know I am dirty. I don't want him to know that part.

He turns around and looks at me. He is still mad. I tell him I am sorry. I don't say anything. I go away to the ditch for a cigarette. I don't tell him about what my dad does. He is mad at me. He will think I am just bad.

Fifty Seven

I try to be good for Mr. Royal. I don't do anything bad at all. When me and Lewis have been to the ditch to smoke our cigarettes, I go to my form room and read or do my homework. Mr. Royal is always there too. We talk sometimes now. But not like before. I made it all bad now. I am sorry that I made it bad. I didn't mean to. I try my best to make it better so he likes me again. I wish I could tell him I am sorry.

I do well in all my classes. I try my best to get good marks. When I get my merits, Mr. Royal doesn't joke about them anymore. Maybe I made him mad at me forever. Maybe he knows why I didn't come and he thinks I am disgusting because I made my dad do things.

When it is Friday and Mr. Royal has done the register and everyone has gone away to their class, he asks me to wait. He wants to talk to me about something. It makes me scared. I don't like when people say they want to talk to me. Usually it means I have done something bad. "There's a sailing trip," he says to me. I know about it. But I wasn't allowed to go. My dad wouldn't pay all that money. It's for a week. I wish I could go. "There is a spare place. It is paid for, you just have to pay £5. Do you want to go?"

£5? That isn't a lot of money. I have that from my paper round and things. Maybe my mum and dad will let me go. They don't have to pay for it. I will pay myself. I tell Mr. Royal that I want to go, but I have to ask my mum and dad. He writes me a note about it and says they can call him about it. I tell him thank you.

When school is finished, I am very excited. I can't stop thinking about the sailing trip. I hope they will say yes. I promise God I will believe in him if he just lets them say yes to this. I don't mean to be mad at him all the time. I'm sorry. "Please let me go on the trip," I ask him and I promise I won't ever ask for things again.

My Nan is coming today. I will ask when she is there. My mum and dad don't say no when she is there. I will tell them I have the money. They don't have to pay for anything. I can go all by myself. I think about it when I do my paper round. I say it to myself while I ride my bike so I can practise what I say to my mum and dad. I am excited. Maybe they will say yes. I haven't ever been on a long school trip before. Just little ones that last a day. I don't tell my mum about those, though. I can sign her name. Writing is like drawing. So I practise her signature and write it on letters. I pay for those too.

When I have finished my paper round, I take my bike around the back and put it in the garage. My Nan is there. I am happy about it. She is in the kitchen. My dad is there too. I run upstairs to get the letter from Mr. Royal and then I get my £5 too and a pen so my mum can sign it and I can put it in an envelope. I run downstairs to my mum, dad and Nan. I stand and wait until they have finished talking.

"What do you want?" my dad asks me. I give him the letter. I say it is only five pounds and I tell him that I have the money. I saved it. I ask him. Please, please can I go? My Nan looks at the letter too.

"It looks like fun," she says to me. I nod my head and tell her I get to learn how to sail a boat.

My dad looks sad about it. He sighs big. "My brother died in that river sailing," he says. I ask my dad please. I won't die. I can swim. I have my teachers there too.

My Nan says it is supervised and I should be okay. He doesn't have to worry. She tells my mum and dad they should let me go. My mum looks mad at her. She doesn't like it when my Nan tells her what to do.

My dad says it is okay. Then he signs it and I take it away before he gets mad and rips it up. I put the money with it in the envelope and then I hide it upstairs until Monday. I can't wait. The trip is next week.

The week takes so long to go away. Lewis and Chris aren't coming sailing. They didn't want to. Peter is going, though. He talks to me about it. He is excited. But he doesn't go with me. He has a new best friend called Lee. I don't talk to Lee very much, but it is okay. Peter says I can sit with them on the bus if I want to. But I tell him no. I want to read my book instead.

I pack all my things myself for the trip. I pinched my dad's sleeping bag out of the attic again. The one I used when I ran away. I walk to school with Rachel in the morning when it is the trip day. She thinks the trip is great. She doesn't go on sailing trips with school, but they go to other places. She wishes she could go with us. She says she will miss me while I am away. I tell her I won't be a long time. It is just a week.

I miss Rachel too. I wish she was a boy and then she would go to my school and she could do all the same things as me. Maybe then she would like Lewis and Chris and we could all be friends.

The sailing place isn't far away from school. It is near where my mum and dad lived a long time ago. When I didn't live with them and had to go to the play place. It is over the high bridge that goes over the river. We are staying in a building which is on the edge of the river. We have rooms there and bunk beds. We have to share the rooms. The bunk beds have our names on them when we get there. I get the top bunk in my room. I like bunk beds. I haven't had one before. My friend, Faye, has them in her room. I want to sleep high up.

There is a boy called Karl. He has the bunk under me. We have to share the room. Me and Karl aren't friends. He isn't mean. I just don't talk to him. He isn't in my form and he isn't in all my classes. I used to sit next to him in geography when I was in the first year of senior school, but now I only sit with him in cooking class because he sits at my table. But I don't talk to him.

We get there in the afternoon. We are not going sailing by ourselves on the first day. We do get to go on the big boat all together so they can show us all the sailing places we are allowed and where we aren't allowed too when we are in our boat. After we have done that, we go to the building to make dinner. We have to help cook and then we have to wash up. There is a list and we have to take turns. After dinner we go into the shed at the back. There are tables in there and lots of fish tanks and buckets with lots of things inside that we can look at.

The man that lives at the place shows us a fish thing. He takes it out of a bucket. It looks like a puffy pom-pom. It is funny. I have never seen one before. It has a hole in the middle. He says that is its mouth. He asks one of the boys to put his finger in. It doesn't have any teeth so it doesn't bite. The boy does and then the man says, "You know it uses its mouth as its bottom too?" We all laugh at him because he put his finger in the fishes bottom. He pulls his finger out very fast.

After we have learnt about some of the fish, we are allowed to mess around outside. We have to stay together, though, and we aren't allowed to go off the land. The teachers sit outside and drink coffee and watch us. When it gets dark, the teachers light the fire outside and we can have some hot chocolate and supper. We have to go to bed at ten because we have to be up early in the morning for the tide. I am glad I get to go on the trip. I am very happy.

I have to share the bathroom with Karl. We have to get ready for bed. I use the bathroom to get changed. I don't want him to see me get changed. He might know about what my dad does. He gets changed in the bedroom. But I am faster than him. He is a slow coach. I am fast because my mum and dad get mad if I take too long. When I come out, Karl isn't finished getting changed. He has no top on. His back is all sore. He has lots of cuts and bruises and marks on it. "What happened to your back?" I ask him.

"Nothing" he says, and then he puts his top on very fast and runs into the bathroom. I get my things out ready for bed. When we are done, the teacher comes around and checks on us and tells us to go to bed. I don't say anything to Karl about his back when he comes out of the bathroom. I don't know what to say. But I think about it. Maybe he is like me and he is bad too. Maybe his dad does mean things.

"Please don't tell anyone," he says to me.

I promise I won't. I climb onto my bunk bed at the top and lie on my front. Then I can hang my head over and look at him. "Did someone hit you?" I ask him.

He rolls on his side so I can't see his face. He doesn't say anything. I don't move. I stare at him. He starts to cry, but then he rolls back over and nods his head. He pulls his sleeping bag up so he can hide his face. I don't like it when people cry. I don't know what to do about it. I wish I could make it better so he doesn't cry. I don't like when people feel sad. It makes me feel sad and makes me want to cry too.

I climb down off my bunk and get him a tissue. Then I go in my bag and get some crisps. My Nan gave me money to buy things. I ask Karl if he wants some. I don't say anything about his crying and we don't talk about it. We talk about school and things. He has a funny accent. He tells me about where he used to live with his dad. But now he has to live with his mum. That's why his voice is funny. I like the way he talks.

"Tomorrow can I be on the boat with you?" he asks. I nod about it. I don't have anyone to be on the boat with. No one likes me because they are all the popular people. I am not. No one talks to me. I make them scared. I can't wait until tomorrow. Me and Karl go to sleep.

Fifty Eight

In the morning, we all have to get up early and then some of us make the breakfast and some of us clean it all away. It is a huge breakfast. I don't get breakfast at home. It is a breakfast like Graham gave me a long time ago with eggs and sausage and some bacon. I have toast and cereal and some orange juice. There is porridge too, but I don't like that. We ate that at the play place and I don't eat it anymore. They used to make it with lots of lumps in it and they didn't use milk so it tasted like water and it was disgusting. The porridge here smells nice but I still don't want any.

Me and Karl sit together in the corner. We talk about lots of things. When breakfast is all gone and cleaned away, we have to go to the other building at the back. We have to wear special waterproof clothes and some boots to go in the sail boats. Me and Karl go to get ours. The shed stinks so bad. It smells like fishes and water. It is disgusting and makes me and Karl screw our faces up.

We get a boat. They are lined up and we have to pick one. I pick number three before anyone else. Karl doesn't care which boat we go on, they are all the same. We have a teacher with us. We get to have our physical education teacher on our boat. We have to wheel it down the jetty and get it into the water. It doesn't have any sails on it. We have to get those and then drag it around the side and tie it to the pole with a special knot so it doesn't float away. Out teacher shows us everything before we are allowed to sail the boat out and then we get to take it in turns holding the sails and making the boat turn and things. It is windy today and we laugh because one of the other boats turns upside down and they all land in the cold water.

We have to stop for lunchtime and then we get to go out again in the boats until it is dinner time. We have lessons on all the different things in the boat and how to use them. We have to learn lots of different words so that the other people in the boat know what we mean. After dinner, when it is all cleaned up, we get the lesson in the other shed again and we all have to write in our diaries about today and what we learnt. Then we get to hang around for an hour or so before we have to go in to go to bed.

I am very tired from the sailing and things, but me and Karl hang around together and go onto the beach. I like the beach. I used to play on it with Rachel a lot. I tell Karl about it and the games we played. Maybe he would like Rachel too. He tells me he isn't allowed to go onto the beach. They live near it. They live next to the pleasure beach. He is very lucky. I like the pleasure beach. It has lots of rides. I went there with my Nan lots of times. But Karl shakes his head. He hasn't ever been to it. He watches it out of the window, but his mum doesn't let him go there. She can't afford it.

Karl has lots of brothers and sisters. He has four sisters and one brother. He lives with them and his mum. "She comes home in the middle of the night," he says to me. "Then she is sick all over the floor and my sister has to clean it up. Then we put her to bed, but she is heavy."

His mum goes to the pub and she drinks every night. She gets mad because when she comes home, the house is a mess. Then she hits them. She doesn't like Karl. I don't know why; he is nice. I don't tell him that my mum and dad don't like me too.

"My mum got mad," he says. "She came in from the pub and she peed all over the floor. I had to clean it up, but I didn't get it all." He lifts his sleeve up and shows me his arm. He has a bite mark on it. It is red and has lots of teeth marks in it. She must have bit him very hard. It has a yellow bruise around it too. It makes me feel sad about it for him. She shouldn't bite him. Maybe he cries when she does it. I don't like his mum. She shouldn't do that to him.

Peter comes over with Lee, so we don't talk about Karl's mum any more. He tells me to shush. Peter asks us if we have seen the jellyfish that is on the other side of the jetty? He tells us that it is huge. We say no and we go with Peter and Lee. There are lots of people there and it is very big. They poke sticks in it. It is dead. We poke sticks in it too.

Me and Karl spend all week together at the sailing school. I like him very much. We don't talk to the others. We don't like them. They are mostly mean anyway so it doesn't matter. They talk about stupid boring things like the television. Me and Karl don't watch it when we are at home. He isn't allowed to either. When it is nighttime and we are supposed to be asleep, we write lots of notes to each other and pass them down the side of the bunk bed. When the teachers come, we pretend to be asleep. Karl tells me lots about his mum. She is very bad.

She goes out at night and gets drunk. Then she brings people home with her so she can have sex on the sofa. He doesn't like when his mum does that. He doesn't like to watch so he hides under the pillows. I don't tell Karl about my mum and dad. But I don't like it when they have sex too. I don't like to see it. I don't write it down. I don't want him to think I am bad.

He lives in a flat with his mum. It only has one bedroom and a living room. His mum sleeps in there on the sofa. Him and his brother have to share the big room with their sisters. He doesn't like it. His sister is bossy and mean too. She cooks them all dinner and thinks she is the boss of them all, but she isn't.

She looks after his mum, though, when their mum is drunk. Sometimes, his mum can't get to the toilet and the alcohol makes her have diarrhoea. "It gets all over her," he says. "Then we have to clean her and it smells so bad. Sometimes she is sick too." I screw my face up. I don't like it when people are sick and things. It smells too bad. Then it makes me want to be sick too.

He cries sometimes when he tells me about his mum. His mum hits him lots of times. She hits him with a stick. That is why his back is so sore. She hits all of them when she gets drunk and mad. She swears and she hates him. "Sometimes the boyfriends are mean too. They get drunk with her and then they think it is funny to hit us too."

He swears when he talks about his mum. He hates her. I hate her. She is so mean. I hope she dies and goes away. "She is a stupid bitch," he says to me. "I hope she gets drunk, falls down and dies." He tells me about his sister. It was the weekend before the sailing. She started her period. The big sister was trying to help, but then his mum came home and she got mad. She beat the sister and then she and her boyfriend made her lie on the floor and they shoved ones of those tampon things inside her. She screamed when they did it. It made her cry. Karl had to hide away. They didn't want to see it.

I don't know what to say about it when he says it to me. But it doesn't matter. He just says lots of things about her. He doesn't know where his dad is. "He pissed off years ago with some slut," he says to me. "I hate him too."

I don't tell Karl about anything with my mum and dad. But I ask Karl if he smokes. He says no. I ask him if he wants to sneak outside with me while I smoke. He says okay. I sneak out when Karl is asleep and he doesn't know. No one knows about it. But maybe Karl won't tell on me.

It is easy to get out because the teachers sleep at one end and we just have to go to the stairs and get out. When we are outside and I light my cigarette, we hide at the back. I ask him if he wants to try smoking. He says yes. I tell him he has to do it slow or he will cough too much and then we will make a noise and get caught.

He knows what to do, though. His mum smokes and he

watches her. He puts my cigarette in his mouth and then he sucks it in. I laugh and tell him to shush when he coughs really badly. He puts his hand over his mouth and tries to keep the cough inside, but it sounds like he farts in his mouth and we laugh about it.

It's easy to sneak back in too. We have to be careful in case anyone got up. But they didn't and no one catches us. The other kids sneak out too to smoke. I don't smoke with them. I don't like them. They think they are special. I just like Karl. I am sad that the week is over and we have to go home again. I like Karl. But he isn't allowed to hang out after school or on the weekends.

We are still friends, though, when we are in school. We see each other lots of times and I sit with him in the classes that we have the same. He likes Lewis too. We all go to the ditch together to smoke. Karl likes to write stories. Sometimes, me and Karl sit in the form room together and write them down. Then we read them to each other when we are smoking. Lewis doesn't like them. He thinks it's for babies, so we don't tell him about it. We just read them when he isn't there.

Fifty Nine

On school days, Karl meets me at the corner shop in the morning before we start school. He gets there before me because he lives so far away he has to catch the early bus. We buy cigarettes there and then we go and meet Lewis, and sometimes Chris, at the ditch. Chris doesn't come a lot, though, because he just likes to have Lewis to himself.

We smoke our cigarettes and talk about girls and things like that. Lewis has a girlfriend. She is in another school near his house. He tells us all about it. Chris is going out with her sister. They go out and get drunk on the weekends and have sex and things like that. "We go to this house," Chris says to me. "There is a girl there called Michelle. She is a friend of Rebecca's." Rebecca is his girlfriend. "Her mum is great; she lets us hang around and she lets us have parties in the caravan at the front. You two should come down one weekend. Michelle would like you. We could get some friends and all go to the Pleasure Beach."

I didn't have a girlfriend before. I have had sex before with girls. But it was a long time ago at the play place. I was seven. Then I had sex with girls all the time. But I haven't done it with them when we have been in senior school. Just with my dad or his friend. I don't say it though. I tell Lewis it sounds like a good idea.

Karl is quiet today. Maybe it is because we are going to go to the Pleasure Beach and he can't go. When we talk, he just nods at the things, but he doesn't smile and he doesn't really say anything. He looks sad. When Lewis and Chris go away, I ask Karl what's wrong, and he says nothing so we go to class.

We have art first in the pottery room. I hate pottery. It's boring and the things we make always fall to pieces. I don't like how the pot feel in my hands too. It is hard and scratchy. We always make stupid pots too. I don't know why. They are grey and ugly and have funny shapes. It is boring because we have to stick them in the kiln to go hard. I sit with Karl in art. We can sit and talk, though. So it isn't that bad. I don't like the chairs in the pottery classroom. They are tall and hard and sometimes it hurts to sit on them if I have been with my dad the night before. Then I get told off for fidgeting because sometimes it gets itchy and I don't want to do anything so people see. It annoys me.

"I have to give my mum £2," he says to me suddenly. "There was some money on the window ledge and it has gone missing. My mum says I took it and I can't go home if I don't bring it back." He doesn't look at me, but his eyes look like he is going to cry. They are all wet and red on the edges. "I don't have any money," he says.

"Someone stole it?"

He shrugs his shoulders. "She was mad about it and she shouted and ran around the house and smashed everything up. She told me to get out and not to come back until I have it."

"We can ask Lewis," I say to Karl. Lewis always has lots of money. He works for his mum at the weekends. He will lend it to Karl if I ask him. He is good like that. But Karl doesn't want to. He doesn't want Lewis to know about his mum. I promise we won't tell Lewis. "I will pretend I want to borrow it," I say to him.

I ask Lewis at lunchtime. He says he would, but he doesn't have the money with him. I can have it tomorrow if I want. He will bring it in for me. But Karl has to have it today or he can't go home. If he does, his mum is going to hit him. She said so when she was shouting about it. She doesn't want shitty thieves in her house. She didn't raise them to be scroungers. That's what Karl says and he puts her voice on when he says it. He sounds like a demented witch. "I can't wait until I can leave home," he says. "You and me can live together and then everyone else can piss off." I think that's a good idea. I can't wait either. We have two more full years left of school after this one. It is forever.

I say to Karl that maybe we could ask a teacher for the money. Maybe we can say he lost his lunch money and then when she lets us borrow it, he can use that. He thinks it's a good idea and we go to the office. He makes himself look sad about it and he tells the secretary he forgot his lunch money.

She smiles at him and says it's okay. He doesn't have to worry. She goes into the other room and then comes back with a book. She writes him a note about his lunch money and he has to sign it. Karl smiles. Maybe he can get to go home now. But the secretary doesn't give Karl money. She gives him a lunch voucher. "Take that to the canteen," she says. "You can have anything up to £2."

He says thank you and takes the voucher off her. It didn't work. It gets to the end of school and Karl doesn't have the money for his mum. I know I can get it for him. I just steal it off my dad instead. But he has to come to my house and I can sneak into my mum and dad's room and they won't notice. My dad will be at work anyway and my mum will be in the kitchen or something like that. I steal all the time and they are so stupid, they don't notice it.

I can't take Karl into my house, though. He has to wait outside around the corner. I tell him I will meet him when I get my paper round. But he needs more than £2 because he missed the school bus. Now he has to pay for the tram to get all the way home too.

When I get home, my mum is in the garden. I run up the stairs and go to my room and get changed very fast. I listen for my mum downstairs. I bend down and look through the secret part, but she isn't there. I quickly go into my mum and dad's room and run to the sink where my dad keeps all his change. I take the money for Karl and run out and close the door again.

My mum comes back out the bathroom when I go downstairs. "Were you in my bedroom?" she asks me.

"I thought I heard a noise," I say to her, and then I tell her

I have to do my paper round and I run out of the house before she can ask anything else. I get my bike and the papers from the shop, and then I go and meet Karl.

Karl is so happy when I give him the money. He looks like he is going to cry again. He helps me with my paper round. He says thank you to me many times. I tell him it is okay. I am happy to give him the money. I like to help him. When my paper round is finished, I walk him to the tram stop on the promenade and we smoke a cigarette and wait for the tram. When he gets on it and goes home, I watch it until I can't see it anymore. I hope he gets home safe and I hope his mum isn't mad. My dad would be if it was me. He would hit me and make me sit on the dinning chair for hours because he's an idiot. He doesn't even know I take his money.

I go to the part where the rocks are and lock my bike up. Then I climb over the railing and sit and smoke my cigarette. I don't want to go home yet. I want to sit and watch the sea. But I know I can't be out too late, because my mum will tell my dad, and he will ask why it took me so long.

When I go home, my dad is there. He is in the lounge. He doesn't talk to me. He doesn't even say hello. Maybe he knows I came in and stole his money. But he doesn't say it to me. I don't ask because then he will know I am a thief. I just go to my room instead. I don't see my mum or dad all evening. I don't want to in case they know. It feels like they do. I stay there all evening and later my dad comes upstairs and he opens my door. "Did you see some money that was on the side?" he says to me. "I shake my head. "It's missing."

I feel scared inside. Maybe he knows it is me. Sometimes he asks when he knows and then I am in trouble because I lie too. I ask him if he is going to bed. He says yes. I ask him if I can come too. He says yes and he holds the door open. He doesn't shout when I have sex with him. He won't ask about the money.

I am bad and disgusting. I wish I could go away forever.

Sixty

I like cooking class. I like to learn how to do things and
then maybe I can make them at home when I am allowed to
cook. But my mum doesn't eat them. Not even when I bring
them home from school, because I made them and I am dirty.
She thinks they will be infected. I am not allowed to touch food
at home that she is going to eat. Just things in tins. I have bread
and cereal that is mine. It isn't special, but it means I don't have
to touch any of the others. It doesn't matter, though. I don't eat
much anymore. I am too fat. I eat too much and I make
everything wrong. Sometimes my stomach rumbles and I laugh
at it. It is good when it rumbles, it means I am hungry and then I
don't eat anything at all.

Today we are making pizza. We have to make it
ourselves and pick what goes on it. We have to make a poster for
it too, for a new pizza. Then people will want to buy it. Me and
Karl are making our pizza together. Chris and Lewis make theirs
too. We all sit around the same table.

Me and Karl just make ours with lots of different things
on the top. We couldn't bring anything in to put on it. My mum
and dad don't like to buy food for school and he didn't ask his
mum. So we get things from the canteen to do it. Chris says it
looks like Karl's face. Karl has lots of spots. I tell Chris to shut
up, he has rabbit teeth. "Maybe your mum humped the rabbits

when no one was looking," I say to him.

Chris always says nasty things. Sometimes I just wish he would get lost. I like to say nasty things back to him to make him shut up. I always win the arguments because he says stupid things that don't make any sense. Sometimes when me and Chris see each other, we race and then see who can hit who the hardest and first. I punch him in the stomach. I hate it sometimes when he does it to me and it hurts because my dad had sex with me the night before. Then it makes me feel sick from it. Everything hurts. But I usually get Chris first and then he can't hit me.

Karl doesn't say anything about Chris saying his face was like pizza. It would make me mad if it was me and then I would hit Chris. He is just stupid. I don't say anything else. Me and Karl make our pizza and I ask him to put it in the oven because it hurts a little bit when I walk from my dad. I don't want to bend down. I don't want it to start bleeding and then it goes through my pants and everyone sees it.

Karl picks up the tray and walks to the oven. He bends down very slowly. I can see his face. He looks like he is going to cry again. I ask him if he is okay. He nods and puts the pizza in the oven. "It is just hot in here," he says to me. But I don't believe him. I think he is going to cry. When we go back to our table, Chris thinks it is funny to throw water at me. I throw it back at him and then I move fast behind Karl. I catch his back by accident. I don't mean to. I don't want to hurt him, but he jumps from it and shouts. Then he runs out of the classroom.

I didn't mean to make him upset. I run after him out of the classroom. I don't listen when the teacher tells me to stop. Karl goes all the way to our ditch. He is very hard to catch because I can't run very fast today. When I get to the ditch, he is crying. He tells me to go away. I stand at the other side and ask him what is wrong, but he says I have to leave him alone. He cries so much it gives him the hiccups.

I climb across the ditch. "I'm sorry," I tell him. I didn't mean to do something bad. He says I didn't. It was an accident. He lifts his shirt and jumper up and turns around. Then he pulls it back down and looks down. His back is all red and cut and bruised. He has many marks from his mum. I am sorry. I didn't mean to make them hurt. I didn't know that his mum had hit him. She has hit him very bad. They look like they are bleeding. I tell him we should go inside and clean them up. We can go in the toilets and put water on them. He nods.

We climb out of the ditch and sneak in the door that is next to the science block. It is dark in there and no one will see us. We lock the door so no one else can come in and see us. Then Karl takes his shirt and jumper off. He has marks at the front too. He has them on his arms.

"I tried to stop her hitting me," he says. "But she hit my arms."

"She was mad?"

He nods. "She wanted to go out, but my sister isn't well so I had to make dinner. I don't know how to do it. I made beans on toast. She didn't want beans on toast so she chucked it at the wall and it made a mark," he says. "It is all my fault." He tries not to cry, but his eyes get red again and some of it comes out.

I tell him it wasn't his fault. "Your mum is just mean." She shouldn't hit him. I wish she didn't. It makes me feel sad inside about it. Maybe he cries when he is all alone and no one helps him. I wish he could live at my house and live in my room too, and then she can't hurt him anymore. He could be my brother and no one would hurt him.

"I am too scared to go home," he says.

"Maybe we should tell Mr. Royal," I say to him. "He is very nice." I tell him that his mum isn't supposed to hit him. He is scared about telling Mr. Royal. But it is okay. Mr. Royal is nice. Karl doesn't want to get into trouble, but I tell him he won't. Then his mum will have to stop the hitting. Maybe she will get to have someone help her.

I wish I could tell Mr. Royal about my mum and dad. But I don't. I am not brave like Karl is. Karl doesn't want to tell Mr. Royal. I say I can tell him. He doesn't have to say it. He doesn't want to get his mum into trouble. He starts to cry again. I don't like it when he cries. I see lots of people hug other people when they cry. But I don't like to do it. It makes me feel funny inside because I don't like to touch people. What if I try to hug him, and then he tells me to go away because he wants me to get my filthy arms off him like my mum?

I wait for him to finish crying and I get him some tissues.

I help him to put his shirt back on because he can't move his arms all the way back. We walk to Mr. Royal's room. Karl stays behind me. He doesn't want to see Mr. Royal. I knock on the door. He doesn't have any class to teach. Mr. Royal tells me to come in. Karl hides and stays outside.

I tell Mr. Royal I want to tell him something. He sits down and I stand there. I don't know how to say it. The words are very hard to say. I wish I could tell him about me too. Mr. Royal says it's okay; whatever it is, I should just say it. I tell him about Karl. I say that his mum hits him. Karl is at the door. I wave for him to come in. He does, but he looks at the floor. He doesn't look at us. I pull Karl all the way into the classroom and turn him around, then I lift up his shirt and show Mr. Royal. "His mum hit him," I say to Mr. Royal.

"Did your mum do that?" Mr. Royal asks Karl. "It is okay to tell me." Karl nods and then he starts to cry again. Mr. Royal gives him some tissue too, and then he tells us to sit down and he pulls out some chairs. I tell Mr. Royal all about it and Karl nods and says some things, but he doesn't say a lot.

"We have to go to the office," Mr. Royal says to me. "Will you be okay to go back to your classroom?" I nod. He writes a note for me and tells me to give it to the teacher. I walk with Karl and Mr. Royal for a little bit until we get to the main part of the school. Mr. Royal says that I did a very good thing in telling him. He says thank you to me for it. I feel sad inside. I wish I could tell Mr. Royal about everything. I wish he looked after me too.

Maybe I can say the words, but I don't know how to. I can't make them come out of my mouth when I try. I don't want my mum and dad to get into trouble, and I don't want them to go to jail. Karl's mum should go to jail. She is very bad. But my mum and dad aren't bad. They just do bad things.

I can't tell anyone because they don't understand. They will think my mum and dad do things because it is on purpose. But it isn't. It is because of me, because I am so fat and stupid, but I try to make the fat go away and I try not to be so stupid. I go back to my class.

When my cooking class is finished, Mr. Royal comes back to get Karl's things. I have put them all in his bag anyway. Lewis had taken our pizza out of the oven. I put half in a box and give it to Mr. Royal for Karl too. "Is he okay?" I ask Mr. Royal.

"Yes," Mr. Royal says, and he tells me that Karl won't be in school tomorrow, and he might not come back. I ask if I can say goodbye and he says yes.

I Feel sad because Karl is going away. I wish he didn't have to. I will miss him very much. I walk home from school and I try not to cry about it. He has gone away. He knew what it was like to have bad things too.

Sixty One

(Age Fourteen)

It is strange that Karl isn't at school. I walk to the shop in the morning, but he doesn't come. I do it every day because it feels strange not to do it. But he isn't ever there. It's been many weeks now and he has left school. He writes to me too, I know he isn't at school, but I keep thinking maybe he will come back. Maybe he will surprise me and be there.

I feel sad about it because I know he isn't coming back. I hang around with Lewis. But it doesn't feel the same. It feels like something is missing. Karl is living with his uncle in Scotland. He told me all about it in his letter. I was very excited when I got it. Him and his brother and sisters all have to go to a new school.

I write him a letter back too. I tell him all about school and what everyone is doing. I am glad his mum doesn't hurt him anymore. She didn't go to Scotland. She went to London instead. Mr. Royal says he is very happy I told him and he is very happy I could.

I go to school and it is form time. Mr. Royal does all the normal things, then he asks me to stay behind before I go to class. It makes me scared inside because he says he wants a word with me. When people say that, it means bad things. My dad says it and then I am in trouble. Everyone goes to their classes and I go to Mr. Royal's desk. I stand back so then he can't hit me if I am in trouble. I try not to do anything bad. I don't want to make him mad again like the maths presentation.

He turns around in his chair, but he doesn't stand up. "This is going to be my last year here," he says to me. "I have another job near where I live. I wanted to tell you myself before I tell other people."

Mr. Royal lives near the city. He has to drive a long way to get to school. I smile at Mr. Royal. I don't say anything bad about it. I tell him I hope he likes his new job. It feels bad inside that he is going away. It makes me want to be sick and cry. But I don't tell him. He says he is very excited about it. I keep smiling. I wish he didn't want to go. I don't want to cry. I don't want it to come out and then I look like a baby.

I didn't know Mr. Royal wanted to leave. It makes me want to cry inside because it is like a secret. Like my mum and dad do. They arrange to go out and don't say anything about it. Everyone always wants to go away. No one ever stays. Karl went away too. I walk to my class; I wipe the tears away that keep getting out. I have two more years of school left and there will be no Mr. Royal or Karl. I don't tell anyone, though. Not even Lewis. If I say it, it will make me cry. They say I am Mr. Royal's pet, but I don't care. I like to be. I don't tell him I am sad at all.

It went very fast after Mr. Royal told me he is leaving. I didn't tell anyone and I didn't talk about it. It makes me sad when I think about it. He only has two months left now. It has gone too fast. We have our options appointment today. I am excited about that. I worked very hard so I could pick all the right subjects to get into medical school. I have A's in everything so that I can pick all the right subjects on the options sheet.

I stand outside the office. I am very nervous about it. The teacher shouts me in and says it's my turn. She tells me to sit on the seat next to her and she asks me what I want to do when I leave school. I tell her I want to be a doctor. I am going to get my A-levels and then go to medical school. She smiles about it. She has my school report. It has all the A's on it. "You are one of the highest students in the year," she says to me. "A lot of the subjects you have chosen have a big queue of people for them. So we haven't been able to give everyone what they want, but we have tried our best."

She shows me the list with the number of places and the number of people that want to choose them too. "We looked at your grades," she says to me. "You do well in every subject so you have two choices. We believe you will do well in whatever subjects you take."

She tells me I can take the higher science. But if I take that, I have to take different lower classes and not the subjects I chose. Or I can take the higher classes my subjects and not do the science. But I need the higher classes for all of them. I need to get A's. I can't get A's in the lower classes. I need all the subjects.

I don't know what to say to her. I need them all. I need the science. Doctors have to have science. But I need all the others too, or I can't go to medical school. I have to do higher Maths and English. My mum's doctor said so. I ask her if I can please do the science with the Maths and English and change the others. "I really need it."

She shakes her head. "We have already set the places out."

I can't stop shaking inside. I want to cry, but I don't. I keep it away. I can't go to medical school if I don't have the maths, English and science together. I whisper that I will do the others and not the science. She smiles at me and gives me the paper I have to sign. I don't want to sign it. I don't want to do any of it. But I do. My hand shakes when I try, I am going to cry, but I don't let her see it.

I tell her thank you, then I leave the office. I don't talk to anyone. Karl has left. Mr. Royal is leaving and now I can't go to medical school. I run down the stairs and out of the school. I don't stop when someone shouts my name. I don't care it isn't home time yet. I run out of the gates. I run as fast as I can. I run so fast it makes my legs hurt, but I don't care. I run along the road all the way to the end, and then I run up the hill. I am crying when I run. My legs ache, but I don't stop. "Stupid, stupid. I hate you," I say to myself. "I am stupid. I don't get to do anything, ever. Because I am me. Because no one likes me. I can't be a doctor.

I can't breathe when I get to the top. I try, but my throat is dry and it makes me cough. I am nearly sick from it. I hate everyone. I hate me. I go into the Rock Gardens that is next to school. It is a big place. Sometimes me and Lewis go there at lunchtimes so the teachers don't see us. We hide in there and smoke. I run in there and all the way down the hill. The hill is steep and sharp, but I don't stop. I don't care if I fall. I don't care if I fall from the path and die.

When I fall over at the bottom, my hands bash down on the path, it hurts, but I don't care. Good. It should hurt. Everything should always hurt. I wish I bashed my face and not my hands. I wish I smashed my head in. I want everything to hurt. I crawl to the side and lie there and cry until I can't breathe. It is all gone.

Sixty Two

I don't care that I left school early. I am not supposed to, but it doesn't matter. What is the point in school? I was just there so I could go to medical school and now I can't. I go home instead after I have sat on the ground at the Rock Gardens for a long time. Maybe school called my mum and dad. I don't care if they did. Maybe my dad will get mad like always. It's all he ever does. Even if I breathe, he gets mad. I hate him. I hate all of them. They just all do what they want and they don't care.

I go to my house and I use the front door. I don't care about that, either. My stupid mum can get mad all she wants about it. She can hit me and shout. I am not bothered. I run up the stairs and get changed. I get all my books. I get the ones that Mr. Royal gave to me for science. I put them in a backpack and then I go to the attic where my dad keeps his wine. I get two bottles of it. One in each hand. I put them in the bag too.

I don't see my mum when I go down the stairs. I don't know where she is. Maybe she went out. Maybe they all did. Maybe she is in the bathroom being stupid and thinking about the doctor that doesn't really love her. I don't care where she is. I go to the garage and slam the door behind me. I tip the books on the floor and I open my dad's wine. I light a cigarette and I drink the wine from the bottle. I drink it fast. I drink it so fast that I can't breathe and it burns my throat.

I put my cigarette out on one of the books. It makes a burn hole in some of the paper. I light another cigarette and then I hold it to the corner of some of the other papers. The paper starts to smoke and then it sets on fire. I watch as the flame grows from a little light to some fire and then the fire goes all the way up the page. I get another page and rip it out and do the same. I hold it until it nearly burns my hand. I do it with the next one and the next one. I rip all the pages out and I burn them all. I do it until they are all gone and the wine is all gone too.

I drink both bottles of wine. I make sure it is all gone. I make sure everything is all gone. It has gone dark and I didn't notice. I sit in the corner and smoke. I am not crying anymore. My head feels funny from the wine but I don't care. I try to stand up but I can't because my legs are wobbly and my head feels like it is asleep I laugh at myself. I can't even walk. I wouldn't be a good doctor anyway. It is a good job I couldn't get the subjects I wanted. My mum is right. I would have killed someone.

I go to my bag and get my homework out. I haven't done it yet. I set that on fire too. There is no point in doing any homework. No one cares, no one will help me and make it better and I can't go to medical school. Mr. Royal is leaving and Karl went away. He got away from his mum. I didn't. I have to stay here because I am bad and I made them this way. I make them all bad. I make them hate me.

I hear the kitchen door bang closed. Someone is coming from the house. It's probably my dad, but I don't care. I tip the bottle to my mouth so there isn't any wine left at all. Not even the drips, then he can't take it back. It's gone and he can cry like a baby because I drank his wine that he made. He comes in and turns the light on. There is smoke everywhere from my papers.

"Are you crazy?" he asks me, and then he walks over to the pile of papers and stamps on them with his boot. "There is petrol in here, you could have taken the whole place down."

I don't care. I wish I did, then I could go away and it wouldn't matter. My mum comes out to the garage too. She comes in the door and swears about what I was doing. She asks my dad what he is going to do about me.

I don't know why they can't leave me alone. They should let me stay in the garage and I can go away. They won't miss me. They don't want me. They just want my perfect brother. I am no good for anything. My stomach rumbles inside because I am hungry. I laugh about it. My mum and dad were right about that too. I don't deserve food. They knew all the time and I didn't believe them.

My hand is swollen from where I fell over at the Rock Gardens. It looks bruised and when I move it, it hurts. But I do it on purpose. My dad is shouting at me, but I can't hear him. I just look at my hand and laugh because it hurts so bad. I hope when I look in the mirror, the boy is crying. He deserves it. I hope he is hungry and it all hurts.

I kick the ash from my books and take the bottle with me. I don't care when I walk past my mum if she is going to hit me, it's what she usually does. Or she gets her nails and digs them into my neck until I fall onto the floor and cry for her to stop it. I walk right past her and out into the back garden towards the house. She shouts my name. "Get back here right now," she says to me.

I swear at her and stick my fingers up. My mum follows me. My dad is at the garage; he has some ash in the bucket. My mum grabs my arm and makes me stop. She digs her nails in and hits me in the face with her other fist. It doesn't hurt.

I try to shake my arm so that she has to let go, but she doesn't. "Let go," I say to her. I shout it at her many times. I start to swear. My dad moves closer.

"Watch your mouth," he says to me. I swear at him too. What's the point? What's the point in anything now? It's all gone and they don't even know it. "Is this what you did? We got a call from the teacher. You left school and came home? What did you do? Decide you can come back here and have a right to get pissed on my wine?"

"You don't know anything," I say to him. He doesn't. He doesn't care like other people's dads. My dad just shouts at me some more. But I don't hear him because I shout back. I try to shout louder than him; it hurts my throat. He puts the bucket down to walk to me. I know what he is going to do. The big, hard man. It's all he ever does. He'll hit me or have sex with me so it hurts, because that's all I am good for.

He moves closer. I get the wine bottle and I lift it up. I

want to throw it at him. I want to hit him with it. I hold it up and my dad stops. I shout at them both about everything. I don't even know what the words are, because I can feel my head is all messy inside from the wine, like the petrol, but different.

"Are you going to hit me with that?" he asks me. But I don't answer, because I want to. I want to hit him so hard with it. I want to smash it in his face and then I want him to cry about it and say he is sorry. I want him to feel sorry. But I don't throw it. It hurts my wrists to hold the bottle high up.

I turn a bit so it doesn't hit my dad. I throw it as hard as I can. It makes me scream because it hurts my wrist to do it, but I throw it and it hits the wall near my dad and smashes. He jumps. I tell my mum and dad to get lost. I tell them I hate them. I wish I was dead. I wish they were.

My mum lets go of my arm and I storm into the house. I go to my room. I slam the door but the glass doesn't break. I wish it did. Then I sit on my bed. So what if it gets a mess and isn't perfect. It can have creases all over it. I lie down, but the room spins around. It feels like when the dentist gives me gas to make me fall to sleep. I try to roll on my side but I know I am going to be sick. I get up and run to the sink in the corner. I am sick in there. My mum will be mad about that. It doesn't matter. I go back to my bed.

I feel sick again. But I can't be bothered to move and go to the sink. It doesn't matter. I just let it come out while I lie on my back. It is hard to get out of my mouth and makes me cough from choking. It goes all down the side of my face and down my neck and under my head. I have to turn my head to spit it out. I don't get up.

My mum and dad haven't followed me. I can hear them shouting, though. I can hear my mum asking my dad what he is going to do about me. I close my eyes and don't move. I lie there and wait for my dad. But he doesn't come. I fall asleep. I don't wake up until it is morning. I don't even know what day it is. I know I am going to be in trouble. I can smell the sick. It is cold and around my head and in my hair.

I move around. My mum or dad didn't come in my room last night. My curtains are still open. I am glad. My mum would have been mad about the sick. I try to move but it hurts all inside. It makes me want to be sick again. My head thumps. I try to sit up to take my top off, but I can't. I roll away and go to sleep again. I don't care if I miss school again. I don't care about anything. It is all bad. All the time. I wish God was real and that he would not let me wake up again.

I ask him please don't let me wake up. I go back to sleep.

Sixty Three

I try to get up when I wake up again, but I lean on my
hand and it makes my wrist hurt. It makes me cry and I have to
get off it fast. It hurts as if someone put fire inside it. I look at it;
it is swollen and bruised. I get out of bed. My hair is all stuck
from the sick. I don't feel very good. My mouth feels very dry
and my head hurts too bad. I wish I could sleep forever.

My dad has gone to work when I go downstairs. My mum
isn't in. I don't know where she is. The doors are locked. Maybe
she went to the shops. She does that at lunchtime. I look at the
clock. It is lunchtime. I missed school. It doesn't matter though.
School doesn't matter at all now. I have nothing anymore.

I get mad when I think about it. I feel it inside and my
stupid teacher that didn't let me have the subjects. I hate her. I
wish she would get lost too. I go to the bathroom and get a
shower. It is hard to do because my wrist hurts so much. I hold it
in front of me so that I don't move it and make it worse. I try to
wiggle my fingers, but even that hurts.

I stand in the shower for a long time. I think about school
because I can't help it. I cry. I cry hard until it makes my head
hurt some more. Everything is gone. When my shower is done, I
get dressed in some clean clothes and ball up my dirty ones. I
have rinsed the sick out of them in the shower and then my mum
doesn't get mad about that. She will be mad about the bed,

though. It is covered.

She is in the kitchen when I come out. I didn't hear her come in when I was in the shower. She doesn't say anything to me. I ask her if I should put my clothes in the basket or in the machine, but she doesn't answer me. So I put them in the basket and walk out of the kitchen. My mum goes over and gets them and puts them into the machine.

My dad comes home. He is early. I don't talk to him. I move back out of the way so he can get past me. I hug my arm up so he doesn't hurt it. "What's up with your arm?" he asks me.

I shrug and tell him I don't know. I hurt it. He asks if he can have a look. I put my arm out and he gets my hand and wiggles it around. It makes me cry. I tell him to stop it, but he turns it over and does it again. "I don't ever get a minute's peace," he says to my mum. "Get your shoes on," he tells me.

He takes me to the hospital. He says he thinks my arm is broken. He isn't coming in with me, though. He doesn't have time. I have to go myself and I can walk home if I am stupid enough to break my own arm. He drives up to the hospital and tells me to get out. Then, he drives away. I don't even know where I have to go. I just go in the big doors and ask the woman there. I tell her I think my arm is broken. I show it to her. She tells me to sit down.

My wrist is fractured. That's what the doctor says. I have to have a special thing on it to keep it still. He gives me some medicine to make it stop hurting. I have to walk home by myself.

I don't really know the way. I know where school is, though, so I walk towards that and then I can find my way home.

My mum and dad don't say anything about my wrist when I get back. I just go to the garage and don't talk to them. I sniff the petrol and smoke my cigarettes and go to sleep there. I don't have anything else to do.

I thought I would have been in trouble for the wine and for shouting at my mum and dad. But they didn't do anything. They just didn't talk to me. But that's normal. They don't talk to me unless it's to tell me what sex thing they want me to do. Probably the only time my mum talks and smiles all at the same time with me. My mum didn't even get mad when she cleaned my sheets up. She told my dad all about it, but he didn't come and hit me for it. He didn't say anything at all.

I hear my mum complaining all the time to my dad. Maybe he is sick of me now. He doesn't come and shout at me all the time. School has finished now for the summer. It all goes very fast. I only have two more years left. But they don't matter anymore. I don't want to go back to school ever again. I don't want to be there and do the work. I wish I could just die and make everything go away. I wish it didn't feel so bad inside.

I'm not going to be a doctor anymore. I don't tell my mum or dad, though. They will be happy about it. I don't tell them anything. The only time my dad comes near me is at night to have sex with me. He does that every night, then he doesn't talk to me when I go back to bed and to my room. I don't know why I can't be like my brother. I don't know why my dad can't love me like that. I don't know why I am so bad. I wish I made them happy. I wish they liked me.

Maybe all I am supposed to be is for sex. Sometimes my dad tells me to go to the bathroom, then he comes too and he does it there and watches in the mirror. I don't look. I don't want to see. I'm not good for anything else.

I don't even make dinner now. I don't eat. I laugh when my stomach complains that it hasn't had anything for a while. It's good when I am hungry. It's what I deserve. When I see Lewis, we drink cider. My stomach shuts up then. My mum and dad were right all along. I don't deserve to eat. I don't deserve anything. Maybe I don't get to be a doctor because of God. Maybe he is real. I have sex with my dad and God sees, so he knows I am bad and now, he takes everything away. Maybe I really am from the devil like my mum says.

She tries to get rid of the devil part still. She tries to get rid of the bad man. She says she sees him in the house. She gets her church people there. I don't like them. I don't like when they are near me. I remember their faces but I don't know why. They look at me and I feel bad inside about it.

Three of them come; I don't know their names. I don't care either. I have to sit on the dining chair in the middle of the room. Everyone has to sit around me. It is so stupid. But my mum wants the bad man to go away, so he doesn't get my brother too. She says I keep him in the house. My Nan bought me a Stephen King book. I liked it and read it. I bought some more. My Nan always gets them from the jumble sales where she goes. I like to read them. I like how he talks. My mum wants me to burn them. "They are evil," she says to me. "They keep the evil spirit here." But I don't care. I am not burning them. I hide them so she can't see them. So, then, she had to call the church people to do an exorcism to get rid of him because he doesn't go away. My brother saw him in the mirror in his bedroom.

I sit in the chair. I don't really know what they are doing. One of the men splashes water at me. It's so stupid; they think the water is from God. It's from the tap and they waved their hands over it. The man tells me I have to think about something called a chakra; I don't even know what one is. Maybe it is a flower? He says I have to think about sitting in it, and then it closes and the evil spirit is outside; he can't come in. The chakra keeps me safe and severs the ties.

I try not to laugh. They tell me to close my eyes. I think about the bad man and his face, his nails and his teeth. I don't like when I can see him. It makes me remember all the things from my Nan's house when I was little. It makes me think about the bad things he did. He used to count on the wall. Every time he came in, he scratched it on the wall above my head. I remember when he did it. His long, dark fingers with his sharp nails. I couldn't get away because he was behind me and he held me tight. He had sex with me like my dad does. Sometimes he used other things too. They made me scream and cry, but my mum didn't ever come. Then he "would bite" my shoulders and dig his nails in really hard until I couldn't stand it anymore. I think about that when the men tell me to think about the chakra.

I am crying when I open my eyes. I didn't know I was. The man smiles. "It worked," he says. I let go of my arms. I didn't know I was holding them. I have dug my nails in as hard as I can. They are all red.

Sixty Four

I'm meeting Lewis today. I haven't told anyone. Not my mum or dad, or even Rachel. I just told her that I couldn't see her this weekend. She doesn't mind, though. She hangs around with her friends from school anyway. I am glad. Then she isn't upset. I don't see her a lot now anyway. She has new friends and a boyfriend. Sometimes she comes around, and we talk when I am on my paper round.

Rachel is different to me too. She doesn't like to smoke and drink. I do. She still likes me, but she doesn't like those things. My mum hates me too. She doesn't talk to me either. Only when I have done something bad. Then she wants to shout at me or moan to my dad that I am too bad. She doesn't understand. Neither of them do. They don't have dreams about things. They don't want to do things. I wanted to be a doctor and now it is gone, and all my mum and dad do is shout about everything I do.

I don't care anymore. I get on the tram to meet Lewis. Today, we are going to the Pleasure Beach. It always reminds me of Karl because he lived next to it. I wish he would come back. I miss him. He is lucky because he gets to live somewhere else. He was supposed to come with me to meet Lewis. He was supposed to meet one of the girls. Now it's just me. I am meeting Lewis's friend, Michelle. I am nervous about it. But I am excited.

The tram feels like it takes a long time to get to the other end, to the Pleasure Beach. It is miles away, but sometimes it feels fast. The tram is full because it is the summer holidays and there are people everywhere. They go to the town and the tower and all the different things here. I can see Lewis before the tram stops. I get up and press the button so the driver knows I want to get off at the next stop, but he will stop anyway, there is a big queue of people.

Lewis is there with Rebecca, and Chris is there with his girlfriend, Wendy. There is another girl there. I guess she is Michelle. I nod at all of them as I get off the tram and walk to them. I take a cigarette out and light it so I don't look at them when I walk; it makes me nervous.

"This is Michelle," Lewis says to me when I get to them. I say hi to her. She says hi back and smiles. Me and Michelle follow the others, but we don't talk as we go into the Pleasure Beach. Michelle talks to me about things. She asks me about things I like. Music and films and lots of things like that. She is nice. I like her. We laugh at people that walk past us. We go on lots of rides all day. Lewis says he has a ride he knows we should go on. Chris jokes about it, because it is the tunnel of love. Me and Michelle laugh at it when we see it. It's all pink and full of hearts and flowers. We all sit in the same boat together and go on the ride. I sit with Michelle. I try not to sit very close to her. I don't want her to know I am bad. My dad had sex with me this morning. I can smell it. When I move, it is there. I look at Michelle to see if she screws her face up, but she doesn't. Maybe if I don't sit close enough, she won't smell it on me.

When we run out of tickets, it is the evening, and people are coming to go on all the big rides in the dark. I don't want to go home yet. It isn't time. Michelle says we can go back to her house if we want to. Her mum doesn't mind. She lives just along the long road. We all say yes. "We can get some cider in," Lewis says, and we all say yes. We put together all the spare money we have to get some.

Me and Michelle walk behind everyone to her house. Lewis and Rebecca walk at the front. It doesn't matter, because they know where Michelle lives. They go there all the time. We laugh a lot when we are walking, and Michelle thinks it is funny when me, Lewis and Chris all mess around. We see a motorbike shop. I look at it. Michelle asks me if I like bikes and I tell her about my dad's bikes. She likes them too.

She asks if she could see my dad's bike one day. I tell her yes, but I don't think so really. He won't let her. He only takes my brother with him because he is perfect and I am not. I haven't ever been on my dad's bike before. I am not allowed to touch it. When I can drive, I am going to get my own bike.

Michelle's house is big. It's on the outside of the town. Her mum has a caravan at the front on the driveway. "This is mine," she says to me. "My mum lets me hang out in here." It is so nice inside. I thought it was going to be like the garage, all dusty and damp. But she has a television in there and a sofa thing. There is even a bed in it. "It keeps me from getting on my mum's nerves," she says to me.

We all go into the caravan. Michelle's brothers and sisters come outside and say hello. They are nice. Her oldest sister is disabled. She talks funny. She asks if she can give me a hug. I let her but I don't like them. She smiles at me. "I like you," she says to me.

"She has epilepsy," Michelle tells me. "She had a fit and burnt her arm." I look at her arm and see it is all wrapped up. She had a fit near the chip pan and knocked it off. It must have hurt very badly.

Rebecca tells Michelle to put the record on. They have a special one they all like. I laugh because then, Michelle and Rebecca and Wendy all start singing. Lewis runs into Michelle's house and gets some cups.

I ask if I can use the bathroom while he is inside. I don't like to go into people's houses. But Michelle tells me to just go in. "They don't mind," she says to me. "It's just at the top of the stairs. " After, me and Lewis stand outside and smoke a cigarette and drink some cider. We drink a lot of it and it makes me feel drunk a little bit. But it doesn't matter. As long as I am home by nine, then my mum and dad don't care what I do.

Michelle's mum and dad come out to see us. Her dad smokes too. He offers me a cigarette and I take it. He asks me about school and things like that. He asks where I live and what my mum and dad do. He is nice; I like him. He puts his arm around Michelle's shoulder and hugs her tight. "So, are you going to ask my daughter to be your girlfriend?" he says to me. I laugh and don't look at him. Michelle's face goes all red too. He laughs, but it makes him cough. He has the smoker's cough.

He asks me if I want a beer. I haven't ever had beer before, but I don't tell him that. I say yes. He gives it to me and I drink from it. It isn't very nice. But I drink it anyway. They are gypsies he tells me. He tells me all about them. They have six children. He wants them all to have six children too. He asks me what I am going to do when I leave school, and I tell him I wanted to be a doctor. I don't tell him about the school, though. I can't say the words. But he thinks it is great. He shouts Michelle's mum. "We could have a doctor in the family," he says. "If our Michelle plays her cards right."

I stay at Michelle's until it is nearly nine. Then, I have to go home so I don't get into trouble. Lewis asks if I am going to come back tomorrow. I say yes. Michelle asks if she can walk me down the road to where I have to catch the bus. I tell her she can. I like her very much. She is pretty. When we walk and we are away from the house, I reach and hold her hand and she lets me. She smiles at me. "I will see you tomorrow?" I ask her.

She says yes and I smile about it. I really want to kiss her. I think about doing it. I have kissed Rachel lots of times. I didn't kiss anyone else, though. Michelle squeezes my hand, and then I put my arm around her. We stand at the bus stop and wait for the bus for me. She puts her arms around my waist. I kiss her and she doesn't say no. I kiss her for a long time. It makes me late, but it doesn't matter that I miss the first bus. I catch the second one, though. I say bye to her and then I get on it.

I smile all the way home. I watch her. She stands and watches the bus. It feels funny inside. Like I have butterflies. Maybe she likes me. Maybe she doesn't think I am bad. I like her. I like to kiss her too. I wave at her. I can't wait until tomorrow.

Chapter Sixty Five

I still feel drunk when I get home. Not as drunk as I was with my dad's wine. But it is there. It makes my head feel fuzzy and I know I can't walk very straight. I am nearly half an hour late. I go around the back to let myself in. Maybe they didn't lock the kitchen door yet. I don't want to sleep in the garage tonight. I feel tired, but I can't stop smiling. I keep thinking about Michelle and that I kissed her. It makes me feel happy inside.

The back door isn't locked when I get to it. My dad is in the dining room. He is sat with his glass of wine and he is reading a book. I say hello to him, but I say it quiet and then he won't get up and start yelling at me for being late and if I don't say hi, then he'll yell because I am rude and ignorant. So I say it quietly and then hope he doesn't shout. I walk past him and I try to do it straight, so he doesn't know I am drunk. "Would you mind sitting down?" he says to me before I get out of the dining room. Maybe he can see I am drunk. It makes me scared inside, but I do as I am told.

"Where have you been today?" he asks me. I tell him that I was out with Lewis and that we went to his house. "You know people like Lewis like to drink and take drugs?" He slides the newspaper over from the other side. "Do you see how many children go out and get drunk and end up in trouble with something bad happening to them?" He shows me the paper and the article, it's about teenage drinkers. He tells me he doesn't want me doing those kind of things. I promise I won't. I just hang around with my friends. I don't know why he is showing me. He doesn't ask about me being drunk. He hasn't got mad about it. Maybe he doesn't know. Maybe he knows what I am thinking. Maybe he can tell.

I try to say all the words properly so he can't hear it when I talk. He doesn't say anything about it so maybe he doesn't know. Maybe he is guessing. "Maybe you should get ready for bed," he says to me. "I'll finish my drink, and then I'll be up in a moment. I know what he means. I sit for a minute and stare at him. I don't know if I want him to do it. I don't know if I want to tonight. He reads his book and doesn't look at me anymore. I get up and go to the bathroom.

My mum is in the bath. I know and tell her I have to brush my teeth. I hate when she is in the bath. She lies back and talks to me and then I see everything and I don't like to see her naked like that. Sometimes, my dad asks me about seeing my mum naked. Maybe I like to, but I don't. I don't say anything when my dad says those things. It makes me want to scratch all my skin off. I feel it all inside.

I try not to look at my mum in the bath. I try to just brush my teeth. I have to use the toilet and I have to do it while she is there. I try to stand so she can't see me, but she sits up. I hate when she does that too. I wish they all stopped it. "What have you been doing today?" she asks me. I tell her the same as I told my dad. Then I tell her I have to go to bed now. "Is there a girl?"

It makes me scared inside. I don't know how she knows or how my dad knows. Maybe they can tell. Maybe they watch me. Maybe they can see inside my head and know about everything like the bad man did. I nod and tell her there is a girl called Michelle. "She is nice," I say.

"Have you had sex with her yet?" she asks me, and I shake my head and look at my feet because I don't want to look at my mum. "I haven't had sex with the doctor yet," she says. "But then that's all he wants. It's all you men ever want. Have you seen him recently?" I don't lie to her today. I tell her I haven't. She washes herself. I stand with my hands down and I don't watch her. I don't want to see it. But I know I can't go yet. She didn't say so and she is talking to me. It is rude to leave when parents are talking. "Can I meet her?" she asks me.

I shrug my shoulders.

"I think I should," she says. "I want to know who you're with."

"Okay," I say to her, then I ask her if I can go to bed now. She says yes. I leave the bathroom and go to my room and get changed.

My dad comes up too. He comes into my room when I am getting into bed. He gets in too and I don't stop him. I don't say no when he takes my clothes off. I don't say no when he rolls me over to have sex with me. I don't say anything when he is finished and then he gets his pants back on and goes to his own room.

I try to swallow a lot of times because it tastes bad in my
mouth. I keep doing it, but the taste from my dad doesn't go
away. I don't think about Michelle. I don't want to. I kissed her
and now my dad made my mouth taste bad. The crying makes
me feel like I choke at the back of my nose. Michelle would
know I was disgusting if she knew about all this. I let my dad
have sex with me. I let him put it in my mouth. I let him do
anything. She would tell me to get lost. She wouldn't understand.
I don't even write about it tonight. I roll on my side and I don't
even let the crying come out. I just fall to sleep.

In the morning, I go to Michelle's again. I go early
because I don't want to go in my mum and dad's room and do all
the games with them. I hate when they do that. Then my mum
makes my dad stand there naked, and I have to pull him around
the room by his thing. Then they have sex and they make me join
in. I don't want to because I don't want Michelle to know about
it.

Lewis and Rebecca will be at Michelle's later. Chris isn't
going to come. He doesn't like Michelle that much, but I don't
care about him. He can do what he wants. I am very excited,
though, when I catch the tram to her house. I hope she didn't
change her mind. Maybe she did. Maybe she knows all the things
like my mum and dad do.

It makes me scared when I get off the tram and walk
along the long road to her house. What if she doesn't want to see

me? What if she doesn't like me? What if she thinks I am bad inside?

I light a cigarette and stop at the corner near her house. I lean against the railings outside the school. I am too afraid to go yet in case she tells me to go away. My mum and dad don't want me; why would she? I try to smoke my cigarette slow so that the time goes away. Someone shouts my name and when I look, it is Lewis and Rebecca. I am happy to see them because then I don't have to walk to Michelle's by myself.

"We decided to come early," Lewis says to me. "Michelle and Rebecca were talking. It's a nice day. We're going to take Michelle's brother's moped to the sand dunes and ride it. You like bikes, right?"

I laugh at Lewis. "That isn't a bike; it's a hairdryer on wheels."

He tells me to shut up and he laughs too and takes a cigarette from me. We walk to Michelle's. She is outside on the wall. She smiles when she sees me. I wish I could run to her, but I don't. I walk to her and I say hi. She says hi back. I wish I could kiss her again, but I don't. I don't do anything. I don't want Lewis and Rebecca to see. Maybe they will laugh at me. Or maybe they will laugh at Michelle because she kisses me.

"We're going to take this out for a ride today," she says to me and points to her brother's moped. "Do you want to come?" I nod. I can't wait.

Sixty Six

I spend every day at Michelle's house. I go there in the mornings and then I come home again at nine in the evening. My mum and dad don't notice when I am drunk or I have been smoking pot with Lewis. Sometimes I don't go right in the house. I just go to the garage and read and go to sleep. I know the back door is locked for the night when the light isn't on in the kitchen. Then my mum has finished and I am too late. it doesn't matter though. The garage is like a second bedroom. I even have covers and pillows in there from when it was winter just to keep me warm.

Sometimes it gets so cold in there I sleep in my coat with some gloves on because my fingers hurt so bad. I stole my dad's thick socks and put them over my own socks. My mum and dad didn't notice. Sometimes I have bad dreams about the garage. It goes all black and I am stuck in there and then the bad man comes. He hasn't ever really been to the garage, but my dreams like to think about it. Maybe he watches. Sometimes I wake up and I think he is sat in the corner watching me. I get afraid because it feels like he is right there. I don't move all night when it is like that. Then he doesn't know I am awake and doesn't get me.

If the light is on in the kitchen, then I check the door. It's usually unlocked, but then my dad is mad at me because I am five minutes late or something, but I don't care about that, either. He's an idiot. So what if I am late? It isn't like he cares where I am. All he cares about is if I get back and then he can have sex. If I'm late and my mum locks me out, then he doesn't. Sometimes, though, he comes to get me into the house.

I fell asleep one time on the sofa, because I had been drinking with Michelle and Lewis and Rebecca. I didn't mean to. I had been home early for a change and sat on the sofa and just fallen asleep. I woke up with my dad's thing in my mouth. He'd done it while I was sleeping, and I woke up just at that moment when I was choking. Of course, I was sick with it too, because I wasn't ready. My dad hit me because I was sick on the floor. I can't do anything right.

Sometimes, if I am drunk, maybe he knows I am. He does everything harder then. It's hard when he does that to hide it. I go to Michelle's the next day, but it hurts to walk and I feel so bad inside. I try and wash it all away, but it doesn't want to go. When I get drunk again or smoke a joint with Lewis, it doesn't matter, though.

I get a ride home from Rebecca's brother, Alan. He's older than us. He works in a lock up near Michelle's house. He has the most cool cars. I want them like that when I am grown up too. He works as a DJ in the pubs and things. We have to meet him there at nine. When we are in his car, he puts the music on so loud that I can feel it inside, and it makes my ribs bang. I like how it feels. He knows all about music.

I get him to drop me off at the corner shop near my mum and dad's house, and then I walk from there. I don't want him to come to the house in case he sees my mum or dad, and they tell him how bad I am. I like Alan. I don't want him to know that I can't get things right ever. He won't give me a ride home if he knows. He is married and he lives near my mum and dad's house. His wife is nice too.

Today I am going to Michelle's, but Lewis and Rebecca are going to be late. Rebecca has been staying with Alan because her mum went on holiday, and she is back today, so Rebecca wants to wait for her. I go to Michelle's by myself early. It still makes me afraid when I have to go alone; maybe she will decide she doesn't like me and just has me there because of Lewis and Rebecca. But I like her and I like being there.

We sit in the caravan on the bed and just talk. She is easy to talk to. She doesn't like to talk about the things I do. Sometimes, I think she isn't really that smart, but it's okay. She doesn't read very well. But sometimes, I lie down with her, and I read to her. She likes when I do that. She lies on my shoulder and listens and falls to sleep. We have the music on. Michelle has the curtains shut because it is too bright. Michele's mum says we have to have them opened so she can see in the caravan and knows we aren't getting up to no good. But she didn't say anything about it today.

We lie in the bed and she kisses me. I kiss her too, and then she doesn't take my hand away when I put it inside her top, and she doesn't stop me when I lift it up to take it off. She hasn't had sex before. She is a year older than me. She is fifteen, but she is still a virgin. She doesn't tell Rebecca, though, because Rebecca has sex with Lewis. Michelle told me to keep it a secret. She doesn't want Rebecca to know because she will laugh. Lewis and Rebecca have sex all the time.

She doesn't say no when I unfasten her pants. I know how to have sex. I did it all the time when I was seven and at the play place. Michelle doesn't know, though. She thinks I didn't ever have sex before too. I don't want to hurt her, though, like at the play place. The girls and boys cried, but I had to do it or they did bad things to me. It makes me scared inside that maybe I will make Michelle cry too. When she says it hurts a little bit, I ask her if she wants me to stop, but she says no.

We do it every day after that. She doesn't think I am bad. But I don't tell her that when I go home, I let my dad do it to me too. I don't know why it keeps making me cry. Sometimes, I cry when I am with Michelle, but I don't let her see. Maybe I am just dirty. Maybe it is me that is bad because I have sex with Michelle, and I like to do it a lot of times.

Sometimes, when Lewis and Rebecca are there, they lie on the sofa and we lie on the bed. We watch films and drink cider and smoke joints. Me and Michelle hide under the covers so Lewis and Rebecca don't know what we are doing, and we have sex. We know Lewis and Rebecca do it too, on the sofa, but we don't say anything to them. Me and Lewis laugh about it when Michelle and Rebecca aren't there. They would get mad if they were.

I go back to school on Monday. I don't want to. I have two more years to do and I don't want to do them. I hate it. It's all pointless now.

Sixty Seven

After school, every day, I do my paper round, and then I go to Michele's house. Alan still brings me home too. School is boring. I hate to go there. I like to hang around with Lewis and sit at the ditch. Sometimes, at lunchtime, we just walk out of school through the rock gardens and go there to smoke a cigarette or sometimes a joint. It doesn't matter. The teachers don't even notice.

I am going to meet Michelle and Lewis and Rebecca at the park after school today. We are going to get some cider and have a play around on her brother's moped again. It's so old, but it's fun to do. We ride it around the lake there as long as the park security doesn't see us. But they just sit in the office.

Michelle's mum and dad don't say anything, either. They buy us the cider if we give them the money. I like her mum and dad. They make me laugh. When I go there after school, her dad gives me his mug, and then I have to go and make him a mug of tea. So many people are there. Sometimes there are so many cups in a line on the side that I have to make two lots.

On Sunday, they are going to a fair. They ask if I want to come. Lewis and Rebecca are going too. It's an agricultural fair. Michelle's dad loves them. He likes to watch the tractors racing and things like that. I haven't ever seen one before. Not racing. Where my mum and dad used to live when I didn't live there, there were farms and tractors, but I didn't see them race before. I say yes.

It is an accident I don't go home all weekend. We go to the park and ride the moped and drink the cider. When it is too late, we have to take it back to Michelle's house and give it back to her brother. But it isn't time to go home yet so we go into the caravan and listen to music and smoke. I didn't even know I was so tired and that I would fall to sleep. When I open my eyes again, it is the middle of the night. Michelle is asleep too. Lewis and Rebecca have gone home.

I jump up fast and swear. I make Michelle jump. I am going to be in so much trouble. My dad is going to hit me. My head hurts and I try to move, but my chest is tight. Everything feels like it bangs inside. "Oh God," I shout many times. I have no idea what to do. My dad is going to beat me so bad because I didn't come home. "I have to go," I say to Michelle. "I have to go home." I am nearly crying, but I don't let her see.

"It's too late now," she says to me. "Stay for the night and go back in the morning. You're already out all night."

I look at the clock; it is nearly 5am. I don't ever sleep that long. I am shaking. Michelle tells me to come back to bed. I try to, but I feel too bad inside about it. She hugs me very tight and then she tries to kiss me again, but I can't stop thinking about my dad. I know what he is going to do when he sees me. I know he will make it hurt. I can't keep the shaking away. I try to hide it so Michelle doesn't see and then she doesn't know. She tells me it will be okay.

I lie next to Michelle and don't go to sleep. Michelle does; she falls right to sleep. She doesn't bother when I sit up or when I get out of bed and go outside to smoke a cigarette. It is so early even the milkman comes. He says hi to me when he walks up the path to put the milk on the doorstep. I ask him if I can buy some orange juice off him. He says yes, and I sit and drink that and smoke outside.

It makes me feel sick inside. I haven't eaten any food. But I don't eat a lot of food anyway. I am too bad to eat. I don't deserve it. I laugh at my stupid stomach when it rumbles. It makes me happy when I can feel it. At least then I won't be fat like my dad says. When Michelle wakes up, she comes outside too.

"What do you want to do today?" she asks me.

"I have to go home," I say, because I know I am in so much trouble. I can't go to the fair. My mum and dad won't let me come back now. I ruined everything because I was so stupid and fell asleep.

Michelle says I am already in trouble I might as well go home later. She can get her mum to call my mum and dad to say where I am. I don't like them talking to Michelle's mum. What if she says how bad I am and her mum tells me to go away? But I nod at Michelle. My dad is going to hit me anyway. It makes me afraid when I think about it.

We go to the fair. It's good fun. Lewis and Rebecca come too. There is a beer tent and Michelle's dad buys us some beer, but we have to behave with it. "No pissing about," he says. We don't. The day goes very fast, and Michelle's mum asks me if I want dropping home on the way back, but I tell her no. I can get a ride off Alan. I am not ready to see my mum and dad yet.

I try not to think about it.

When it is time to go, Alan gives me a ride and drops me at the usual place. I think about the police because I am two days late. They didn't call them because they aren't outside, but it makes me afraid that they might have. I wonder why they didn't call them. I wasn't even late when they did.

The lights are on in the house. The car is in the driveway. The house looks normal. I stand at the corner and watch it and smoke a cigarette before I have to go in and die. I know what's coming. I know what is going to happen to me for not doing as I was told. I don't want to go in here. I look down the street and wonder if I can just keep walking. Maybe no one will notice. But I don't. I finish my cigarette and take a deep breath. Then I walk down their drive to the big back gate. It is locked. I have to climb over it. I used to climb it all the time. But I have been drinking today. It makes me wobble when I climb onto the wall.

I stand on the wall between us and next door. Then I pull myself up onto the large concrete beam. When I was little it was so very high. But it is only six foot and I am nearly that too. I jump down onto the other side. The garden is dark. My mum isn't in the kitchen. She has finished. Maybe I have to sleep in the garage tonight if she put the key in the lock so I can't open it.

But she didn't. I try it. I know I have to because I am so late.

I wish it was locked, then I wouldn't have to see them. But it opens and I go inside and lock it behind me. I can see my mum and dad through the glass walls. My mum is lying by the fire. She has the television on and my dad is on the sofa reading his book. They don't look at me when I come in.

I walk through the dining room and into the lounge. I am so scared. I try to make my breathing slow, but it is hard and I feel sick. "If you're getting a shower, do it now because I want to get a bath," my mum says, but she doesn't look at me.

I stand and think about it for a minute. I don't know why they aren't shouting at me. My dad doesn't even look at me. Maybe he doesn't care. I don't say anything and go to the bathroom to shower and brush my teeth. When I close the door, my dad knocks on it. I didn't know he was behind me. I open it and I move to the other side of the bathroom and look at my feet. My hands start to shake because I know he will hit me now and I am stuck.

He leans against the mirror and folds his arms. I try not to look up at him. "Get your shower," he says to me. I try to see if he is going to go away, but he isn't. He stands and waits for me to start taking my clothes off. I don't know why I start to cry when he watches me. I can't get the buttons open because my hands shake so bad. I wish I could leave the room.

"Are you enjoying having sex with Michelle?" he asks me. But I don't know what to say about it. I shrug.

I take all my clothes off except my underwear. I wait for him to go, but he doesn't. "The rest too," he says to me. I take them off and then my dad unfastens his belt and takes it off. I don't want him to hit me with it. It hurts and makes me bleed when he does that. "Come here," my dad says to me and I do, but I don't look at him. He pushes me down so I am on my knees, and then he puts my hand to his pants. I have to open them myself and put it in my mouth. He puts his belt around my throat. It makes me scared. They did that at the play place, but my dad didn't ever do it before.

My dad pulls the belt and I have to move. He uses it to make me stand back up again and then when he has sex with me, he uses it to pull my head back so I can see him in the mirror behind me. I don't want to see, though. I don't want to know what he does, then I have to see Michelle and she will know too.

He puts his hand on me, and he pulls my head so my face is next to his, he leans over my shoulder. "Does it feel good to have sex with her?" he says. He asks me lots of things about it. He does it until I get to the end when I make all the sounds and he tells me I am good. He catches it all in his hand and then he puts it to my mouth. "Open your mouth," he says to me, but I don't want to. I try to turn my head away, but he pulls the belt and it makes my mouth open, he puts his fingers inside. I don't like how it tastes.

When he is finished, he gets the belt off my neck and puts it back on his jeans. He gets dressed and opens the door. "It's a good job we called Michelle's mum to ask where you were," he says to me. "Or we wouldn't have known where you were." He goes out of the bathroom. I stare at the stupid face in the mirror. I hate that face. He ruins everything. I get my nails and I make them scratch all down his neck. I dig it in as deep as I can. I make it hurt until he starts to cry, but it doesn't work. He has to hurt. I want him to hurt.

I get my dad's razor instead like when I was little. I get it and I cut under his eyes like stripes. I watch the blood fall down his stupid face. I make another line and another until there are three and then he is crying like a stupid baby. I am glad. He deserves everything.

Sixty Eight
(Age Fifteen)

When I come home from school the next day, my mum is acting very strange. She has nice clothes on, her hair is done nice and she has makeup on. She is in a good mood and she smiles at me. She only wears nice things when she is seeing the doctor. But I know she isn't seeing him because she makes me go with her when she does so that I can remember everything he said, and then we can talk about it.

The house is nice and neat too. She has cleaned everything up. I don't ask her about it. I just go inside to get changed and then go to do my paper round. When I come back, I am going to get the tram to see Michelle, but my mum asks me if I will set the table for dinner. "Don't forget to set a place for your brother too," she says to me. I don't ask her about that, either. He doesn't usually eat at the table. He has his on his special tray in front of the television.

I don't know how many seats to put at the table. I put three. If I put four and then my mum didn't make me any dinner, she will say I am greedy. It doesn't matter, though. I don't want the dinner anyway. I haven't eaten dinner in a long time. It is good that I am hungry. I deserve it.

My mum serves the dinner onto plates. She shouts me

and asks me to help take the food out. I try to stand away in case I have done something bad and it is a trick. Sometimes she does that, and I am stupid so I fall for it, and then she hits me or gets her nails in my neck. She has four plates. She sees the dining room. "How come there are only three settings?" she asks me.

I tell her I didn't know I was having some dinner too.

"Why wouldn't you be? What do you think I am? Do you think I starve you?" I don't say anything, but I go and get the mat and set another seat. I tell her I am sorry, that maybe she thought I was eating at Michelle's house or something.

We all sit at the table. My mum has made a big salad with chicken. It's been a long time since we all ate at the table. We don't even do it at Christmas. It's very strange. I know something bad is going to happen, I can feel it. It feels too strange. Maybe I have done something really bad and I don't know about it. I try to hug myself tight so that if my dad hits me, it doesn't hurt too bad. He sits next to me. My brother sits at the other side of me and my mum sits opposite. I don't like it. I can't move. I feel trapped.

"How is Michelle?" my dad asks me. I tell him she is okay, then I ask him about his work, and if he is busy there. I don't want to talk about Michelle with him. I don't want him to start asking all the questions about sex with her. I hate when he says it. He makes it all feel very bad.

My mum starts to ask me things, though. Like what school she goes to and what does she want to do when she leaves school, but I don't want my mum to know about Michelle, either. I tell her I don't know. "We just hang out," I say.

"I want to meet her," my mum says. It makes my stomach ache when she says that. It's not going to be good if she meets Michelle. Nothing good will happen. My mum will meet her and be nice and then when Michelle is gone, she will say bad things about her. I don't want my mum and dad to tell Michelle about the things I do with them. Then she will go away because of how bad I am. "If we can't meet her, then you aren't going to see her again," my mum says when I haven't said anything to her.

"And don't think about just taking yourself there. There are places we can send you to stop that," my dad says.

"Tell her to come here Sunday. She can have dinner with us," my mum says. "But you aren't to see her until then. I know you and the schemes you'll come up with to get out of it. It's like you're ashamed of us or something."

"Are you ashamed of us?" my dad asks me. "Is that why you can't behave all the time? You should count yourself lucky at what you have. Other children have it bad. They'd give anything to have the life you have."

My dad eats his food. I stare at him and wish he could hear all the things that I say inside my head, but he can't. I watch as he chews. I hate his mouth. I hate the sounds he makes when he is breathing. They make me think about when he has sex with me. I can hear it then, the way his lips make a noise when they go together like he has too much spit in his mouth. He makes me feel dirty, and I can't wash it away.

I don't answer my dad about the week. I just nod and look at my food. I don't want to eat it. It's been days and I haven't eaten a lot. If I eat it, it will make me hungry and then my stupid body will want more and more because it's greedy. I don't want to feed it.

The whole week has been very strange. I don't really know why. It feels like I've been in a daydream. My mum and dad talk sometimes, but I can't hear them. They sound far away. I try to answer them. When they shout, I don't feel it inside. My mum is making dinner. She has made it for me every day. My dad shouts at me when I don't want to eat it. I give it to Sheba when he isn't looking. I hide it in my sleeves and things. He doesn't know because he's blind and stupid.

It's Sunday and my mum is making roast chicken because my Nan is coming too. So is Michelle. "Can I go to the toilet?" I ask my mum.

She looks at me with her stupid, shocked face that she does. I wish I could hit her when she does that. I hate that face. I hate most of her faces. "Why are you asking me?" she says to me. "If you want to go, just go."

I try to keep my laugh inside. If I just went when I wanted to, all hell would break loose, and I'd be bounced around the room, no doubt peeing myself as they did it, and then punished because I messed up my clothes and made to stay in them so everyone could smell what a failure I was.

I hate them this week. I don't know why. I keep saying bad things to my mum. It just comes out. I don't mean it to. My mum is making me scared about her meeting Michelle. I try not to go near my mum or dad because I know they will hit me or something.

Yesterday, my dad grabbed my arm. "What's your problem?" he said to me. But I didn't know what he meant. I told him I didn't have one. "You're acting like we never cared for you," he said. I just told him I was sorry and that I don't mean to. But I don't understand. It makes me feel like I am not real. Maybe everything is a dream and I am asleep. Maybe they aren't bad and I just made it that way?

Michelle rings the bell. She is early. I answer the door, but my mum is behind me. "Wait before you open the door," she says to me, and then she looks in the hall mirror and makes her hair straight. I open the door and Michelle turns and waves at her mum. My mum squeezes past me and looks down the side of the house to where Michelle's mum is. She leans out and waves at her. Michelle's mum waves back.

Michelle comes in and we stand in the kitchen while my mum finishes making dinner. She talks with her stupid high voice. I want to tell her to shut up. I hate when she talks like that. It's fake and like a baby. She thinks it's cute. I think she sounds like an idiot. My Nan comes and she talks to Michelle too. We all have dinner at the table and my mum and Nan talk to Michelle. When it is all gone, and I stand up to take the plates away, my mum says, "It's okay, I'll do that. You two go off and do something."

My mum is acting strange, but I don't say anything. Michelle's mum comes to pick her up again when my Nan is going home too. My mum goes to the kitchen to wash the dishes and my dad tells me to go and dry them for her. I know I am going to get told off. I wonder what it is that me or Michelle did wrong. There will be something; there always is.

"How is school?" my mum says to me while she starts to fill the bowl. I tell her that it is okay. "Are you doing okay there? Nothing bad you need to talk about?"

"It's all fine," I say to her.

"We do love you, you know?" she says to me, and then she stares when she says it. It makes my stomach feel sick inside. It turns over and my eyes fill up. I don't want her to say that to me. I don't. She can't. I try to stop from crying, but it is too hard and the tears come out and go down my face. My mum starts to cry. "Do you think we don't?"

I can't talk. I try, but the words are stuck. I open my mouth but they don't come out. I can't say anything. She dries her hands and then she comes towards me. She is going to hug me. I move backwards. I don't want her to touch me.

"You're my son," she says to me. "Sometimes, at night, when I am alone, I cry because of how things are. Craig made me afraid when they took him. I didn't want to love you. Maybe they would take you too."

She puts her arms out to try and hug me, but I don't want her to. I want her to say sorry. I don't want her to love me. I don't want her to say that. I am sorry. I am sorry I made her do all the bad things to me. I can't keep the crying away. I didn't mean to make my mum and dad do lots of bad things to me. I am sorry about it all.

She wants to hug me, but I can't let her. I don't want her to touch me. I am bad and she is crying very hard. She cries loud. I tell her I am sorry. "I have to go to Michelle's," I say to her. I know it is Sunday and I have school tomorrow, but I have to go. She can't hug me. She can't love me.

She can't.

Sixty Nine

I spend all my time at Michelle's house. I like it there. I like her mum and dad and her brothers and sisters. They let me do things. They treat me as if I am part of their family. They don't get mad at me and don't shout at me. I even spent Christmas and New Year with them. Michelle's dad bought me a bottle of rum. My dad got me nothing.

I stay there a lot. Sometimes I don't go to school. I don't really care. I get E's in my lessons now. I am not even allowed in my religious Education lesson. The teacher banned me from the lesson and then I had to drop it. I don't care. Who believes in God anyway? They tried to ban me from French too, but they can't. I have to take that. I am not allowed in the classroom, though. When I get there, the teacher puts my desk and chair outside and I have to sit there out of sight and do the work she gives me. I write all the answers in English. She says if I don't stop it, I will fail French. I shrug. I don't care.

My physical education teacher wants to me to get out of her class too. She didn't like it when me and Lewis played with all the gym equipment, and then he sat on the trolley and I pushed him fast all along the gym and let go. He crashed into the frames. She tried to make us stand without hands on our heads in the corner. I told her to piss off. She can't do anything to me. No one can. Then I walked home.

My PE teacher banned me from playing sports too, because of a stupid boy called Christian. He hit me with a tennis racket. He said it wasn't on purpose, but I know it was because he laughed about it. I hit him in the face with a hockey stick. He deserved it.

My teachers don't want me in their lessons. No one wants me really. They just put up with me because they have to, but when I go away, it makes everyone happy. I just like Michelle and her mum and dad. They don't make me feel like I should go away. They let me and Lewis and Rebecca stay around there and have fun. I can smoke pot and no one says anything about it. I don't get hit for it. So I go every day. Sometimes, I don't go to school.

My mum is so stupid, though. She doesn't even know. I asked her to sign something, and I learnt how to do her handwriting. Now, I can write notes to school so I don't have to go in, and I can sign them. Then the teachers don't call her and ask her where I am. It's easy to write like someone else. Writing is like drawing, and I draw all the time in my books. So, I just draw her handwriting and say sorry he wasn't in yesterday. No one asks about it.

When I don't go to school, I just wait at Michelle's house until she finishes. I help her mum and dad with things, or I just sit with her dad and we smoke and watch westerns. He likes them. He falls asleep sometimes, and I just sit there and read. He loves horses and carts. On Sundays, he takes me to the pub around the corner and it's all he talks about. He wants horses and a farm of them. It sounds great.

Michelle isn't here today. Her mum and dad have gone out too. He has a hospital appointment or something. I am allowed to be there when they are not there. They just let me go in. They don't lock the front door. As long as I look after the dogs, it doesn't matter. I don't stay there today. Instead, I go to the rock gardens near the house and school. I can meet Lewis at lunchtime, and we can have a smoke. It's a nice day, even though it is just April. It isn't raining and it isn't very cold. I take my book, and I sit and wait for Lewis. Sometimes, I like to do it and just be quiet. When Lewis comes, I ask if he has a joint on him. He usually does. We light it and smoke it and talk about nothing, and then he goes back to school for the afternoon, and I tell him I will see him later.

I don't want to sit there all day. The Rock Gardens are on the top of a long hill. I walk down that. At the bottom of the hill is the golf course, where me and Rachel used to hang out together. I wonder if all our things are still there. Maybe I can look. I have lots of time before I have to go home to get changed.

I don't hear the car beeping at me at first. It just sounds like a noise in my head, but then it gets louder and makes me jump. It's my mum. She doesn't drive a lot. She doesn't like to. She thinks things will fall over, like the street lamps, and then they will crush her. She played with the Ouija board and the bad man came out. Many things try to kill her she says to me.

I think about turning and running away, but she pulls over and opens the window more. There isn't any point in running away. She has seen me, and she will just get me when I get home. I sigh and walk over to the car.

"Get in," she says to me, and I do. I know I am about to get yelled at. "Why aren't you in school?" she asks me. I tell her I don't know. I'm just not. I stare out of the window and she drives. She says lots of things to me, but I don't say anything back. She is getting mad. I can hear it in her words. She smacks the steering wheel. "Will you answer me, so I am not talking to myself," she says to me. But what is the point? She won't listen anyway.

"What's wrong with you?" she asks me. "Why are you acting this way? Why can't you be more like your brother, or your friend, Aadi?"

"Shut up," I say to her. I don't want to hear her stupid voice or the stupid words.

"Shut up?" she asks me. "Shut up?"

"Yes, shut up. Clearly, you heard me. Stop saying it."

She says it many times and gets really mad about it. I fold my arms over and look out of the window again. Whatever.

I don't know what happens. It goes slow. Like I am dreaming. I can't move. I watch it coming, but I can't speak and say anything about it. It's blue and getting bigger. I don't realise it is a car. I just watch it and it gets closer. I don't know what I am watching, or why it is coming this way. I can't think. It bangs so loud in my ears maybe they have popped. It's like an explosion, and we slide sideways, and then we stop.

I sit still. I don't move. Nothing moves. My mum doesn't move. The car door is bent inside. The blue car is against ours. My mum's head is at her window, and then, I don't know. Maybe I go away. It is all black and I can't remember. Maybe I fell asleep like I used to when the bad man came.

Someone knocks on my door. There are lights everywhere and I am cold. I shiver and it makes my teeth rattle. A man talks to me, but I don't know what he is saying. There are police everywhere. I can see the lights and lots of people around. The man says he is an ambulance man. He opens my door and tells me to stay still. "You've been in an accident," he says to me. "I'm going to put this on your neck to help you." He slides something around my neck and fastens it. I don't understand.

He asks me my name. I know what it is, but I don't know how to say it. I try to look at my mum. It is hard because of the stupid thing he put on my neck. "Look this way," he says to me. "Keep your eyes on me." He asks me lots of questions. Stupid questions about school and my friends. He asks me when my birthday is. They get me out of the car and put me on a trolley and put me in the ambulance. I don't say anything. I don't know what happened.

Maybe I fell asleep again. I don't really know. I open my eyes and I am in hospital. I am sat up in my bed. My mum isn't there. No one is. There is a nurse. I ask her where my mum is, but she says my dad is on his way. I should get some sleep.

It feels like hours.

Seventy

I don't know what time it is. My dad is here. Maybe it is dinnertime. I can smell food. It smells like old cabbage and coffee. It reminds me of when I go to the place my Nan goes to. It smells like old people's dinner. I can hear trolleys, and people are moving around. I see them through the window in my room. They pull the big trolley out. It has sliding doors, and the nurses come and take plates that have blue covers on them. They take them into other rooms. The nurse knocks on the door at the other side and takes some food in. I don't know why I got put in this room.

I can see my dad out of the window. I sit up so my legs hang off the edge of the bed. I haven't seen my mum yet. I don't know where she is. Maybe she is in one of the other rooms. She will be scared all by herself. She doesn't like strange places. Maybe she is already home and I didn't know. I don't have the neck thing on anymore. My chest hurts. I have a bruise there from the seatbelt. My tongue hurts too. I bit it a little when the blue car hit our car. I think about it. I can hear the smash noise in my head. It makes my ears full so I can't hear anything else. I don't even hear my dad when he says something to me.

I hug my knees up and put my arms around them. "Where is my mum?" I ask him. He doesn't answer me. He stares at me as if he is mad. "I'm sorry," I say to him. Maybe she told him about me not going to school. Maybe she is too mad at me. "I didn't mean to shout at her. I didn't mean to make her crash the car. It's my fault. I made her mad."

I know it was me. If I had gone to school, she wouldn't have crashed. Now we don't have a car anymore, and it's my fault.

"It's your fault?" he asks me. I nod my head. I know I will be in trouble when I get home. The car is gone. That's a lot of money. "It's your fault she's dead?" he asks me.

Dead? I don't know what he means. I try to ask him again, but he is mad. "Is my mum dead?" I ask. He says yes. I don't say anything at all. I don't talk. I don't look.

"Get your things," he says to me. I feel funny inside. It isn't real. Someone else died. Maybe they got the name wrong. I need to go and see my mum. We can't leave her at the hospital by herself; she will be scared. She doesn't like to be in places by herself. What if she cries about it? What if she needs to go home because she gets too worried, then she can't walk because her car is smashed up, and it is all my fault. We have to go home.

I walk behind my dad out of my room and along the corridor. They are green like before. I don't say anything to my dad. I didn't mean to make the car crash. Maybe my mum is outside in my dad's car and she is waiting.

I rub my neck. It feels funny from where the foam thing was. They took it off because I don't need it. "Not a scratch," the nurse said. She said I was lucky. Many people walk past us. I don't know why they are there. I wonder if they know why I am there. Maybe they can see that I made my mum mad, and now she is dead. They look at me when we walk past them, lots of them. Some smile and some look sad. I wonder if they know anything. I feel like I am dreaming. All the sounds make echoes in my head, and I am sure I am not real. Not really real right now. If I close my eyes, maybe I can open them again and wake up. Did I get drunk?

Maybe if I touch my dad, my hand will go through him like a ghost. I reach my hand out to him, but I don't touch him. What if he is real and then he hits me? All the people that walk past us will see, and they will know that I made my mum crash the car.

We go outside and my dad has his work car. My mum doesn't like to sit in that one. My dad uses it for work. He wears his overalls, and it makes the seats black. It is old and tatty. It has a door from a different car and patches where my dad fixed bits of it. It is raining now. It wasn't before. I look up and it goes in my eyes. Maybe I am really awake. I think about my mum at home in the kitchen. I try to think what it will be like if she isn't in the kitchen.

My dad drives along the main road to go home. Every time he stops behind a car, I think it's going to hit it, and then I hear the crash in my head. My dad stops at some traffic lights. It makes me scared. I look around at all the cars. Maybe one will hit us. The car feels like it will just break. All the cars are going to hit us because they don't fit on the road, or they don't see us.

Something bad is going to happen. It makes it hard to breathe. I feel it all inside. It makes my head feel funny. I grip the edge of the seat in case we crash.

My dad stops. He pulls over at the side of the road near some shops. Perhaps my mum asked him to get her something. I close my eyes and tell myself it is okay. I will be home soon, and then it all goes away. But I feel scared inside. My dad doesn't get out of the car. He said something, but I didn't hear him. I ask him to say it again.

"Get out," he says to me. I ask him why. Maybe I have to go to the shop for him. "I don't want you near me," he says. "I don't want to have to look at you. I don't want you in the car with me."

I tell him I am sorry. I didn't mean to make the car crash. "I'll be good, I promise," I tell him. "I'll sit still and won't make any noise."

"Get out," he says it again.

I start to cry, I can't help it. I don't want to get out of the car. "Please don't make me," I say to him.

He reaches over and smacks me in the face with the back of his hand. "Get out," he says to me again. He makes his words so mad that he is nearly spitting when he says them. I put my hand to my face where he hit me. I try to make the tears go away, but I can't.

"Please," I cry at him. "I'll be good." He lifts his hand up to do it again. I cry so hard that I can't even make it all come out.

It makes my eyes and head hurt. I don't know how to make him know that I will be good. I won't do anything bad. I just want to go home and see my mum.

"Out," he says to me like he is growling. I open the door and get out of the car.

"Please don't go. Please stay." I don't want him to leave me there. I didn't mean to make the car crash. I didn't mean to make my mum dead. "I'm sorry." It makes me be nearly sick because I cry so much. "Please dad," I say, but he pulls the door shut and puts the lock down.

He drives away. I put my hands over my face again. My nose is bleeding, but I don't care. I just want my dad to come back. I watch for him. I watch the car go along the road. Maybe he will come back. Maybe when he gets to the roundabout, he will turn around and come and get me. It's just a trick because I am bad. "Please come back," I say.

I run to the end of the road and shout dad. But he turns off the road and then he is gone; I can't see him. I bend over and put my hands in my hair and pull to make the crying stop. I don't want people to see me. I don't want them to know what I did. I stay there for a long time. I don't have anywhere else to go. No one wants me. Not when they know. I think about Michelle's house and her mum and dad, but I can't tell them that I made my mum die. I think about Rachel, but I haven't seen her, and she has lots of new friends now. Maybe I can just go to the garage, and my dad doesn't know I am there. I won't get in his way.

I walk slowly. I look for his car in case he comes back, but I know he won't. He doesn't want me. Not really. I am sorry I made her die. Maybe it should be me. I ask God many times to not let me wake up. Maybe I can be dead instead.

Seventy One

It is late when I get back to my mum and dad's house. I go around the back like always. The gate isn't locked. I can see all the lights on. Maybe I can go inside. Maybe my mum didn't finish in the kitchen again. Then I remember. She is gone. I go around the kitchen to the back door. I look through the window in the dining room. I can see all the way to the lounge. My Nan is there. There are some people from my mum's church too. They all have cups and are talking. I can't see my dad.

I try to see if the door is unlocked. It is. I open it slowly. I don't want to make my dad mad if I come banging into the house. It always makes – made - mum mad when I did that. It would make her jump and scared.

I don't realise my dad is in the kitchen. I didn't see him there and couldn't see him through the windows; they are too high up. He slams his hand down on mine that is still on the handle. He squeezes my fingers around it. It is metal and it digs in. I can feel it. It feels like my bones are going to break around it. He squeezes as hard as he can. I put my hand over my mouth to keep my scream inside. I don't want to make any noise, then my Nan will hear and then my dad will tell her what I did.

"Look at your Nan," he says to me. "Go in there and look at her face and see what you have done. When you have looked, don't you dare stay. You go to your room and you don't move. I don't want to see you. I don't want to look at you for one more minute."

He lets go of my hand. I put my other hand down and some of my tears come out. I nod at my dad, but I don't look at him. I wish he knew that I am sorry. I wish I could tell him that I didn't mean it. I wipe my eyes and squeeze my hand together because it hurts. I walk through the dining room and into the lounge. I can see my Nan has cried too. Her eyes are all red. I am sorry. I didn't mean to do it. I don't say anything. I wish I could go away. I wish my mum came back.

My Nan and everyone stops talking when I come into the lounge. My mum is supposed to be there, but she isn't and it's my fault. I look at the pile of magazines on the floor next to the fireplace. She lies – lay - there reading them. But not now. My Nan says my name and holds her hand out for me, but I shake my head and look away. I turn and run up the stairs away from everyone. I'm sorry.

I go to my bedroom and close the door. I kneel on the floor and lean on the bed, but I don't want my mum to shout at me because I make the bed a mess. I try not to. I try not to cry. I don't do anything. I listen to all the people downstairs. I can hear them talking. I don't know what they are saying; maybe they are talking about me. The boy that killed his mum. I really am evil like she said.

I fall asleep there. My chest hurts when I wake up. It is dark and everything is quiet. I try to move and get up but everything is stiff. I can hear my dad. He bangs and swears and then he comes up the stairs. He bangs into my room. He makes me jump because he can't stand properly. He is drunk. "Downstairs," he says to me. But I don't want to go past him and he stands at the doorway. I know he is going to hit me. Maybe he will do it hard.

I don't stand. I don't want him to get me. I crawl to the door, and then I try to squeeze past him, but he kicks me in the side and it makes me cough and cry. "Take your clothes off," he says to me, but I shake my head. He tries to reach down and grab my hair, but he misses. He puts his bottle down on the floor. It is one of his wine bottles. He reaches down, and then he grabs me and pulls me up. "Dining room," he says to me. He pushes me and I nearly fall down the stairs, but I catch myself, and then I go down them fast and out of his way.

He follows me down. He is shouting and swearing. "Your mother was right," he says. "You really were a bad child all along. I should have listened to her." I don't stop him when he pushes me. I don't stop him when he pulls my pants down and his own. I don't stop him when he has sex with me, and it hurts so bad because he is angry with me. He puts his fist in my back while he does it and he swears at me about how bad I am. I try to count. I wish I could go away.

When he is finished, I pull my pants back up, and then I lean against the wall. The tears go down my face, and I don't wipe them away. My mum is dead and it's my fault.

My mum is dead and it's my fault. I say it in my head so many times. It makes me cry. My dad has pulled his pants up. He smacks me across the face. "Don't you dare cry," he shouts at me. I try not to. I try to hold it all inside. I hold my breath so I don't cry. It makes me shake and I can't help it.

He hits me over and over. My nose bleeds and my mouth hurts. I try to make it go away. I slide down the wall away from him, but he smacks me, and my head hits the edge of the window ledge. "I said stop crying."

I hug myself when I am down on the floor. I wish he would stop. Maybe he can make me die too, and then it won't matter. I lean against the radiator and my dad tries to hit me again, I put my arms up above my head so he can't. He hits me many times. He swears at me.

The dining room door opens, and my dad stops. It is my brother. He is crying too. He says he has been sick in his bed. It makes my dad madder. My dad shouts at him so loud until his voice is scratchy, and it makes him cough. He hates us kids, he says. My brother says he is sorry. He didn't mean it. My dad runs over to my brother and then he hits him really hard and he falls over. He cries very loud about it. He cries because he wants my mum too. My dad tells him it is tough. "She isn't around anymore." He hits him again, and my brother curls up to make it stop.

I shout at my dad; I tell him to stop. I try to get up, but I don't want to make him mad at me again. But I don't want him to hit my brother. He is just ten and he is little. He has wet his pants too. I can see it where he curls up.

"Stop it," I shout at my dad. He does, and my brother tries to get up, but my dad pushes him hard and he falls into the lounge. Then my dad stops. He starts to cry. I haven't seen him really cry before. He goes into the lounge, and then he falls on the sofa and puts his head in his hands. He cries very loud too. I don't move. My brother doesn't move. We watch my dad for a long time.

I just let the tears go down my face. I don't cry like my dad. I just lie there until my dad falls to sleep. I crawl to my brother and I give him a hug. I tell him he has to go to bed. I hug him very hard to make his crying go away. But it doesn't. It makes me cry too. I try not to lie on him. My dad is still sleeping when my brother starts to be sleepy too. I don't take him upstairs. I put a cushion under his head, and I get a blanket off the sofa and put it on him.

I leave him on the floor and go to the garage. I know my dad doesn't want me there. I get my dad's petrol and smell it until I go to sleep too.

Seventy Two

It's been a week since my mum died. Everything feels
strange to me. I keep thinking that she is going to be there. When
I walk in the kitchen, I expect her there, or when I walk in the
lounge and look at the empty space by the fire. She isn't
anywhere. I don't know why she isn't there. It doesn't feel like
she died. Nothing else changed. Just she isn't here anymore.

I close my eyes sometimes and try to think about the
crash. I can hear it. It's so loud when the blue car hits ours, then I
can't remember. Just the man talking to me. I didn't see my mum
because he didn't let me.

When I go to school and sit in the class, or the teachers
talk to me and ask me if I am okay, I tell them I am. Why do they
keep asking me? My mum isn't dead; she just isn't at home. I
don't understand it. I walk away when they ask me. I don't want
to talk about it. They all look sad and have that stupid voice
people do when something is 'aww' and so cute. It makes me
want to smack them in the mouth and tell them to shut up. Don't
they realise how stupid they sound?

When I am at home, I feel like I am invisible. My brother
lies on the sofa. Sometimes he cries. He says mum, and then he
remembers, and he cries again. If my dad is there, he looks at me
with his red, drunk eyes and tells me to look at what I did. I just
leave and go to the garage. I sleep in there. Then my dad leaves

me alone. Except when he remembers I am there. Every night, he remembers at some time, then he comes in. I don't argue with whatever he wants. Once he's had sex with me, he leaves.

Luckily, because my mum has died, I don't have to do all my lessons. My grades are so shit I can use that time to catch up. I'm glad. I don't catch up, though, I just read. But with no PE, no one sees the marks from my dad. I can cover it all away and no one notices. I'm the creepy creature in the corner with my book and black coat, so no one sees anything. Only Lewis talks to me. Sometimes, I wish even he would shut up. I don't tell him, though. He sits with me and passes me a cigarette, and then we don't talk. He tries to, but I have nothing to say to anyone.

My dad needs to shave; his face is all full of his stubble. He looks like a tramp. He hasn't even showered. All he does is get drunk and shout. The house is a mess too. When he is asleep, I put the cans and bottles outside, and I sneak in and make some food. I make it for my brother. It is just stuff from tins, but he can eat it. Then, we wash the dishes and put them away, and my dad doesn't know I have been inside the house. Then, I go back to the garage and read or sniff the petrol and wait until he has woken enough to remember I am there.

Yesterday, I was such an idiot. I sniffed the petrol too long and fell right to sleep. I didn't even feel what my dad did. I didn't know he had come in until I woke from the pain of it. I use the bathroom in the garage to clean myself up and wash away the blood.

Rachel came around to see me, but I didn't want to say anything to her, either. We just sat outside on the edge of the kerb, but we didn't talk. I didn't know what to say. I couldn't tell her I was living in the garage, and it was my fault about my mum. She told me her mum was sorry about my mum. I told her to tell her mum thank you, but maybe my mum isn't really gone.

I smell her sometimes; her perfume. And then I turn around and look, and she isn't there. I just need to wake up. When I do, she will be there again. When I think about it, it makes my chest hurt, and then I can't breathe again. I don't believe she is dead. She can't be. She is my mum.

I talk to Michelle on the phone, but I haven't seen her. I don't want to in case my dad gets mad at my brother. He's too small when my dad gets drunk and wants to hit him. Then he cries for our mum, but she doesn't come, and it is my fault.

It is my mum's funeral today. It feels strange to say it. My dad has been drinking. I think he is drunk already. My Nan came around, and we all got changed into black clothes. We have to go to the church. My dad isn't driving, so we are going to get a taxi there. We get there before everyone - even my mum. No one is there. Maybe she isn't dead.

My dad stands with my brother, and my Nan stands at the side waiting. She tries to talk to me, but I don't want to. I make her cry because I killed my mum. I move away so I am behind them all. I lean on the wall and look at my feet. I wish it was me that was being buried today.

The hearse comes around the corner. I stare at it. It has my mum inside, but I can't see her. She is in the coffin. It is brown and wood and shiny. It has gold handles on the side. Maybe she is asleep. Maybe she is scared. It stops next to us, and I go over to it. I put my hand on the glass. It is cold. I wish I could tell my mum I am sorry. I didn't mean to make her mad.

I feel sick inside, and I can't make it go away. I can't make my mum come back. I made her go away. Why didn't I just go to school? It catches in my throat, but I don't cry. I can't cry. Then my dad will say it is my fault; I did it. He is right. I know. He says it all the time. I made her go away.

My mum gets carried into the church. I sit at the back of everyone. I don't want to sit near people. They look at me. They know I did it. After we have listened and sung songs and said prayers, my mum gets put back in the hearse, and we have to follow. My brother and dad and Nan go in the big black car. I know I am not allowed in it. I hide at the back, and then my Nan doesn't see. When it drives away, I stand at the kerb and watch it.

There are people from my mum's church there. "Do you want to come with us?" one of them says to me. I don't really, but I have to. I don't like him. It makes me think about being tied to the table and then they made it hurt. I don't like his face. I remember all the blood and lots of things that make me feel very sick inside. I don't want him to touch me. He smiles with yellow teeth, and he smells like old cigarettes. He did lots of things at the church. But I get in the car. I sit next to him, and I try to hug myself tight so I don't touch him.

There are flowers on top of my mum's coffin. They say mum. My brother wrote a card to put in them. I looked at my dad, and then he looked at me, and I knew I wasn't allowed to write one. I didn't ask. That's what happens when you kill your mum. You don't get to say goodbye. I wish I could tell her I am sorry. I wish I could make her come back. I didn't mean to do it.

When we get to the cemetery, I don't walk with my dad. My Nan walks behind them, and I walk behind her. I look at the ground. I cry because I made everything bad. My Nan cries. I am sorry. I didn't mean to make her sad. Maybe she will hate me like everyone else. Maybe she will think I am disgusting because me and my dad have sex.

The vicar says nice things about my mum. We have to throw rose petals on her coffin. We get them from a basket and then we pass it around. I don't look when I throw them. I don't want to see the people looking at me. I don't want them to know what I did and that I am bad and evil.

When it is finished and we go back to my dad's house, I sit on my chair in the dining room and don't move. I know I am not allowed to. I am not even allowed in the house really. When everyone goes away, I will go back outside to the garage. My dad has his whiskey, and he sits on the sofa with his friend. My Nan makes everyone drinks and talks to people. She tries to talk to me too, but I tell her to go away. I don't want to.

I sit there all day until my legs go numb and my feet feel fat. My Nan sees everyone out and says goodbye to them. She says thank you for coming. She does the washing up when they are all gone. My dad has fallen asleep on the sofa. My Nan hugs my brother. When she tries to hug me, I turn away so she can't see me. She tells me I should go to bed. But I don't answer her. I don't say anything at all. Maybe I can pretend she isn't there, and then she'll go away.

She sighs because I don't answer. She has to go home. She calls a taxi and then she goes. She asks me to please go to bed. She kisses the top of my head. I don't let her see that I cry. I'm sorry I made her so sad. I try to keep it inside. But it makes my face scrunch up and my bottom lip shake.

My dad wakes up when my Nan goes away. I hug myself tight. He is going to be mad because I am in the house, but it is cold outside. I know I should have gone to the garage. He doesn't say any words to me. He is mad right away. He walks and then he hits me his hardest and I fall off the chair. I don't get up, but I hug myself and try to cover my head. But he doesn't let me. He grabs my arms and makes me stand. Then he hits me again. I tell him I am sorry. He hits me and I can't breathe because he does it fast.

I try to get away, but he pushes me and I nearly fall over. He pushes me with both hands towards the lounge. I try to put my hands out to stop him, but he doesn't. I beg him to stop it. "Please dad, I'm sorry," I say to him, but he swears at me.

"Fuck off," he says to me, and then he hits me hard again and I fall backwards. I try to catch myself, but I can't. I fall into the glass on the door, and he pushes me again. The glass breaks and cracks, and I go right through it. I land on the floor with the glass. It hurts so bad. I try to get up, but my dad comes through the broken door and presses me down onto the glass. I ask him to stop, but he doesn't. I try to push him off, but he is bigger than me, and he holds me down.

He gets up after, and then he drags me to stand up too. He digs his hands into my arms. It hurts real bad, but I don't say anything. Maybe if I shut up, then he will stop. He pushes me away and walks up the stairs.

Seventy Three

I watch as he goes up the stairs. Maybe he is going to bed. I can hear him banging upstairs, though. I start to pick the glass up. My back hurts and my hands are cut too. I cry because I don't know what I am supposed to do. Maybe I should go to the garage and leave it all. Maybe I should stay inside. I don't know. He didn't tell me. I try to make the crying stop. I hold my breath, anything that makes the tears go away, but they don't.

My dad comes back downstairs. I hug myself tight in case he is going to hit me again. But he doesn't. He walks past me and then I hear the front door bang open. He does it so hard it makes the house shake. I can hear lots of bangs and swearing. I try to look through the glass door to the hallway, but I can't see.

Then my dad comes back in and goes back upstairs and then comes down again. He has my things. My books, my pictures, my clothes. He storms past me again, and then he throws them outside onto the ground as hard as he can. I hear some of the things break. My hands shake when I try to pick up the glass off the floor. I bite my lip, and then I don't say anything or cry. But it happens anyway.

My dad does it a few times. Then he comes down with my school bag, and he throws it at me. "Get out," he says to me. I don't move. I don't know what I am supposed to do. He stands at the door. I am scared he might hit me when I walk past him.

He takes two big steps towards me. I grab the broken

door next to me. He hits me fast. I didn't know he was going to do it. I fall over and let go of the frame. I fall backwards and land on the floor. My nose is bleeding again. My whole face is sore; it feels like it is fat and swollen. I try to wipe the blood away, but my dad steps over me and then he yanks me up by my jacket. I try to grab the door again, but my dad is stronger than me, and he drags me to the front door, and then he pushes me outside into the rain. I try to grab many things, but he pulls my hands off. I land on my things, he closes the door.

I don't move at all. I watch the door. Maybe he will come back. Maybe he didn't mean it. I crawl to the step and sit there and lean against the door. I hear my dad go into the back garden. I hear him go to the garage. I hear him lock the gate so I can't get back in. I hug my knees up. It is cold. The lights go out in the house. My dad is going to bed. I'm sorry I made my mum die. I miss her so bad.

I roll onto my side and cry. I cry very hard, and I can't make it stop. It makes me have hiccups. But no one is around, and no one can hear. When the crying is all finished, and my face hurts and it's all puffed up, I get my things and stuff them in the bag my dad gave me. I don't put it all in; it doesn't fit. I put the rest on the step so it doesn't get too wet. Maybe my dad can put them back inside.

I don't know where I am supposed to go, but I know I can't go into the garage. My dad knows I go in there, he will check even if I climb over.

My nose is blocked from the bleeding. I have to breathe through my mouth. I have bits of glass in my hands. I try to pick them out. I don't remember getting them. I have some in my back too. I pick those out. I go out of the driveway and stand at the kerb. I think about going to Michelle's house, but then she will know my dad doesn't want me. I could go to my Nan's, but then I have to tell her it is all my fault, and she won't want me too.

I just walk. I don't know where to. It doesn't matter. The night is forever and very long. I walk along the road that is next to the golf course. It is very dark there. I am too scared to go all the way to in. I hear a car coming. I run to a garden and pretend that I live there so they don't stop and don't take me back to my dad.

I walk near school and down the hill. My mum is just there. I don't know why I go to the graveyard. It's just the way I walk. I stand at the gates and look inside. I am not scared of graveyards. My mum lies in there. She is all alone and it is raining. She doesn't like the rain. It makes her scared when it is loud. We put the television on so she can't hear it. The storms make her scared too. I hope she isn't scared all there by herself.

I don't go into the graveyard. I tell my mum I am sorry for what I did. I go to the bus shelter just outside. It smells like pee and beer. It makes me want to be sick. My mouth opens and I retch, but I am not sick. At least the bus shelter is dry. I sit in it against one of the walls in the corner. I hope no one see me. The walls are green and dark.

My back hurts a lot when I try to lean on the wall. They are hard. I try and rub it and then lean slowly. When it doesn't hurt, I shut my eyes and hug myself to make the shivering stop. Maybe God can take me away when I go to sleep, like my mum. I ask my mum to forgive me for what I did. I am sorry.

In the morning, a milk wagon wakes me up. I hear it rattle and it makes me jump. My eyes snap open and I sit upright. I forget that my back hurts, but then it hurts very bad, and I try not to cry like a baby about it. I try to pull my shirt away from my skin, but it is stuck there. It feels like I pull tape off when I try to move it away.

My clothes are nearly dry, though. I feel very horrible. Like when I have a cold and it makes my legs ache. My hands hurt from the night. I move them and try to make them not sore. I open and close them many times until it feels wet. They are bleeding again. I watch the blood. My head feels dizzy. I know I have to get up soon. It must be six in the morning because the milkman is out. Soon, people will come to catch the bus, and then they will ask why I am there, and someone will make me go home to my dad. But he doesn't want me, not anymore.

Seventy Four

I look in my bag for some things. My dad had thrown some clothes too. I try to take my shirt off. It makes me bite my lip because it stings, but it is dirty and horrible. When I get it off and look, the back is ripped. It has holes in it and there is blood in it. Maybe my back is all cut. I get a t-shirt from my bag and put that on.

I don't leave my shirt at the bus shelter. What if someone finds it, and then knows it is mine? Then they will be nosey and find me and take me back to my dad, but he doesn't want me, so he will get mad and hit me. I put it in my bag instead. I can throw it in the bin later when no one is looking. I put my jacket around my waist; it is too hot to wear it.

I don't know where to go. I just walk again. I walk until my legs are too tired, and I swing my bag because I can't be bothered to carry it. People walk past me and go to school. The roads get busy, and then they get quiet again when everyone has got to school and work. My throat feels dry inside. I haven't had anything to drink for hours. I haven't had anything to eat, either. My stomach rumbles, but I don't have any money.

I walk to Michelle's house. I haven't seen her since my mum – I haven't seen her for many days. I don't care right now if she is mad at me. Everyone is, but I am too tired. My head hurts so bad. When I walk, it bangs when I take a step, and sometimes I have to stop just so it does, but then I feel dizzy. I just want to go to sleep. I don't feel very well inside. I stand outside her house. It feels very strange to look at it. Perhaps they will all tell me to get lost.

She sees me. She doesn't come out at first. She stands and stares at me, and maybe she wishes I would get lost, but she doesn't. She smiles, and then she runs over to me and hugs me. Then, she stops and looks at me. "What happened to your face?" she asks me.

"It's nothing," I say to her. I don't want her to know. I don't want to tell her my dad did it. She wouldn't understand. She would think he is bad when he isn't. It's me. It's all my fault. I ruined everything. I deserve what he did. I am the bad one. I make it all bad.

"Tell me," she says.

I sigh. "I just got into a fight, that's all."

Lewis and Rebecca are at Michelle's house. I didn't know they were there. I didn't even realise it was so late. I have been walking all day. I guess school is finished. They don't say many things to me. Maybe they don't know what to say. I ask Lewis for a cigarette and he gives me one. "Do you have cider too?" I ask.

He grins at me. "Of course." He goes to get me some and brings it out to me. I close my eyes for a second and smoke my cigarette. Lewis hands me the mug, and I drink the cider too. "You didn't come to school today," he says to me.

I shrug. "I will another day," I say to him. I don't care,

but I don't tell him that part. We sit and laugh and joke about lots of things. I try to smile, but then I think about things, and my smile goes away, and I have to remember to do it. I sit and listen and smoke instead.

"Are you getting a lift with Alan?" Rebecca asks me when it is almost nine. I hadn't thought about it really. I hadn't told them I have nowhere to go. They would think I was a loser. They would know I made it so we crashed and my mum died.

"Sure," I say to her. I wish I could tell her the truth, but I know she won't understand. Maybe she would let me stay if I told her, but maybe her mum would call the police or something, and then they would take me back to my dad. So I don't say anything. I say goodbye, give her a kiss and tell her I will see her again tomorrow.

I go with Rebecca to Alan's lock up, and then he gives me a ride to my dad's or the street next to it, like always. I walk up my dad's road, but I do it slowly while Alan is still there. When he drives away, I turn around and walk the other way. I just walk again. My feet hurt and I am so tired, but I have to walk to somewhere.

I go to the park that is near my Nan's house. It's next to the junior school I used to go to. There is a slide there. It is tall, but it also has a tree house at the top. I climb all the way up to that and curl up with my bags. I stole some bread from Michelle's house when I was making tea for her dad. I also stole some milk. They didn't see. I hope they don't notice it. I hide in the corner, eat some bread, drink some milk and fall asleep where no one can see me.

I sleep many nights in the park. It isn't too cold. Just when it rains and there is wind. But if I curl right up, then it doesn't come in so much. I don't like the bus shelters so much. They smell like pee and sweat. Alan gives me a ride home every night, and then I take all day to walk back to Michelle's house while she is at school. At the weekend, I get to stay there and sleep and eat and have a shower. It makes me sad on Sundays when I have to go again, because they think I go home.

When I am walking to Michelle's, I go into the shops. I go different ways every day, so it's different shops every day. I take food and water. I don't take a lot because then they might catch me, and my dad will find out, and then I will be in trouble again. But I am good at shop lifting; I don't get caught.

Two weeks go past very fast. I walk to Michelle's every day, steal food and water, and then I get a ride home from Alan, just so I can sleep in the park and then start walking again. I haven't been to school, and I haven't done anything. I haven't seen my dad or even my Nan. I miss her very bad. I wish I didn't make it all wrong.

Alan drives me home like normal. He takes Lewis home first, though, and then he takes Rebecca home. He says he has to do something near my house so if it is okay, can he take me home last. I say it is. I don't mind. But it makes me a little bit afraid because we are alone in the car, and it is dark. But he stops the car near my dad's house where he normally drops me off. "Wait," he says, though, before I get out of the car. I stop and look at him. He doesn't look angry, but maybe he is inside, and maybe I did something wrong. "What's going on?" he asks me.

I don't know what he means. I shrug my shoulders. "Nothing."

"I don't believe you," he says. "If you don't start talking, I'm going to drive to your parents' house and find out what's going on."

I stare at the road that goes to my dad's. I don't want him to go there and ask. It makes me think like when the fisherman took me home. Everyone has to get in everyone else's business all the time. I don't know why. I want to run away, but I know I can't. If I do, then he will go to my dad and my dad will tell him. I try not to cry about everything. I know I have to tell him.

"You can tell me, you know." He opens the glove box and gets out some cigarettes. They are his wife's. He gives me one and I light it. "I know you just lost your mum."

I smoke the cigarette, and I watch the ash on it get longer. I don't look at Alan. I don't want him to know I am too bad. "My dad threw me out," I say to him.

"When?" he asks, and I tell him a few days ago.

"You should have said. I could have given you a lift . Where are you staying?"

I don't answer him. I don't want to tell him I sleep in the park. I am stupid and no one wants me.

"You aren't staying anywhere, are you?" he asks, but he doesn't wait for an answer. "Do you want to come and stay with me?"

I nod at him after a minute, but I still don't look at him.

His house is nice; it is small. Not like my dad's. It just has a couple of bedrooms. His wife shows me to the spare room at the front. It is just little. It has a bed in it and some drawers; that is it. She gets me some of Alan's clothes and tells me I can use them. They are a little too big, but they are clean. She asks if I want a shower or something to eat. I nod at her, but I don't say anything. What if she gets mad and tells me to go away?

When I have had a shower and some coffee and toast, I say I will go to bed. His wife shows me to the spare room again. I get in bed, and she turns the light off. I don't know why, but I cry. I don't mean to. It just comes out, and I cry until I fall to sleep. I sleep all night.

When I wake up, Alan and his wife are already up too. They are downstairs. I can hear them. I make my bed and fold my clothes. Then I go downstairs too. I stand at the door so they don't get mad at me, but his wife tells me to come in and asks if I want something to eat. I look at my feet and nod.

They ask me about my dad, and if I want to go back there. I tell him no. I don't tell him I made my mum die, and now my dad hates me. I just say that we fell out, and I can't go back. They ask if I want to stay there. Maybe they can ask my dad. Maybe it will make things better if me and my dad just get on each other's nerves all the time. I say yes.

A few weeks later, my dad signs the papers. He signs me away. He doesn't ask any questions. He doesn't ask me to stay. He doesn't even look at me. He just signs the papers and leaves.

He just gave me away.

Seventy Five
(Age Sixteen)

It has been nearly a year since my mum died. I think about her all the time. I am sorry she is gone. It's gone very fast. It's just been her birthday too. I don't like February. It makes me think about her, and then no one can get her anything. She is all alone still.

I have nearly finished school. Just five more months and then it is done. I can't wait. My marks are so bad, though, so it doesn't matter. I don't care. I live with Alan. When I leave school, I will get a proper job. I just have a paper round at the moment. I don't give it up because then I have to ask Alan for money, and I don't like to.

I like living with him and his wife. He is nice. But I miss my dad and brother. I don't speak to them really. I didn't speak to them on my birthday or Christmas. Maybe they had a good time because I wasn't there. Sometimes, I talk to my dad on the phone. Sometimes he is nice. When he has had too much to drink, then he says he misses me. I don't let him hear me get sad about it. Then, he tells me I should have died and not my mum. I know that too. I try to wish it, but it doesn't happen.

He tells me about my brother and all the things they have done. Sounds like they have a real nice time now I am not there. I always knew they would. Sometimes, I wish he would take me too, but I don't ask. Sometimes, I wish he loved me, but I know he doesn't. I don't tell him about things I am doing. He doesn't want to know anyway, and he doesn't ask.

He tells me about the places they go to or where they are going. "Maybe you can come too?" he says sometimes, but then when it gets to the day, he forgets and doesn't come and get me. I wait. Many times I stand at the window and his car never shows up. I don't ask him about it next time. Sometimes, he even calls me the night before to make sure I still want to go, but he hasn't picked me up, not even once. I'm such an idiot I think he will.

Maybe it is me that gets it wrong? Maybe it is just because I wish he would take me, or I get the day or time wrong. I am a fool to believe that something will change, and my dad will want me to be in his family. I am nothing.

He promises again, and I make sure I remember it. I say it over and over and write it down like I had to do for the doctor with my mum. Then I know I don't get it wrong, but still he doesn't come, and I waited so long. I sat at the chair in the window and waited. I don't tell Alan about it, though. He would think I was an idiot too. Not even my dad wants me. Then Alan would know I must be bad.

I just go to Michelle's house instead. I go there every day, and Alan brings me home still. I like Alan's house, but I don't like to be in his way, or maybe he will get sick of me and tell me to leave. So I hang out with my friends. Lewis makes me mad sometimes. He says stupid things about his mum. At least he has one. At least she loves him. Not like me and my mum. She didn't love me. Not once. It makes me mad when I think about her. She was stupid too. All the things she used to say. When I think about them, they make me mad. I wish she was here so I can ask her about them. But she isn't, and that's my fault. Why would Alan want me around too?

Me, Lewis, Rebecca and Michelle sit in the caravan and we smoke pot and drink cider like we do every night. At least I have that to look forward too. Lewis opens the cider and asks for Rebecca's cup so he can fill it up for her. "No thanks," she says to him. "I'm a few days late."

Lewis sighs about it and I do too. She does this every month. But she isn't ever pregnant. He doesn't bother about it now. He says she does it all the time so he is used to it. Sometimes we talk about it. He laughs because she is on the pill, so she can't get pregnant. He says she just likes to do it for attention. He doesn't really like her anymore, but he doesn't know how to tell her.

He asks for Michelle's cup. She looks away. "Maybe I shouldn't have any either," she says. Then she looks at me. She whispers, "I am three months late."

Rebecca starts swearing. She jumps up from her seat and says, "Oh, my God" so many times I want to tell her to shut up. I just stare at Michelle.

"I am already a week late for the fourth month," she says to me. Rebecca asks so many questions, and she is so excited about it that she jumps up and down. Me and Michelle might have a baby. I am only 16. I can't.

Lewis gives me a cigarette, and we go and stand outside. I don't know what to say. I don't even know what to think. My brain can't make it all make sense. I keep seeing it in my head. She is late. I know she is. I didn't get told to stop anytime because it was that time in the month. I didn't even realise. I didn't notice. I stand with my cigarette and lean against the side of the caravan.

We wait until Saturday to buy a test. Then, I can get the money from my paper round and with Michelle's pocket money. We catch the bus into town to get one. I don't want anyone to see us if we buy it near her house or Alan's. Then they will know, and maybe Alan will throw me out too, or my dad will know, and he will get mad at me for it.

We go to the main town and buy one in the big shop. But we don't get it right away. We get one off the shelf and look around in case anyone sees us. Maybe there will be people from school or something, and then everyone will know, even if it is negative. When we buy it, we run out of the shop as fast as we can and all the way back to Michelle's house.

I am so nervous inside. I haven't eaten today. I didn't sleep last night. I can't. I can't do anything but think about that stupid test. Even at school, I think about it, and then I miss what the teachers are saying. Not that that matters; I don't listen anyway. Lewis and Rebecca are there. They wanted to be there. I think I smoke all of my cigarettes in one go.

Rebecca asks if she can go to the bathroom with Michelle while she does the test, but Michelle says no. If she goes with her and her mum comes home, then she might come up too. So Michelle does it by herself, and I stand outside with Lewis. Rebecca is talking so much about how great a baby would be and what we can all do. I just wish she would stop talking, but she doesn't. Not until Lewis tells her to just shut up.

I don't know what I am supposed to do while we wait. I stare inside the house and up the stairs and wait for her to come out. It takes so long. My hands shake because I am so afraid. I try to light another cigarette. I wish she would just hurry up so then we know.

Michelle opens the door, and then she comes down the stairs. It feels like she walks very slowly. She doesn't look at me while she walks down the stairs. I don't need her to say the answer. I already know. I can see by her face that the test is positive. She isn't crying, but she looks scared when she comes outside. We walk to the end of the garden, and she looks around in case her mum or someone comes. She shows me the test. "I'm pregnant," she says to me.

I don't know why, but I can't help but smile. I am scared and I don't know how to look after a baby. I don't know anything. I am just 16. I put my arms around her and hug her very tight. She hugs me back. I am happy. Maybe it isn't really real. Maybe I am just dreaming.

Seventy Six

It feels like a dream; no part of it is real. We took the test away from the house, and I put it in a public bin far away. It was stupid, but it felt like maybe someone would find it, and then they would know it was ours. I even check no one would see when I put it in the bin, but we wrapped it up in a bag and lots of paper, and no one will really know what it is, but I feel scared they will.

When it has gone in the bin, we all walk back to Michelle's house again. "Was it really positive? We read it right? You're sure it was?" I ask. She says yes, but I try to remember. Maybe we got it all wrong.

Nothing feels real at all. Even when I go home to Alan's house, I can't believe that she is pregnant; that she has a baby inside and I will be its dad. I can't be someone's dad. It's too strange. I don't tell anyone; just Lewis knows about it at school, and Rebecca. She is happy about it. She can't wait. She says she is going to be Aunty Becky.

Monday comes and I go to classes with Lewis and hang out with him at the ditch and smoke, but we just talk about normal things. He tries to ask me questions about the baby, but I am not ready to talk about them yet. I change the subject. I don't want anyone to hear, either. Then it would get back to my dad or someone, and I would be in huge trouble.

After school, I do my paper round, and then I go to Michelle's house. "I told my mum," she says to me straight away when I get there, and suddenly I feel very scared. "I can't hide it for long," she says, and she shows me her belly. It wasn't flat anyway, but I can see it when she stands and sticks it out. She gets my hand and puts it there. "My mum says it's hard because the baby is in there." It feels funny. A week ago, I didn't think about her belly like that.

"What did your mum say?" I ask her, but I am afraid. Maybe she called my dad.

"She said there wasn't anything she could do about it now. Now we just have to deal with it." She looks down at her hands. I am a little mad with her that she didn't wait for me or ask me if it was okay to tell her mum. Her mum waves at me from inside the house, and I wave back. "Are you okay?" she asks me, and I nod my head. "My mum says you have until the end of the week to tell Alan, or she is going to do it."

My stomach turns upside down inside. The cold goes all the way down my back and in that moment, I want to run away. I can't breathe. What if he makes me leave?

"My mum says it's only fair he knows." She is right, but I don't want to tell him. I don't like that Michelle's mum says I have to tell him. It makes me scared and mad. I will tell him when I want to.

I try all week to tell him. Sometimes, when he is in the kitchen cooking or just making coffee, I stand and stare at him.

The words are in my mouth, and I just need to spit them out. But I can't, they won't come. They jump back down my throat and go away. I'm so afraid. What if he tells me to leave? I can't go to my dad's. I haven't heard from him for weeks, so he doesn't care. I don't want to live on the street again. I only did it for two weeks, but it felt like a long time.

I don't tell him. Michelle says she will come with me on Friday, and we can tell him together. I have my paper round first, and then she is going to meet me at the house, and we can tell him together. I go to Michelle's for the weekends. She says maybe if we tell him Friday, then he has all weekend to calm down about it. It still makes me scared, though.

When I finish school on Friday, I can't even look at Alan. I rush in, get my bike and go deliver my papers. I can hardly think as I ride. Normally, I put music on in my stereo, but even that isn't working. All I can think about is Alan and that I have to tell him. I do the paper round as fast as I can. It's a huge round. Sometimes, it takes me two hours to do. When I am done, I take my bag back to the shop and then cycle back to Alan's. I hope Michelle isn't there yet. I am so afraid. I feel sick inside.

I go to the house and open the front door. Alan is there. "I want a word with you," he says to me. Michelle is behind him. She has told him. I want to run away. Maybe I can just go. My stomach turns over. I don't want him to be mad at me. I put my head down and tell him I know. My hands shake and my mouth is dry. I try to get my bike in the house. I watch where he is in case he decides to hit me when I don't expect it, but he doesn't.

"I'm not mad," he says to me. My dad used to say that too, then he would hit me. But maybe Alan won't in front of Michelle. When I go into the lounge, I try to make myself not very close to him, then I can get away if he tries anything. He doesn't, though. He sits on one of the chairs. Michelle and I stand by the television. "What do you want to do about it?" he asks us. "Have you thought about your options? Abortion?"

Michelle shakes her head. "I don't believe in abortion," she says. "I want to keep the baby."

He looks at me. "Do you want to live here still? Or are you going to move in with Michelle now."

I don't really know what to say. I want to stay with him, but maybe he doesn't want me to. Maybe that's why he asks. "I want to stay," I whisper. He smiles.

"Well shit, you got yourself into a good old mess this time, didn't you?" He isn't mad at us. He doesn't shout at all. He says he will help whatever we decide to do, but I have to sort myself out at school and college. "You're going to be someone's dad; you can't just not do schoolwork like you have been. You're a smart kid."

I know he is right. I just don't know how. I don't have school anymore. I can't be a doctor now. I don't have anything else.

Seventy Seven

Everything is crazy and busy. Everything just goes too fast. I haven't told my dad about the baby and soon it's going to be here. I haven't seen him, though, but I don't actually want to tell him. I don't want to listen to him when he gets mad about it. Then he'll just come around and hit me or something. So I haven't said anything to him. I am sure he doesn't care anyway.

Michelle's mum says the pregnancy has been real easy. I don't know what that means. I didn't know it could be hard too. But all Michelle does is sleep. When I come home from school and do my paper round, then I go around to her house. But at six she is asleep, and I lie there and read until I have to go home at nine. I have exams soon so I don't mind. I know I can't get good marks now, and I know I can't be a doctor, but maybe I can try to pass them a little bit.

Alan asks me why don't I think about art school. I like to draw. I show the pictures to him sometime times. I make comic books and draw all of those. My mum always said it was stupid. No artist ever gets rich, is what she used to say. But Alan thinks maybe I can do something with it. I just have to get through my exams.

I haven't done any of the assignments in the last two years. I can't even catch them up because the deadlines are all gone. All I have are the exams. Maybe if I get full marks in those, I can get some C's. Alan says don't worry if I can't, I can always do them again at college - my maths and English anyway. He says I need those, whatever I do.

We get to July 15th, when the baby is due. The day comes and goes, and me and Michelle and her mum and Alan can't wait. I saved up my pocket money and bought the baby a crib. It rocks and is made from wood. We got it from the secondhand shop, but it doesn't matter. I sanded all the paint off it, and then Alan let me buy some varnish for it, and I painted it. It looks real cosy now. Michelle's mum got some special blankets for it and bumper things for the side. She says babies have to have those, or they roll over and bang their heads.

Michelle can't wait for him to come. We don't know he is a boy, but Michelle says he feels like a boy. We have been to scans and things, but he hides. Alan says he is being a pain like me, but he laughs about it. We're going to name him William, or Will for short, but if he is a girl, then maybe we will call him Callie. I hope it is really a girl, then maybe she isn't like me, and she doesn't have bad parts in her like I do.

It's the 18th of July today. Michelle has had her hair done. Her mum wanted to do it to cheer her up. She is getting sad because the baby doesn't come. Yesterday, she cried because it started to rain. She is very tired, though. She says the baby has made her wet herself many times today. It lies on her bladder, her mum tells us. I laugh, but she smacks me in the arm and tells me I am mean.

We lie on the bed, and Michelle watches the television while I read. I have a couple more exams to do, and then it's all done. Michelle makes me jump. She gets out of bed so fast and then runs into the house. I don't even know what's wrong. She runs up the stairs, and I run after her and wait on the stairs and listen. Maybe she just needed the toilet, but then she starts to shout for her mum, and she runs up the stairs too. Her mum goes in the bathroom; her waters have broken. Her mum asks me to go and get her some clean pants. The baby is coming. I am afraid.

They go in the car, and we put her bags in there. I go on my bike. I have school in the morning. I race to hospital; I can get there faster because I can ride through the park and take the shortcut anyway. I lock my bike up next to her mum's car, and her mum goes inside to get someone. The porter comes outside with a wheelchair for Michelle. I help her to get up, but when she moves her water breaks some more and makes her pants wet. Her mum tells her not to worry, it's supposed to happen.

We go into the room, and we help Michelle get onto the bed. She has to wait for the nurse to come and look at her. The nurse takes a long time, but when she does come, she says we need to go to the delivery suite because Michelle is already far along, and she would like to get her comfortable. We follow them. They wheel her to this other room; it is big and there is a bed that is kind of funny shaped because the feet part comes off so she can hang on the edge. There is a chair next to the bed, and then there is a plastic baby crib. It has blankets and a name sticker. I stare at it. There's going to be a baby in there soon. It feels so strange. I tell myself I am going to be a dad, but it doesn't sound right.

Michelle has to have a thing around her belly. We can hear the baby's heartbeat. It sounds like a fast train. She has another one too, which says when the contractions are coming. The line on it starts to go up, and then me and her mum know to stand up and hold her hand.

For eight hours, I stand there next to her. She is tired. I am tired too. It is almost 3am. I don't like when she has contractions. Her mum watches the machine. Michelle says she wants to push, and the nurse tells her to if that's what she wants to do. Her mum holds her other hand. There is another nurse; she holds her leg. She crushes my hand, and I try to hug her at the same time. I watch as his head comes out. He comes out very fast after his head, and the nurse slides him all the way out and puts him on Michelle's belly. He is messy. He is a boy. It is 2:54 a.m.

I am a dad.

It all happens very fast after that. They take him away to the other side of the room. They have to clean him and weigh him and things, but Michelle is bleeding. She is bleeding a lot. The nurse shouts for someone, and she has to change the bowl under her. Many doctors come in. They run around, and the blood is everywhere. Michelle tries to fall asleep, but her mum tells her to wake up.

It makes me scared inside. What if she dies? I watch them

all; they all run about and try to stop the bleeding. There is so much. It just pours out and goes everywhere. I don't want her to die. Her mum starts to cry. Michelle doesn't know; she just tries to sleep. The doctor comes over. "We have to take her to theatre," he says. "We have to remove the placenta manually; it's making her haemorrhage."

He leans down to Michelle and tells her they have to take her to fix her. He is very nice. He asks her if she wants to sleep, or if she just wants to be numbed from the waist down. She says sleep. She says she is so tired. Her mum gets upset about it. They can't put her to sleep.

"She's been eating and drinking all day; she can't have any anaesthesia."

"If we don't take her to theatre right now, she is going to die," he says. They lower the top of the bed and wheel her away.

Her mum stands back, and then she puts her arms around me. She is crying. All the nurses go away except a couple. "She will be okay," one of them says to us. "Would you like to see your son?" she asks me.

My son? It feels so strange that he is here. I nod at her, and she brings him over in his little plastic crib thing. He has a blue blanket wrapped all around him and a little white hat on. I look at him. I want to touch him, but I am afraid. His hand is out of the blanket. I touch his fingers, and they are so small. He opens his eyes and is looking at me. They are blue. I lean on the side of the cot and watch him. I smile at him, because he is so perfect and I love him so much. I didn't think I would, but I do. "Hi," I say to him. I touch his cheeks and his nose. His skin is so soft; it feels like feathers and cotton wool. He opens his mouth.

"Do you want to hold him?" one of the nurses says to me. I nod, but I am scared. I might drop him. I might hurt him, and he is so little. She reaches in and picks him up, and she tells me to go and sit in the big comfortable chair in the corner. She tells me to put my arms out, and she puts him in my arms. I can't stop staring at him. I just watch him, and I wish I didn't ever have to move.

I'm going to be the best dad ever. I tell him inside my head. Michelle's mum comes over, and she strokes his face. I ask if she wants to hold him, and she says yes and nods. She is crying again. We take turns to hold him until Michelle comes back. She is asleep. They are going to take her to the ward soon. It is after 6 a.m. I am tired. I have school soon.

"You can go home if you want to," Michelle's mum says to me. "Do you want me to call Alan to pick you up?"

I shake my head and tell her no. I want to ride my bike home. I say goodbye to Will and Michelle. I wish I could stay there forever, but I can't. I walk out of the hospital. It all feels so strange. Like when my mum died, no one knows how my life has just changed again. They walk past me like I am no one and nothing special has happened, but it has.

The sun is shining outside. I go and stand in the sun, I light a cigarette, and when it is finished, I just stand there and cry. I don't know why I do it. I don't even know what I am crying for.

.

Seventy Eight

I am surprised I make it to first break at school before someone sends me home. I peddled all the way to Alan's, got changed and went to school. I told Alan about Will, of course. He couldn't wait to hear when I walked through the door and asked why I didn't call him to come and get me, but I don't really know. I just wanted to ride home. I don't know what I was supposed to do or think; going to school seemed like the easiest option. So that's what I did, and now I'm falling asleep. My head feels so tired and so excited all at the same time.

I'm a dad. I say it so much, but it doesn't make any sense. I tell them at school my son was born, but I don't have pictures yet. It's only a revision class I am in. My teacher comes and crouches beside me. "Go home," she says, and I nod.

I do, of course, but I don't rest for long. I can't. I sleep for maybe a couple of hours, and then Alan asks if he can take me to hospital. He wants to meet Will. "Why?" I ask him.

"Because I'd like to see him," he says, and he frowns at me.

I frown back. "I didn't think you would be interested," I say to him. He looks hurt, but I didn't think he was. It surprises me he takes an interest in my life. Especially the good things. No one ever did before. I tell him I would like him to come. He smiles about it.

Michelle will have to stay in the hospital for four days. I
go and see them every chance I have. I can't stop looking at him.
My Nan came too. She smiled so big that I thought she might
make her face split open. She hugged him so much she squashed
him. I didn't think she was going to let him go.

"Has your father seen him yet?" she asks me, and I shake
my head.

"He doesn't know about him," I say to them, and both my
Nan and Alan look at me and want to know why, but I don't tell
them. When I talk to him on the phone, he is drunk. I don't want
to tell him. He doesn't know what I do in my life. He doesn't
care. He signed me away. He didn't want me. No one ever does.
So why should I tell him? They stop asking about it.

Michelle and Will come home on the Saturday, and I
spend all my spare time there with them. I hate when I have to go
home at night because I miss them so much. But I call her in the
morning, and she lets me listen to him. I love him so much too.
Sometimes, it makes me cry because I just want to go there and
touch him and hold him. I get scared something bad will happen
when I am not there.

I finish school and all my exams. I know I haven't done
very well. I wish I could go back and do it properly, but it
doesn't matter now. Me and Alan went to the art college. I
showed them my art, and they said I could get onto the art
diploma with just that. I didn't need my exams, but I decided that
I would do my maths and English again, and I would take some

art classes at the same time. Alan thinks it's a great idea. I am also going to do media. Maybe with the English and the art, I can do something in media. Then I can get a job and look after Michelle and Will.

When Will is four weeks old, me and Alan are having dinner. Alan coughs like he has something to say, but he looks scared about it. It makes me scared. Maybe he is going to tell me to leave now I have left school?

"I wrote to your dad," he says to me. I sigh and put my knife and fork down. Maybe that is worse than telling me to get out.

My hands shake. "Why?" I ask him.

"I think it's the right thing to do. He is Will's grandfather and your dad. I know you don't get along."

"Did he reply?" I ask.

Alan nods. "He called, he wants to come and see him - on the weekend. He wants to meet him and he wants to see you. He wasn't mad. He was just sad you two had drifted so far apart he didn't know about you being a dad."

I don't want to see my dad. I haven't seen him for a long time. Maybe he will still be mad at me about my mum. I don't know. I don't talk about her when we talk on the phone. I don't want to hear him say it's my fault again. I just let him talk. Sometimes, if I say something, then he starts to shout at me down the phone, so I don't bother, and then he has nothing to get mad about.

My dad comes on the weekend. At first, I think he isn't going to come because he is late. We all wait nearly two hours and he hasn't come yet. Me and Michelle think maybe he isn't going to bother. Maybe he is drunk and forgot, but I don't say that part. He knocks on the door, though, and my stomach gives a flip.

He is here with a woman. I don't know her or who she is. He hasn't told me about her. She doesn't look very old. He says she is called Joanne. She is his girlfriend. He says he is late because he had to wait for her to get ready. I tell him it's okay, and he comes in with her. I try to make myself move away, then he can't hit me again. Maybe he is mad because he didn't know about Will, but he doesn't say it.

They sit on the sofa and it feels funny to see him. I look at him and then I look away again. Alan goes to make coffee, and me and Michelle sit opposite them. I feel like it's wrong that I sit down. I wasn't ever allowed at his house unless he said so. It makes me want to stand up, but I don't. I hold my hands together between my legs and try to hug myself away.

He doesn't really say anything to me. Maybe he doesn't want to be here. He makes me feel scared inside. I think about if he is sorry. Maybe he doesn't remember. Maybe he missed me. Maybe he will tell Michelle and Alan that I made my mum die.

My dad looks different, like he is thinner, but he looks older too. It feels like I went away for a long time and now I have a hole inside. It feels like when I miss my mum, but my dad is just here. He doesn't really talk to me or smile or say anything at all. He puts his hand on Joanne's knee and he doesn't ask me anything about me. Nothing at all. He doesn't care; I know that. Maybe he is always going to hate me for what I did. I am sorry.

"Well?" he says. "Where is he?"

Michelle smiles, and then she goes to get him. He is in the back room asleep in his pram. Will likes it in there; it is dark and quiet. We don't talk at all while Michelle goes to get Will. I look at the floor and my dad looks at the wall. I feel scared inside, maybe he doesn't want to be here.

Michelle brings Will in and takes him to my dad, but his girlfriend takes him instead and she looks at him. She talks about him like he is her grandson, but he isn't. She talks like she is my mum, but she isn't that, either. She tells me they are going to get married. I don't say anything about it.

"We have just bought a building," she says to me. "It was in a fire, but we are going to make it into flats. We were thinking that you, Michelle and Will here would like one of them. It will have two bedrooms, a lounge and a kitchen."

I don't know, but Alan comes in and hears what she says. He thinks it's a great idea and so does Michelle. I don't think I want to live in one of my dad's flats, but I don't know how to say no about it. I just nod, and they all talk about it. Joanne says they will be ready in January.

My dad is also going to the motorbike races next

weekend. "Do you want to come?" he asks me. I haven't ever been to one with him before. My dad seems very strange. He talks funny too. Not like he is drunk, but very fast. Joanne does the same. It is a little hard to tell what they are saying. Her eyes look big and huge.

I tell my dad that will be nice, and he says he will pick me up at lunchtime and not to be late or forget about it. Maybe he will come this time? I hope so. But I don't get excited just in case he changes his mind and doesn't want to take me anymore.

"Now you have a son, perhaps we should be friends again," he says to me. "Build some bridges." He says he is trying to get off the drink. After losing my mum, he just didn't know what to do.

Joanne pats his leg. "I saved him," she says. "I even got him to sell all the old bikes he doesn't use."

I don't say anything about it. My dad hugs Will, and then he brings him over to me. He smells like old whiskey, as always.

"We were at a party last night," Joanne says to me. "We haven't been to bed yet. Your dad nearly fell asleep driving the car home again."

I don't say anything about it. My dad is different.

Seventy Nine

My dad is supposed to come at two to pick me up, but it is nearly four and he isn't here. I keep checking out of the window whenever I hear a car or a bike, but it isn't ever him. I don't know why I check or why I think he is going to come this time. I stand outside and smoke my cigarette just so I can watch for him to come, but he doesn't. I'm sure he has forgotten again.

I should just go to Michelle's. I am supposed to see Michelle and Will after I have seen my dad. He was going to drop me off there, because the bike races are at the sand dunes where me and Lewis and everyone used to take the moped. Then I'd stay until Sunday and Alan would give me a ride back. But my dad isn't here.

I stop looking. I am such an idiot. I don't know why I fall for his stupid lies all the time. He doesn't mean it when he says he will come and take me out. I sigh and go upstairs and sit on my bed for a moment. I will just go and see Michelle and Will instead. I miss them so much.

Someone knocks on the front door, and Alan shouts up that it's my dad. Maybe I got the time wrong; it makes my stomach turn over from excitement. Maybe he meant four and not two. I get so many things wrong. I am stupid after all.

I say goodbye to Alan, and then I follow my dad out. I ask him where my brother is. I haven't seen him for a long time.

"He didn't want to come," my dad says. "He has seen the races every year." It makes me feel a little sad when he says that. My brother doesn't like bikes, but he got to go and I didn't. I don't say that to my dad, though.

I get to the car, and I have to sit in the front next to my dad. My dad's friend is in the back. He smiles at me, but I don't smile back. I don't like him. I haven't seen him for a long time. Not since my mum tied me up, and he was there. He makes me think about that, and I don't like to. I just look out of the window, instead. Maybe I should ask my dad to take me to Michelle's instead of the races. I want to go to them, but I don't want to be with his friend.

We drive towards the sand dunes, because that's where the races are. They always have them there because it's so far back, the tide doesn't really come all the way up, and it's just masses and masses of sandy hills. Me, Michelle, Lewis and Rebecca used to go there all the time, even without the moped. It is just a nice place to go and have a mess around. At times like these when the races are on, though, it's all marked off so people don't get in the way of the bikes and get hurt.

I watch out of the window as we drive past everything. My dad waits at the traffic lights, but when they go to green he doesn't turn right like he is supposed to. "Where are we going?" I ask him, because I have been to the sand dunes a ton of times; I know the way.

"We've had a change of plan," his friend says to me from

the back seat.

"Yes, but where are we going?"

"It's a surprise," my dad says, and it makes me feel sick. I don't like his friend. He did many bad things to me. I don't want him to be here. I don't like my dad's idea of surprises. I know what it means, and I don't want to go.

I don't say anything to them, but I look back out of the window, and I can feel my hands shaking. I don't want my dad to know my face gets hot because I am scared. I know what he is going to do. I stare at the houses as we drive past and watch them; people in their gardens going places, people inside. I wish I could be there. I wish I was them and not me, and then I would be safe and not scared. I try to keep my mouth closed so my dad doesn't hear that I can't breathe properly.

We stop at another set of traffic lights. We are on a lane I don't know. It is the other way from the sand dunes. I don't want to go wherever my dad is taking me. I open my door and unfasten my seatbelt so fast so my dad doesn't have time to do anything, and then I jump out and run. I run so fast. I don't care if I get hit by something. I run right across where the lights are and to the lane at the side. I don't know where I am going, but I don't care. I have to get away from my dad and his friend.

I hear a car coming, and I know it is my dad, but I run anyway. I try to run as fast as I can, but my legs can't go fast enough. I turn to look to see where he is, but my dad stops the car, and he and his friend jump out too. They shout my name, and then they run towards me.

He is bigger than me and he is faster. I run so hard that I am almost crying trying to make myself get away, but it doesn't take my dad long to catch me up. He reaches out and digs his big hand into my arm, and his long fingers squeeze my skin. I try to fight him off, but he stops me from running, and then he drags me back and I can't stop him. I try. I try to shake him off me, but it's too hard.

"Get back in the car," he yells at me, but I try not to. He pushes me but I hold the edge of the roof so he can't make me get into the car.

"Let me go," I shout at him, but he just keeps shouting for me to get back into the car.

Another car stops near us. He was going the other way. The driver gets out and comes near our car. My dad lets go and stops pushing me. "Is everything okay?" the man asks me. "Do you need some help?"

I stare at the man. Yes, yes, I need help. I say it in my head, but I don't say the words to him. They are right there. I want him to help me, but if I say yes, I know my dad will get in trouble. I don't want him to. He didn't do anything bad.

"Everything is fine," I tell the man, and I don't want to cry because I lie to him, and I do want him to help me.

The man stares at us. Maybe he doesn't believe me. "Are you sure?" he asks, and I nod. I get into my dad's car just to show the man that there is nothing bad. The man watches for a second, and then he gets in his own car and drives away again.

My dad closes my door, and I put my seat belt on. His friend gets in the car and sits right behind me. My dad doesn't say anything to me, but when he drives and has to stop, he reaches over and then he grabs my arm so I can't get away again. But I'm not going to. I don't want anyone to see and then maybe get in a fight with my dad.

We get to a house. It is big and white, and I haven't ever been there before. "This is one of my new houses," my dad says to me. "I just bought it." I didn't know my dad was going to buy a new house. I look out of the window at the house. It looks nice, but it has a skip and things outside because I guess my dad is fixing it up.

I tell my dad the house looks nice. My dad leans over me, and his friend gets out and opens my door. I can't run away even if I tried. His friend is in the way. I feel stupid, though, about trying to run away. All my dad wanted to do was surprise me with his new house.

We walk to the door, and my dad opens it, and we go in. He doesn't have a lot of furniture. I don't think he lives here, but there is an old television and an old sofa in the lounge. The rooms are all big, but the paper needs changing; it's all faded and peeling, and I can see the shapes where someone had pictures hanging before.

The room smells like old cigarettes and beer. My dad and his friend come in behind me, and my dad locks the front door.

"Do you like it?" he says to me. I look around and nod at him. I tell him it's nice.

My dad puts his arms on my shoulder and guides me into the lounge. "Sit down," he says to me. Its dark in there, but I don't tell my dad to open the curtains or anything. He puts on the television and asks me if I want something to drink. "I even have cans of coke if you want one."

I nod at him and sit on the sofa like he says. My dad goes to the kitchen and comes back with a drink for me. Then he says he'll be back very soon, and he leaves the room and goes upstairs.

I can hear him and his friend up there. I don't know what they are doing. It feels like ages before I hear them walking. I have finished my can and changed channel on the television, and when they eventually do come downstairs, I don't know what time it is. My dad hands me another can and a glass, but the glass has something in it. It's clear like apple juice. He smiles at me, but it isn't his happy smile. It's that smile I don't like - the one that makes his eyes look funny and I know he is thinking about something bad.

"Drink it," he says to me and sits next to me on the sofa. His friend sits on the other one near me.

I take a sip; it is sweeter than anything I have tried before. I don't know what it is. It's so fizzy the bubbles from it jump from the glass and up my nose. Whatever it is, it tastes nice. My dad keeps refilling my glass. I can feel my eyes get heavy and it's late. I don't know what time it is, but my dad puts the lamp on because it's getting dark.

We had been watching some other racing thing on the television, but my dad turns it over and puts on a porn film. I try to look away because I don't like to watch those with my dad. They remind me from when I was little. I don't like them. I don't even let Lewis watch them, because they make me feel bad inside.

My head feels like it is spinning in circles, and my eyes want to close and go to sleep, but I try to keep them open. My dad gives me a cigarette. I didn't even know he knew I smoked. I light it, and then suddenly it is nearly all gone, and I don't remember smoking it. Time feels funny. I lean over to put it into the ashtray on the coffee table, and I don't know what happens. Something bangs so hard at the side of my head that I have to catch myself to save from falling on the floor.

I turn and look at my dad. I know he has hit me, but I don't know why. I didn't do anything wrong. I don't really know what happens but my dad jumps onto me. My head feels funny and all I want to do is sleep, but it hurts inside my head. I don't understand why he hit me. He didn't shout or tell me what was bad. Maybe it's because I tried to run away and made him look stupid?

I try to get myself up, but my dad is on top of me, and he pushes me so I fall off the sofa and land between that and the table. His friend stands and pulls the coffee table out of the way.

I shout at him to stop it. I ask him what I did and I tell him that I am sorry. I try to shout it all, but my head doesn't want to stay awake. I beg my dad to please stop. I didn't mean to try to get out of the car. I was afraid. "I'm sorry dad, please don't," I say to him, but he hits me across the face, and then his friend comes and holds my shoulders down.

My dad lifts my top up, and I try to stop him. He scratches my skin because I fight too much. They don't take it all the way off, though; just enough, and his friend uses it to tie my hands above my head.

I can't move, and my dad unfastens my belt and jeans and pulls them down. I beg him to stop. I say dad so many times because I know what he is going to do, and I don't want him to. "Please dad," I say, but he isn't listening, and his face is mad.

They make me roll over onto my front, and I hear my dad's jeans. I am crying and asking him to stop, but he doesn't. I don't know how long it takes. It isn't like before. He doesn't say nice things to me. He makes it all hurt. They both do. They both do everything to me, and even when I am sick on the floor, it doesn't stop. I give up fighting them. It doesn't matter. It all hurts too much. Maybe they can kill me. They take turns. I hope I die soon.

I don't remember passing out, but I must have done. I lie there for a moment and don't know how to move. Everything aches and my face feels funny. I don't know where my dad and his friend have gone. I don't think about anything. On the floor is blood and vomit. Everything hurts. My dad's friend bit me many times. I can feel them against my shoulders as I move. I hurt inside. I am bleeding there too, but I loosen my hands and put my top back on, and then I pull my jeans on too. I want to go home.

I don't look for my dad. His keys are on the coffee table. I just let myself out and go home. I don't even know how I get there.

Eighty

Every time I move, it hurts. When I sit, I do it carefully
and hold my breath so no one notices. I haven't heard from my
dad. It's been over a week now. I don't talk to anyone about it. I
haven't talked to my dad. He didn't call to see where I was.

Alan asked about the races. I shrugged. Michelle asked
why I never turned up to see her and Will. I shrugged at her too.
She got mad at me, but I didn't know what to say, so I didn't say
anything. When I see her and Will, I just sit there and watch the
television with them. Everything seems so pointless. It makes it
hard to breathe. Every time I try, it makes me feel like I'm crying
inside my chest. I wish I could just go away, and then nothing
would hurt. Not inside or outside.

I read my books and try to get lost in that, or draw for my
art class so I have a nice portfolio made for when I start. I don't
even know why I do that so much. For Will maybe? He's the
only good thing I have. Sometimes when I look at him, I just cry.
I'm sorry he has me for a dad. I'm sorry he has to be part of my
life. I wish he wasn't here sometimes, and then I can go away
and it won't matter. But now I can't. I don't even ask God to take
me away, because if I die, who will make sure no one ever hurts
Will. I don't want him to ever sit alone and cry about things.

I don't let Michelle see when I cry. I don't tell her things.
I don't touch her or go near her. I'm still bleeding. When I go to

the toilet, or when I get changed, it's there. It smells strange too. I hope it will go away soon.

Michelle and Will are coming to Alan's today. I have to do some sketches, and I think Michelle is happy to come just to get out of the madhouse she lives in, because of all her brothers and sisters. It feels odd when she comes around; more so now maybe. She brings Will in and I look at him. I want to hold him so bad, but I haven't properly; not since my dad. I just lean in to him and breathe so I can smell that scent he has. I'm not good enough for him. I know that. I am sorry. I feel bad that one day, he will grow up and know how bad everything is. I wish he could stay a baby forever.

Michelle asks if I mind watching him while she goes to town. I am just drawing, and she has some things she wants to get from town. Her mum is going there alone, so she can meet her. I tell her it's okay. Alan is here too.

It's maybe an hour later when he starts to cry, and Alan is trying to do some work. I tell him I'll take Will upstairs. It feels strange to hold him when I haven't really for a couple of weeks, but I take him to my room and lay him on the bed after changing him. I lie down next to him, wincing as I move because it all hurts too bad. I cry as I lay with him. I cry because it hurts to move, but I cry because I don't understand, either.

I stare at Will. I wonder what I did to make my dad hate me so much. I couldn't ever hurt Will like that. I don't think I'll ever hit him, either, not even when he is bad. He falls to sleep, and I turn my head into the covers and just cry until my head hurts. I don't want Alan to hear me. I hold Will's little hand and tell him I am sorry.

When Michelle comes back later, I ask her if she minds going home with her mum. "I don't feel very well," I tell her. I just want to sleep I think. Everything feels so heavy inside. I'm not sure I can stay awake another minute. She tries to kiss me goodbye, but I move away. I can still smell all the bad smell from the blood. I don't want her to smell it, and I don't want her to know what my dad and his friend did.

When she has gone away, I tell Alan I am just going to bed to sleep for a while. When I get upstairs and lie on my bed, it doesn't take long for me to feel like I'm drifting away, except its different, and I feel like I'm falling. I feel like I'm falling into some darkness, and when I open my eyes, I can't move my body, just my arms. I try to shout for Alan, but I can't even make my mouth move. I am paralysed, and I don't know why.

It makes me afraid. I fight so hard to make my hands move, and when they do, I can feel my heart beating fast inside my chest. Maybe it was a bad dream. I roll over and close my eyes, but almost straight away it happens again. But this time, I don't get scared and I don't panic. I don't feel any pain; it's all gone. I don't feel sad. I just feel blank. I let myself fall and everything starts to get darker, like I'm slowly floating away, but where I am going, I don't know.

I can hear my name. It sounds like its far away, but I can't tell. I don't want to answer it. I just want to keep falling. Nothing hurts. Not inside or outside. I can feel something, but I don't know what it is. Like something sharp in my arm, but I can't move to find it. I hear Alan shout my name again and again. "Open your eyes," he is saying to me, and I do try, but it is hard.

He stands over me when I do, and there is another man there. At first, I don't know who it is, and then I realise it's the nice doctor. "There's an ambulance on the way," Alan says to me. "Stay awake."

The doctor says something, but I'm not sure what it is at first. "Another hour and he'd have been dead," he says to Alan. I can hear him talking, but I drift off again, and when I open my eyes once more, the paramedics are there.

"He has no temperature and barely a heartbeat," he says to the other man.

"Call my dad," I ask Alan.

Alan looks down. "I already tried. He says he's too busy to come. Do you want me to come to the hospital?"

I shake my head and let them take me away. I want to be left alone.

Septicaemia is what they said I had. We raced along in the ambulance, but I don't remember that much about it. Then, for four hours, I was in the emergency room while doctors ran around and did examinations and things. I don't remember so much. I think I passed out. They put a drip in my arm, though.

It hurts when I try to move. Every so often, one of the nurses comes into my room and pushes something through it. It makes my arm feel cold inside as it goes in. All I want to do is sleep. I am not allowed anything to eat. I have to go to theatre tomorrow. The doctor tried to ask me how I got injured, but I don't want to tell him. He says he has to fix me. He says my skin is ripped inside, and they have to put it back together. I don't want to listen. It just makes me cry. I don't want them to touch me.

At visiting time, Alan, Will and Michelle come to the hospital. I can see them outside through the window. They are talking to the nurse, but I don't know what they are saying. I close my eyes, and maybe I fall asleep again, because when I open them, Michelle is sitting in the corner with Will in her arms. "Alan is outside," she says to me. "Do you want to hold Will?"

I shake my head and roll away from her. I don't want her to look at me. I don't want her to know. I don't want to touch Will. I don't want to make him bad like me. I wish they would all leave.

"Please, go away," I say to her. "I don't want you here."

She says my name, but I say it again. I tell her to go away and leave me alone. She starts to cry. She stands there for a few minutes but doesn't say anything. Then, she leaves and I am alone again. She doesn't see me cry. No one does.

Eighty One

I stand in the lounge with so many boxes around me I don't even know where to start. I'm excited and afraid all at the same time. Will plays with the chain around my neck and giggles happily in my arms.

It's January. I am moving out of Alan's and into my new flat. Alan is here with me. He stands next to me with his hands on his hips, ready for us to start unpacking.

The next part of my life. It feels strange to be facing it.

The flat is owned by my dad and his wife, Joanne. They got married. I didn't go. I've hardly seen him and when I do, we talk as if nothing happened. I can deal with that as long as he leaves me alone. I know I'll never be rid of him; he is, after all, dad.

College starts in a few days for me. I got in late, but they said I still could do it. I just did a lot of the catch up work at home. I'm set to get C's at least. Not A's, I know, but it's better than nothing. Next year, I'm going to start catering. Everyone needs to eat.

Michelle and I have split up, but maybe it was for the best. I was never right for her, anyway. She's expecting her next child. Not mine, though. I hope he does right by her. I'm sorry that I hurt her, but I'll never be sorry I met her. She gave me Will and for that, I'll always thank her.

He's the one reason I plan to live. The one thing to keep me going. I hold him as close as I can. I'm going to be the best dad I can be.

"Should we unpack Will's room first?" Alan says. "At least then he has somewhere to play while we do the rest."

I look at Will, and he stares at me with those eyes. I nod my head and smile. Will, will always be first.

THE END

Also by JD Stockholm

Dear Teddy

Dark Ramblings of the Phoenix

Telling Teddy

Stupid Boy

If I Were To Die Today

Contact

dearmrted@gmail.com

http://jdstockholm.com/

http://www.facebook.com/dearmrted

https://www.facebook.com/JDStockholmTeddy

These two sites have been invaluable to me throughout the last few years. I salute the many people on there, survivors, directors and above all, my friends. Thank you for the support at those times I needed it.

http://www.isurvive.org.uk

http://www.recoveryourlife.com/

FAQ's

I've been meaning to put this page in all of my books, every time I sit, I can't think what to write, so I'm just going to try and if anything crops up that someone wants to know from one of my books, then by all means ask, and I'll do my best to answer.

I get emailed and messaged on Facebook often, not that I mind, I love to hear from people, just it seems if these questions are things many people have, then maybe it's better to answer them here.

1. Who was the bad man and what happened to him?

- I don't know who he was, or where he came from. I can't remember him, other than the vague memories that are in my books. I didn't see him after I was seven years old, but by then the damage was already done and since then, and even until this day, I have flashbacks of his face almost every day. I was diagnosed with PTSD last year. My therapist that I was working with suspects that my mind has shut out his face for a reason, and perhaps its someone I know.

2. What was the medicine my mother was giving to me?

- I don't know what it was she gave me. I suspect it was made of whatever she could find that day. It never really tasted the same, though it was always hot. I think perhaps she put some kind of spice in it. I don't think it was real medicine, but then I don't really know.

3. What happened to my mother, father, brother and nan?

- My mother passed when I was fifteen. I don't really like to talk about that part, maybe when I am stronger I will do.

- My father is still around, though recently I told him to leave me alone, it had reached the point when I couldn't take much more from him. I have to accept, he will never see me how I want him too and he will never take responsibility for his actions.
- My brother is still in my life. He does well and recently qualified as a staff nurse. I'm very proud of what he has achieved.
- My Nan, she passed when I was twenty four. It hit me very hard at the time, and I suffered mental illness due to the loss of her.

4. Was my brother abused too?

- I don't think so, not in that way, though he has his own things and his own issues. I don't think he was abused in the same way. I would be heartbroken if I learned different.

5. When did it stop?

- Officially when I was sixteen years old, after I had been thrown out, but there have been violent incidents since.

Printed in Great Britain
by Amazon